From Carl and Jeannine
Aug. 16, 1979

Crossroads and Coffee Trees

a Legacy of Joe Creason

Crossroads and Coffee Trees

a Legacy of Joe Creason

A collection of
Kentucky anecdotes
with introduction by
Bill Creason

Executive Editor: Samuel W. Thomas
Editor: Nancye J. Kirk
Book Design and Cover Illustration: Joseph V. Rigsby
Copyright © 1975
The Courier-Journal and The Louisville Times
525 W. Broadway, Louisville, Kentucky 40202
Library of Congress Catalog Number: 75-18222
Printer: Consolidated Printing Services, Inc., Louisville, Kentucky
First Printing: August 1975

Contents

"Hey! Hurry up...Creason's telling
another whopper!"

Introduction

"They're saying up around Richmond that Old Dame Luck has claimed the Central High basketball team as one of her very own."

So it all began. A short paragraph, at first glance not too noteworthy, just a routine beginning for a sports story.

But this brief excerpt has some historical significance. The author of the sports report was a young staff writer just four days on the job. His name was Joe Creason. Not Joseph Creason or Joel Creason. Just plain Joe. And the nine-paragraph article of January 31, 1941, was the first appearance of my father's by-line in *The Courier-Journal*.

For the next 33 years (less a two-year obligation in World War II) Dad tried to pass on to his family and the citizens of Kentucky the love and admiration he had for his native state and its people.

Few people knew the state and its citizens as well as Joe Creason. He was a recognized authority on many aspects of Kentucky life. He made it a point to visit each of the state's 120 counties annually if for no other reason than to just keep in the know on things happening throughout the Commonwealth. Partially due to this effort to visit all corners of the state, he became Mr. Courier-Journal to many of its readers.

Jesse Stuart, the noted Kentucky author and a close family friend, once referred to my father as "the foremost ambassador of good will for one of the ten great newspapers in the world." Not only was he an ambassador for *The Courier-Journal*, but he served in that capacity for the entire state of Kentucky.

The purpose of this book is to give the reader the perspective with which Joe Creason viewed his home state and its people. To accomplish this task, I have collected stories he wrote which I believe best personify the kind of man that he was and will always be remembered as being. These stories did not appear in his book *Joe Creason's Kentucky* published by the newspapers in 1972. Dad had planned to do this sequel, and I hope it conveys something of the deep affection he felt for Kentucky and its people.

My father's career in journalism was spent essentially as a Sunday *Magazine* feature writer, an interpretive news reporter, and a daily columnist.

Magazine features probably made the greatest contribution to his name becoming so familiar in Kentucky. During the miles and miles of intra-state travel dealing with these articles, he struck up many acquaintances. Dad estimated he had traveled more than a half million miles in search of the people, places and things featured in his articles.

Even more astonishing to me is the fact that most of these miles were driven prior to the development of the interstate and toll road systems that now criss-cross the state and connect the distant corners of the Commonwealth. A trip to Pikeville that now takes less than four hours used to take six. By car, Paducah used to lie more than seven hours down the road. Now it is five hours away.

During his 21-year tenure as a feature writer for the Sunday *Magazine,* Dad was often called upon to write interpretive news articles for other sections of the paper. The Passing Show section, later renamed Outlook-Environment, and the Op Ed page were his most frequent hangouts when he made good his escape from the pages of the *Magazine.* Although these articles were somewhat shorter than the regular magazine features, they still displayed the typical Creason style and insight.

The intent of many of these articles was the same as his regular magazine pieces—to help the reader better interpret the issues of the day. He once told me that he wrote in such a straightforward fashion because, "often times when I began my research I found out I didn't really know anything on the subject, so I wrote with the idea that there were a lot of other uninformed people like me in the reading audience."

His column, "Joe Creason's Kentucky," began an 11-year run in the pages of *The Courier-Journal* on October 1, 1963. Appearing six days a week, the column soon developed into one of the best-read features in the paper.

In his first column, Dad set down the premise for its existence. He wrote, "All of us at *The Courier-Journal* have long felt that we needed to have some corner of the newspaper set aside for our particular part of the world, for the things that interest us quite aside from the so-called hard news of what, when, where and how. . . . It's to be about this beautiful, often charming, often perverse part of the nation we call 'home.' "

He also wanted his column's readers to participate in the undertaking and to help in collecting material for publication. And help he got. People he knew, and even those he didn't, would write, call, or visit to pass on interesting stories or vignettes which they had heard or experienced. Wherever he went he was ready to take down a novel story or funny tale.

Later called simply "Joe Creason," the column had various positions in the paper. From its initial spot on the page opposite the editorial page, the daily feature moved to the comic page and eventually to its final resting place on the first page of the second section. But wherever the column went the readers followed.

After examining the extensive files Dad accumulated through his stay with *The Courier-Journal,* my first impression was that he must have written about every personage and crossroad in the Commonwealth at one time or another. I could arrive at no definite total of news articles, magazine features, and column items which he was responsible for putting into print, but it is safe to say the number easily passes 30,000.

If there is one dominant trait which runs throughout his 33-year career, it is that he wrote of others and for others. In fact, to look at my father's files from beginning to end, one might get the impression that he lived a quiet, dull life. Quite to the contrary. It is just that he was a great one for reporting the comic stories that involved others. He rarely reported those which he personally encountered, believing that readers weren't interested in knowing about the reporter. He felt that to talk about himself would be an imposition on the time and good nature of the reader whom he cherished very much. When it came to patting himself on the back, my father was a very modest man.

So perhaps it is now time to tell some humorous stories that involved Joe Creason. These anecdotes show that Dad, just like the many thousands he wrote about for so long, had his humorous experiences too.

Two stories occurred early in his travels along the banquet circuit. As many people know, Dad was an accomplished speaker. Few people in the state were in as much demand as a commencement or after-dinner speaker. During the May graduation season it was not unusual for Dad to be gone five nights a week delivering thought-provoking messages to graduating classes around Kentucky and in southern Indiana. Nor was it extraordinary to find him traveling 1,000 miles in one week to make his talks. I guess his biggest problem was saying no to a speaking request.

But such enthusiasm to hear him was not always so prevalent. As a matter of fact, early in his career he was down the list of preferred speakers from the newspapers. Columnists such as Bill Ladd and B. M. Atkinson were the celebrities—and, in turn, were in great demand.

So in the early going, his only chance to speak occurred when a last-minute replacement was needed.

One such instance happened in the late 1940s. Bill Ladd, then the television reporter for *The Courier-Journal,* was to make an appearance before a civic group in Eminence in Henry County. However, Mr. Ladd had to withdraw a day or so before he was to speak. He told the group he would take it upon himself to send someone in his place who would be entertaining, informative, and cheap, and he asked my father if he would like to go.

When Dad arrived he sought out the gentleman in charge of the program and introduced himself. He eyed my father somewhat suspiciously and showed him to his seat on the podium.

After the meal of cold chicken and all the trimmings, the master of ceremonies tapped his water glass for order. Father could feel his ego slowly beginning to swell in anticipation of all the glowing things that were about to be said about him.

"Well," the master of ceremonies began, "we had hoped to have Bill Ladd tonight. But at the last minute he had to cancel. We were fortunate to obtain anyone at all at this late date, so we settled for Joe Creason."

Although the introduction left something to be desired, the audience was duly impressed with the talk, and I think Dad usually returned to Eminence at least once a year to speak and was always well received.

The second anecdote involves B. M. Atkinson, the former columnist for *The Louisville Times*.

My father was to deliver a talk to a group out in the state, and, as customary, the organization had gotten the newspapers to supply biographical material for the introduction.

The fellow who was to introduce my dad either forgot who was to make the speech or was sent the wrong biographical data, because the introduction he read was for B. M. Atkinson, not Joe Creason.

During his tenure at *The Courier-Journal,* Dad had a great rapport with everyone at the paper. It often manifested itself in little gags which the photographers, reporters, editors and others would play on him.

One such prank concerned a picture taken at the 1954 Mt. Sterling Court Day.

The editors of the Sunday *Magazine* had thought my father was getting his name and picture in the paper a little too frequently. It seemed as though whenever pictures were chosen to accompany an article written by him, at least one shot had Joe Creason in it. It never was planned, but it just seemed to turn out that way.

And when the pictures taken at the Mt. Sterling Court Day were examined, the editors, to their dismay, discovered him in a prominent position in one of the photos to be used.

It was then they happened upon a novel idea. Why not disguise Creason? If we have to use this one particular photo, they thought, cover him up so no one will recognize him. So they painted a mustache on him and waited to see what happened. No one noticed for a month.

When it came to the Civil War and the part Kentucky and its citizenry played in that national struggle, Father was a real buff. One aspect of the war which interested him was the facts and stories surrounding the Battle of Perryville, fought October 8, 1862.

On October 9, 1949, my father had a piece in the Sunday *Magazine* about the bloodiest battle of the Civil War fought in Kentucky. In the article he went into some detail describing how the two armies just happened to meet on that October morning, and he had tried to be objective and to give the specifics clearly.

However, around 6 a.m. on the Sunday morning the article appeared, the phone at our house rang. The caller told my father she thought he was sympathetic to the South and the "darn rebels" in the story.

After assuring her he favored no one side or ideology, she hung up, and he was able to return to bed. Or so he thought.

A half hour later the phone rang again. This time it was a man on the line who thought the story had been colored to favor the North.

Father concluded that there is no way to be impartial about the Civil War in Kentucky.

I sincerely believe one of the hardest ideas for anyone to accept about my father was his name. Contrary to what others tried to tell him, his real name was Joe Cross Creason, and not Joseph, Joel, or any other derivative.

In an attempt to get the world educated on the subject and to band together all those who had a similar burden to bear, Dad began a club. Its name was JOES (Joes Only and Exclusively Society). Its membership was comprised of all those who had only Joe for a full first name.

One of the benefits of starting your own organization is that you get to place yourself in the seat of authority, if you wish. My father assumed the title of Head "Joe."

Through his column he publicized the society's existence and urged all those with the name Joe to write for a membership card. Several hundred requests came in including one which was addressed to Joseph Creesin, Head Joe, *The Courier-Journal*.

This confusion over his name went on not only outside the walls of the paper, but inside as well.

When *The Courier-Journal* moved into its present building at Sixth and Broadway in 1948, a marble wall in the lobby had inscribed on it the names of those company employees who had fought in World War I and World War II.

In the group of World War II veterans one can find between the names William O. Coyne and Carlisle Crutcher, one Joseph Cross Creason.

One final anecdote that involved my father is an incident that had Dad cast as an accessory to a crime. Not a major one, mind you, but a crime nonetheless.

Dad covered a story involving the raiding of a moonshine operation by federal agents in Marion County. The article appeared August 8, 1948, and detailed the proceedings of the day's events.

At its conclusion, my father included a common recipe for moonshine whiskey, not only giving the ingredients and their proportions, but also publishing the time each step takes in the process.

Then in February, 1949, a gentleman was arrested in a Louisville suburb for making bootleg whiskey in his garage.

Charged with operating an unlicensed distillery, the local moonshiner pleaded guilty. Federal Judge Roy M. Shelbourne gave him a suspended sentence of 90 days.

When questioned by the judge as to how he ever learned to make moonshine whiskey, the offender said he had learned it from a story that had appeared in the Sunday *Magazine*.

In passing sentence, Judge Shelbourne advised the guilty party, "In the future, you'd better stick to the funny-paper section."

It has been almost a year since my father passed away. I assume I am no different from anyone else when I say a void appears in your life when death claims someone close to you. But I can only feel a warmth when I think of the joy that my father brought to so many people for so many years.

Although he is no longer here, Joe Creason left us all, you and me, a great deal. He made us proud to be Kentuckians. He pointed out to us how diverse and yet how unique the Kentuckian is. He recorded the way Kentuckians live, work and play. He showed us the beauty that can be found in the mountains of eastern Kentucky, the Bluegrass of central Kentucky, and the lakes of western Kentucky. He made us realize that Kentucky is a good place to "hail" from and grow up in.

This pride in being a Kentuckian is the legacy Joe Creason, my father, left to me.

Bill Creason

Preface

The Kentucky flag flew at half mast over the Capitol in Frankfort on August 16, 1974, in tribute to the Commonwealth's most beloved homespun journalist. Two days earlier Joe Cross Creason had suffered a heart attack while playing tennis, the game he loved best.

Before his untimely death, Joe had planned to publish a companion volume to *Joe Creason's Kentucky,* published by *The Courier-Journal* and *The Louisville Times* in 1972. His second volume was to have included longer pieces from his earlier years as a newspaper and magazine feature writer as well as selections from his later columns.

Joe did not have the opportunity to compile the second volume, but his younger son, Bill, took it upon himself to carry out his father's plans. He read through the stacks of clippings his father had written throughout his 33 years with *The Courier-Journal* and selected those that best expressed the Creason philosophy. Bill also wrote the introduction to this volume as well as the introductions to each chapter.

Many Kentuckians knew Joe Creason personally, and many more knew him through his "little stories," as he liked to call his columns. For those who wish to remember the sincere Creason smile, and for those who never had the chance to meet Joe, photographs have been included in this volume. The pictures were selected from Joe's personal collection and from the newspapers' photography files.

Joe was the champion of many causes throughout his newspaper career. He stressed the need to preserve the Red River Gorge in its natural state long before it became a political issue. Joe was one of the first people to see the possibilities of a state park being built in a remote area along the Kentucky-Virginia border. In 1955 these hopes were realized and the Breaks of the Sandy Inter-State Park, funded from the treasuries of both states, was dedicated. Another issue he felt strongly about was the state's tourist industry. During Governor Bert Comb's term, Joe convinced a special session of the cabinet to begin a concentrated effort to tell Kentuckians about Kentucky and its state park system.

The banner Joe carried immediately before his death involved the Kentucky coffee tree and his desire to have it named the official state tree. Joe used his column to urge support of this idea among Kentucky lawmakers at the 1974 General Assembly. Legislation was introduced but was killed in committee.

This book is a tribute to Joe Creason, the columnist and the institution, to all his causes, and to the folk wisdom Joe collected throughout his journey among Kentucky crossroads and towns.

INTRODUCTION   *The art of the comic retort and the timely
one-liner knows no age limitations. Many times children's amusing
comments are not meant to be funny but only spontaneous
reactions to the world around them. My father was well aware
of this delightfully innocent humor, and some of the funniest
anecdotes he recorded involved youngsters, some of whom were
barely beyond the diaper stage.*

*Take for instance the six-year-old hellion who developed a
fatalistic attitude regarding his chances of receiving anything better
than a bundle of switches for Christmas.*

*"There's nothin'," he explained, "I want bad enough to be
good for."*

*Or consider the blunt-spoken fifth grader with whom his teacher,
Mrs. Wade George of Versailles, was having considerable trouble.
After a rather heated run-in, the boy turned to her.*

"Ain't your husband named Wade?" he asked.

"Yes," Mrs. George confessed.

*"Well," the boy sighed, "he shore waded in when he married
you!"*

*With these and the following examples of youthful awareness,
we can rest easily knowing that the type of humor which we have
come to recognize as distinctively Kentuckian will continue to
flourish for many years.*

CHAPTER 1

FROM THE MOUTHS OF BABES

Children, at times, show logic which is both frightening and candid in the same situation.

Consider, for instance, the kid, no more than four, who was waiting in the office of an Owensboro dentist while his mother was having some molar matters taken care of. Nearby sat a kindly woman.

After a while the woman started talking to the child, and before long they were looking through a book filled with color pictures of wheeled vehicles and playing a little game. She would turn to a particular picture and ask the little boy to identify it.

One vehicle was an ambulance with a bright red cross on the side.

"That's a 'happened truck,' " the child piped up as soon as he saw the picture.

"What do you mean a 'happened truck?' " the woman asked.

"Well," the kid replied logically, "when people see it, they say, 'What happened?' "

The little boy W. Gordon Ross of Berea spoke to on the street didn't mince words.

"Hello, son. How old are you?" Ross asked.

"Eight," replied the kid.

"And what are you going to be?"

"Nine!"

Nathan Etheridge is a PK—Preacher's Kid. And he can ask the kind of questions that can give his father, Donald Etheridge, a Baptist minister in Mercer County, and his mother pause to think.

"What is spirit?" he asked his mother one day.

"What do you mean, spirit?" she parried, stalling until she could think of an answer.

"Like when you're eating food," Nathan explained, "you spear it, blow on it and eat it."

When Scott Applewhite, a student at Western Kentucky University, worked at our newspapers as a summer intern in the photography department, he took a picture of two seven-year-old boys in Bowling Green. Since they looked like two peas from the same pod, he could tell they were twins.

"You both have the same last names," he kidded them when they told him their identity. "You must be brothers."

"Nope," answered one of the boys, "we're just twins."

When he was being examined prior to going to camp one summer, Richard Sturgill of Lexington was answering the usual questions about whether or not he had mumps, measles, whooping cough, etc.

"I've also had heart failure twice," Richard, a great sports fan, told the startled doctor. "It was at UK basketball games, and we were behind by one point!"

Children have such big ears and mouths to match that it isn't safe to say anything around them that you don't want repeated.

Early one school year Mrs. Joe Henderson, third grade teacher at Franklin, was approached by a little girl in her classroom.

"My mommy says I'm lucky," the little girl blurted out, " 'cause last year I had Miss Hatton and she's young and pretty and this year I have you and you're old and experienced."

After they'd prepared him by telling him that people go to church to learn how to be good enough to get into heaven, this Lexington family I won't identfiy for obvious reasons felt their five-year-old son was ready for his first full-scale preaching service.

The minister was especially long-winded this Sunday and after half an hour the kid began to squirm. Finally he tugged on his father's arm.

"Are you sure," he whispered, "this is the only way to get to heaven?"

His young grandson, Pee Wee, who lives in Houston, Texas, was helping Edgar Davis of Greensburg dig potatoes, according to Slim Pickens, the upper Green River area recorder of historic events. After a while the kid began to tire.

"Grandpa," he asked wearily, "what caused you to bury these things in the first place?"

There is one thing that characterizes the way Kentuckians sound. It isn't an accent as such, but rather the way so many in this state tend to drop the "g" on words ending in "-ing."

Thus we say someone is "comin' to visit" and "stayin' for a while."

Like their elders from whom they learn, children also fall into this habit, as Mrs. Leon Wesley of Whitesburg illustrates. She is a teacher of a Sunday school class for preschool-age children at the Methodist Church where her husband is the minister. Early one spring she spent a Sunday discussing the signs of spring—grass growing, flowers blooming, birds returning.

"Have any of you seen any robins this spring?" she asked.

"No, ma'am," a little five-year-old boy replied. "I haven't seen any robbins, but on television I saw some beatin' ups!"

No matter how devious we are, we don't often fool children. The wife of an old acquaintance found proof of this among the seventh grade students she teaches in a southwestern Kentucky school.

One boy in the room, Alfred by name, hadn't been a model of deportment. But rather than chew him out for his misdeeds, she decided to use a little flattery.

"I just know it wasn't Alfred who did that," she said, laying it on pretty thick. "Alfred is too considerate and too intelligent to have done such a thing."

"Ma'am," another boy in the room spoke up, "you just don't understand all you know about Alfred."

The April 3 tornado taught people, both in and outside the devastated areas, a lot of things. It provided two girls the chance to learn the meaning of a new word.

One girl (they were both in the eight- to 10-year-old bracket) was visiting the home of the other in the Indian Hills section of Jefferson County, and they were alone in the basement recreation room waiting for the sitter who was supposed to stay with them that evening.

It was just past 4:30 and they were watching TV when the regular program was suddenly interrupted for a weather bulletin.

"A tornado," the announcer said, "is imminent in the Louisville area."

"What does 'imminent' mean?" one of the girls wondered.

"I don't know," the other replied. "Let's look it up in the dictionary."

They went upstairs, found a dictionary, and returned to the basement. Just as they were leafing through the "I" section, they heard the sound like a squadron of jets passing at treetop level. The house shuddered and the lights went out as the full fury of the storm hit.

"I think," one of the girls said in a quivering voice, "that 'imminent' means now!"

If we left it up to children, events rather difficult to comprehend would be easily explained. Take, for instance, school themes written about two of our most illustrious presidents, Abraham Lincoln and George Washington, by second grade students.

As recalled by a Louisville friend, one little girl had this to say about Lincoln:

"Lincoln was one of our greatest presidents. He won the Civil War. He was so glad that he won that he went to the theater to celebrate. That was a great mistake."

Another child offered this theme on Washington:

"George Washington was our first president. When he was a little boy he cut down his father's cherry tree and that made his father very mad. His father gave him a good spanking. That is why he stood up in the boat."

A classic little essay written by a third grade student with his teacher's help—especially fitting around Christmas—appeared in the newsletter of the St. Matthews United Methodist Church.

"God is like Bayer aspirin; He works wonders. God is like Ford; He has a better idea. God is like Coke; He's the real thing. God is like Dial; He gives round-the-clock protection. God is like Pan Am; He makes the going great. God is like Hallmark; He cared enough to send the very best."

There's more than one way to answer the broad questions, so who's to say the country boy I recently heard about was wrong?

Anyway, the kid was named Lake, and one day in class his teacher was reviewing geography.

"Who can name the five great Lakes?" she asked.

The boy's hand shot up.

"I can," he answered happily. "There's Pa, Ma, Bub, Sis and me."

To say politics is taken seriously in Kentucky is about as great an understatement as saying moonshine whiskey has a distinct taste about it.

So serious is politics in Kentucky that almost as soon as a child can talk he is drilled in the basics of the political game.

Evidence of this is five-year-old Kristen Peters of Lexington who was looking at some Christmas cards her parents had received early. One showed Jesus astride a donkey.

"My goodness," she exclaimed. "I didn't know that Jesus was a Democrat."

When the topic of barbers comes up I am reminded of the boy, maybe 10, from far out in the country who was used to the soup bowl-style trims. He came into the barber shop of Chet Gordon in Benton and announced he'd like a haircut.

"How do you want it cut?" he was asked.

Not being one used to such sophistication, the kid simply replied, "Off."

Don't tell me children aren't wise beyond their years. Take the granddaughter of Mrs. Jeanette Abrams who was visiting her Louisville grandparents.

"Grandma," the kid said, "I love you more than I do my other grandma."

"Don't tell your other grandma that," Mrs. Abrams replied, taking the child into her arms. "It would hurt her feelings."

"Oh, I won't," she responded. "When I'm with her, I tell her I love her the best!"

A friend of Mrs. Joe Hagan of Louisville had a three-year-old daughter who became fascinated by the ritual whereby her baby brother was treated to a change of linen. After standing close and watching the baby being bathed and sprinkled with powder from a can time and time again, she made what seemed a reasonable request.

"Mommy," she asked, "may I pepper him next time?"

A rural church in Carroll County was preparing for its Vacation Bible School and one of the members asked the four-year-old son of neighbors if he intended to enroll.

"Yes'm," he replied, rolling his eyes. "I'm a-comin' if I can quit cussin' long enough!"

When Todd Smith of Columbia was seven he was asked by his parents after Christmas if he had received the presents he wanted. His answer would warm the heart of any parent.

"I didn't get what I wanted," Todd replied. "But I like what I got more than what I wanted!"

Three or four years ago tryouts were being conducted for parts in the Nativity Play to be staged by the children of the Second Presbyterian Church. There was brisk competition for all the roles except that of the innkeeper who told Mary and Joseph that he didn't have room for them.

For some reason the kids seemed to think the innkeeper was a sort of bad guy and no one wanted to be saddled with the part.

"But he wasn't really mean," one of the teachers explained to the four-year-old boy chosen for the role. "All the rooms in the inn were taken and he just didn't have a place for Mary and Joseph to stay."

That appeased the boy somewhat, but when the play was staged he felt constrained to underscore the innkeeper's innocence by ad-libbing his lines just a trifle.

"I'm sorry I don't have room for you, I'm really sorry," he said when Mary and Joseph stopped by, "but won't you come in and have a drink?"

To show how tight-lipped some Kentuckians can be, there's the case of Vance Clem of Louisville. Some years ago, when he was 10, Vance announced to his parents, Mr. and Mrs. Robert Clem, that he couldn't see the blackboard in his class at school.

When his school work began to slump, he again blamed his drop-off on his inability to see the board. His concerned parents rushed him to the eye doctor for an examination.

"This boy's eyes are perfect," reported the doctor in due time. "Vance, why can't you see the blackboard?"

"Because," Vance said matter-of-factly, "there are a couple of tall boys in front of me and their heads are in the way."

When Elsie Kennedy was teaching at Murray State University she found herself putting on a few extra pounds. When she returned to the University of Kentucky as an instructor, she decided to join a health spa as a shortcut to a smaller dress size. But after gaining, not losing, two pounds the first month because of the voracious appetite the exercising gave her, she decided to buy a bicycle and peddle off the pounds with a nightly ride through Arcadia Park, the area in which she lived.

Since she hadn't ridden a bike in years, it was with some uncertainty that she embarked on her first ride. But the longer she rode without falling off, the greater her confidence grew.

By the time she was on her second lap around the park, a veritable host of neighborhood children had climbed on their bikes and were trailing behind her.

Starting the third round, her confidence was at about the 100 per cent level. Then what was intended as a compliment by one of the small fry riders following her caused her ego to drop lower than a well-digger's instep.

"You're not doing too bad, Miss Kennedy," said a little fellow who barely had graduated from training wheels. "In a few days you can ride out in the street with the rest of us."

Mrs. James Lechleiter just had time to get to the basement of their home on Lime Kiln Lane with her four-year-old son David when the April 3 tornado hit. When it passed and they came out of the basement, glass from broken windows was scattered all over the floor.

"I," David said in a resolute voice, "didn't do it!"

Children learn early to be quick enough with their wits not to talk themselves into a no-escape corner.

About a dozen or so years ago, Jimmy Robertson, then six, was walking down the street in Mt. Sterling when he met Garnett Chenault, a good friend of his grandfather, Harold Robertson.

"You any kin to Harold Robertson?" Chenault asked him.

"He's my grandfather," Jimmy confessed.

"Is he any account?" Chenault kidded.

"Well," Jimmy evaded, "that depends on what you want him for."

Having had two sons, I can appreciate the story Brucie Beard told in the *Breckinridge Herald News.*

It seems that some friends were having a cocktail party and the five-year-old son of the house wandered into the living room where he noticed a guest pick up an olive and eat it with great relish. He did the same and, since he'd never eaten one before, almost gagged.

However, when the guest took another olive and seemed to enjoy it as much as the first, the kid tried another one. Again he made a wry face, spit the obnoxious thing into his hand, and turned to the guest.

"I guess," he said, "you got all the good ones!"

Ed R. Hulett of Paducah has never forgotten a summation laid on him by his niece, Linda Walker, when she was only six.

"Uncle Eddie," she asked, "did you go to Sunday School when you were little?"

"Sure I did, honey," Uncle Eddie replied.

"I'll bet," Linda sighed, "that it wouldn't do me any good either."

It is the practice in the Episcopal Church that stoles of different colors are worn by ministers in the pulpit as part of their vestments to denote different seasons of the year and special occasions.

A blue stole denotes one season, a purple stole another, and so on.

A few years back in the fall, the Rev. Robert Shearer, then pastor of St. Luke's Church in Anchorage, was questioning the children of the parish about the significance of the different color stoles.

"I am wearing a green stole," he said. "Who can tell me what season it is?"

"This," one eight-year-old volunteered, "is football season!"

A Louisvillian I won't identify for fear of embarrassing the principal of the story took his family on a long western trip one summer. One of the stops was the Grand Canyon.

Among the family members on the trip was a nine-year-old son. The boy was an avid diarist who recorded the day's activities in considerable detail in his journal. Needless to say, the western junket provided much grist for his mill and he spent each night setting down in his diary what he had seen and done that day.

The boy was apparently impressed with the Grand Canyon. When they came to the first observation point, he peered down into the mile-deep ditch with eyes the size of saucers. However, his diary entry that night took only a few seconds to enter, all of which caused his father to wonder if the kid really appreciated what he had seen. So, after he was asleep, old dad decided to peek into the diary.

The entry for the day was tersely written, but the awe that the boy felt in seeing the Canyon came through loud and clear. For, in its entirety, the entry read:

"Today I spit a mile."

I've said it before and I'll say it again—children get right to the point and tell things the way they see them without a lot of buts, maybes, and howevers to muddle the issue.

A story that helps prove that contention is told by Thomas Wilson, a former Cynthiana newspaper editor.

Recently, his story goes, retired Harrison County contractor Carlyle Whitaker was working in a field at his farm near Cynthiana. He had every intention of baling hay, but the baler was exasperatingly regular in breaking the twine that is used in binding the bundles of hay.

Eventually the twine broke once too often and Whitaker made note of the occasion by addressing the machine with a few choice words that about peeled the bark off of nearby trees. His nine-year-old grandson, Douglas McIntosh, who had gone to the field with him, was somewhat taken aback.

"Grandpa," he chided him once things had calmed down, "you'll never get into heaven talking like that."

"I won't have to worry about that," Grandpa grinned. "You'll be there and you can let me in."

"No way," Doug shot back quickly. "If I get to messin' in God's business, He'll throw me out, too."

During one little league baseball season, reports a Louisville father who will remain nameless, his young son was preparing for a game.

"Who do you play today?" the father asked.

"The next to worst team in the league," came the answer.

"Well, then, you ought to win."

"I doubt it," the budding big leaguer replied honestly. "We're the worst team."

A father I know gives his daughter 20 cents each Sunday morning: one dime for the Sunday School collection plate, the other for her own use. On the way to church recently the child dropped one of the dimes and it rolled through a sidewalk grating.

"Oh, God," she sighed reverently, "there went your dime."

Some years ago a little girl in a first grade class at Owensboro didn't want to do her homework like the other children. The principal invited her to his office for a talk.

"Why do I have to learn to color and draw?" the practical-minded kid asked. "I won't do that when I marry."

INTRODUCTION   Kentuckians claim, and rightfully so, that their
home state has made significant contributions to the cultural,
political, and social development of this country. Dad, a Civil War
and Kentucky history enthusiast, often used his space in the
newspaper to delve into the past.

One of his subjects was John Fox Jr., author of The Trail of the
Lonesome Pine, who made the first genuine effort to accurately
depict the Kentucky mountain man as he really was, abstaining
from the more popular motif of using sarcasm and ridicule
to describe the mountaineer.

No other state can lay claim to the fact that it produced two
presidents who held office simultaneously. Nor can many other
states match Kentucky in the number of criminals and rogues who
roamed within its borders.

Throughout the years, Kentucky has supplied her fair share
to the legend and tall tales department, and my father did not
ignore these. Few states can claim the distinction of having an
honest-to-goodness lost silver mine within its borders. Kentucky
can. Likewise, the many Indian stories surrounding the formation
of western Kentucky's Reelfoot Lake rank at the top when it
comes to true folk history and Indian legend.

From Daniel Boone to the McCoy-Hatfield feud and the Floyd
Collins cave disaster, Kentucky has provided this nation with some
of its most exciting and colorful characters and adventures.
The following articles recall some of these bygone days and
personalities which have helped make Kentucky a truly unique
place.

CHAPTER 2

OUT OF KENTUCKY'S PAST

THE McCOY-HATFIELD FEUD   Every now and then something is recovered from behind the hazy curtain of time to renew the interest held for two mountain families who have become part and parcel of the folklore of America.

The families are the McCoys of Pike County, Kentucky, and the Hatfields of Mingo County, West Virginia.

They were principals in the feud that made a bloody battleground of the pinched valleys and rough mountains that fan out from both sides of Tug River, the border between the two states.

It has been around 65 years since the last shots were fired in the interfamily war. The feudists' rifles and long-barreled pistols today are museum pieces, silent reminders of the fighting which claimed the lives of more than 100 men, women and children between, roughly, the end of the Civil War and the late 1890s.

There were feuds elsewhere in Kentucky, and in other states, in those days, but none came near capturing and holding the imagination of the nation as did the McCoy-Hatfield vendetta.

Thus it was that the recent discovery on a Pike County hillside of the supposedly long-lost graves of four McCoy brothers and a sister rekindled great interest. All five were slain in the feud. The graves are marked only by creek stones. They are a short distance across Blackberry Creek, a shallow mountain stream, near where once stood the cabin of their father, clan-leader Randolph McCoy.

The four sons were Tolbert, Phamer (or Farmer), Randolph Jr. (or Bud), and Calvin. Allifair was the daughter.

Tolbert and Farmer, both grown, and Bud, just 13, were killed on an August day in 1882, the aftermath of an election-day shooting that took the life of Ellison Hatfield, a brother of Anderson "Devil Anse" Hatfield, leader of the clan. Allifair, 15, and Calvin, 18, were slain on New Year's night, 1887, when armed Hatfields beseiged and set fire to Randolph McCoy's cabin.

Mountain legend has it that Tolbert, Farmer and Bud were buried in a common grave on the hillside. Legend also holds that the bodies of Allifair and Calvin were laid out in the home of a neighbor, then buried beside their brothers in separate graves.

At any rate, headstones indicated three graves. Only one, that of Calvin, is marked. The name "Cal McCoy" was crudely chiseled on a thick, pointed creek stone. The other two stones are weatherbeaten, partially buried, and show no markings.

The way the discovery was played in newspapers all over the nation late last year proves that the McCoys and the Hatfields have become part of Americana, real life participants in the folklore of this nation. Their very names strike a romantic chord in the hearts of people who have never been near the Tug River country.

It's easy to understand why. The McCoys and Hatfields belong to a long-gone age of independence; an age when blood was very much thicker than water; when families stuck together and lived by the ancient tenet, "an eye for an eye."

When the first families moved into the Tug River country around 1800, they settled in the narrow flats along the creeks. In time, the children married and like as not moved up or down the creek, built a log cabin, and began family life.

Family units were closely knit. And they took pride in "name" and "honor." A grievance against one member of the family became a grievance against every member—the children, the in-laws and cousins once removed.

The law was far away. The county seat was a good two-day ride by horseback up creek beds and across roadless mountains. The only nearby courts were run by "squires" with little or no power to enforce judgments.

The settlement of a grievance usually was a personal matter between parties involved. If they could agree, they settled the affair peacefully. If not, they resorted to guns.

Thus, the mountain clans originated. One strong man emerged as the unquestioned leader, and at his call the clan would mount up and ride across the hills—generally with rifles flung across the saddles—to right a wrong, either imaginary or real.

Clan leaders Rand'l McCoy and Anse Hatfield were rawboned men who commanded the loyalty and respect of their followers. Neither was educated formally, but each had great native intelligence and tact enough to mold their clansmen into armies of sorts when the occasion arose.

They were rugged individualists, the McCoys and the Hatfields, self-reliant men many people like to imagine their ancestors were. They asked no quarter. They gave none. They accepted Nature in its most ungenerous mood and still made a living for large families from thin, unproductive land.

Both families were of Scotch-Irish origin and reflected the character of their forefathers, even reacting in much the same way those ancestors did under similar circumstances. There is a striking parallel between the vendettas of the Scotch Highlands and the Cumberland Mountain feuds.

A fist beating begot a fist beating along Blackberry Creek, a knifing begot a knifing. Finally, there was a killing and retaliation, and no turning back, not until the leaders were old men, tired and ready to rest.

By then both families had been bled almost white. And folks in the remote area stretching down Blackberry Creek to the Tug River and up Mate and Peter Creeks on the West Virginia side had lived in fear and anxiety for better than 30 years.

There are other reasons why the McCoy-Hatfield war fired the imagination of the nation as no other feud did. There was the long period of time the fighting raged. And the feud crossed state boundaries, pitting a family in Kentucky against one in West Virginia.

But most of all, perhaps, there were classic features which none of the other feuds had. Within the complexity of the vendetta was a trace of the Romeo-and-Juliet theme—the tragic story of lovers whose families were mortal enemies.

The true origin of the feud has never been determined, but the ill-fated Romeo-and-Juliet romance between Rosanna McCoy, daughter of Rand'l McCoy, and Johnson Hatfield, son of Devil Anse, did as much as anything else to make smoldering hatreds erupt into violence.

Many old-timers along Blackberry Creek say the trouble started in the Civil War when the McCoys, with one exception, sided with the Confederacy and the Hatfields with the Union. The one McCoy with Union sympathy was Harmon, one of Rand'l's six brothers. He joined a Union Army outfit headed by Anse Hatfield. Also in the band was Jim Vance, a Hatfield cousin.

In 1863, Harmon McCoy was shot and killed mysteriously. The McCoys said Vance did it. For the next three decades the families were at war.

For several years nothing more than fist fights, wild shots and threats developed. However, a dispute over a pig between Rand'l McCoy and Floyd Hatfield, a nephew of Devil Anse, came close to igniting real trouble in 1878.

It was the chance meeting of Rosanna McCoy and Johnson "Johnse" Hatfield two years later that primed the powder for the explosion. The place was a schoolyard on Blackberry Creek where a local election was held. Although it was a Kentucky affair, several Hatfields rode into the state to take part in the drinking and fighting that nearly always spiced the voting.

Also on hand were many McCoys, including Rosanna, a beautiful girl of 19 with red-brown hair. Before the day was over, Johnse had persuaded her to return home with him to be married.

Devil Anse refused to permit the marriage but did allow them to live in his cabin.

Later, still unmarried and expecting a baby, Rosanna returned to her father's home. Rand'l McCoy, then 65, was furious. He allowed her to live at home but, they say, never spoke to her again.

Hatred seethed. Then came the explosion that resulted in four deaths in August 1882.

Once again it was an election day in the Blackberry Creek schoolyard that was the setting. Late in the afternoon Tolbert McCoy and Elias Hatfield, a brother of Devil Anse, began to fight. When McCoy won, he immediately was challenged by Ellison Hatfield, a nephew of Devil Anse.

Being much larger, Ellison seemed about to break Tolbert's neck when 15-year-old Bill McCoy rushed to help his brother. The boy began to slash Ellison with a knife. Ellison, however, picked up a large rock and lunged to strike Tolbert McCoy. Then someone in the crowd pulled a pistol and pitched it to Farmer McCoy.

A shot rang out and Ellison slumped to the ground holding his stomach.

Before further trouble could erupt, John and Floyd Hatfield, both Kentucky magistrates and nephews of the wounded man, arrested Tolbert, Farmer and Bud McCoy, thinking the latter was Bill, the boy who had done the knifing.

Ellison Hatfield was moved across the creek to the home of an uncle, Ransom Hatfield. The prisoners were kept over night at John Hatfield's before starting for jail at Pikeville, the county seat.

Next morning 40 armed men led by Devil Anse Hatfield surprised the group, seized the three McCoy brothers, and galloped across the Tug and into West Virginia. If Ellison Hatfield lived, the boys would go free, Devil Anse proclaimed; if he died, then they, too, would die.

Three days later Ellison died.

Late on the night of August 9, the McCoys were slipped back across the river, tied to pawpaw bushes, and shot. Their bodies were discovered the next morning, moved home on sleds, and buried on the hillside not far from their father's cabin.

The feud was on in earnest after that. In the years that followed, folks throughout the area took up arms with one side or the other.

Kentucky warrants were issued for the arrest of 23 Hatfields, but the governor of West Virginia refused to honor them. The McCoys were deputized and partisans of both families died as they made raids into West Virginia in an effort to capture the Hatfields.

Tragedy continued to stalk the family of Rand'l McCoy. Bill, who had been involved in the election day knifing, died from grieving, they say, over the death of Bud, the brother mistaken for him and executed.

Meanwhile, Rosanna gave birth to Johnse Hatfield's child, a girl, but the infant died at the age of eight months. Rosanna, in turn, "grieved" herself to death in a short time.

The most violent act of the feud remained to be played on New Year's night, 1887. That was when the Hatfields set fire to Rand'l McCoy's cabin, then shot and killed Allifair and Calvin as they tried to escape. They also shot and brutally beat Mrs. McCoy, who died two years later.

The two who died in the siege were buried on the hill near the graves of Tolbert, Farmer and Bud.

Violence continued to flare off and on for years after that, but the end was in sight.

Kentucky renewed its efforts to capture the Hatfield ring leaders. Tom Chambers, Pliant, Sam and Doc Mayhor, Andrew Varney, Alex Messer, Ellison Mounts, Tom Wallace, Val Hatfield (a brother of Anse) and others were seized. Mounts was convicted of the murder of Allifair McCoy and hanged in Pikeville early in 1890.

Johnse Hatfield wasn't arrested until 1898—10 years after he was indicted. He was tried and sentenced to life in prison. Later he was pardoned.

By then Devil Anse had retired to a farm miles from the Tug. There he died in 1921. Rand'l McCoy—with seven of his 14 children and wife victims of the feud—died at the home of a nephew in 1915 of burns received when he fell into an open fire.

In time the surviving McCoys scattered from Blackberry Creek. The bitterness grew less as the years passed. The graves of Calvin, Farmer, Bud, Tolbert and Allifair were lost in the tangle of weeds and sassafras bushes. Their headstones were covered by leaves and soil.

Eventually the location was forgotten. The site was rediscovered a year ago when Wallace G. Smith, a Williamson, West Virginia, banker, learned of the approximate location. Smith and William Blackburn, a Williamson accountant, found the graves hidden under waist-high brush and weeds.

News of the discovery, however, didn't spread far until late in 1957, when an engineer came across the stones in making a survey for a coal company. Now Smith, Blackburn and others are attempting to have the grave site preserved and a suitable marker placed nearby.

For the graves are about the last remaining visible marker that connects the McCoys to the locale where they became part of the folklore of America. (1/19/58)

RELUCTANT REBEL   History, through the words of those who record it, has been known to take an almost grudging attitude toward some of the characters who have played leading roles in the passing parade of human events.

But perhaps in no instance has history been more reluctant to judge objectively one of its own than in the case of Jefferson Davis, the Civil War president of the Confederate States of America who was born in a Kentucky log house 150 years ago.

The sesquicentennial of Davis' birth, then, seems a logical time to review in an unimpassioned manner what may well be a classic example of history slander.

For although some historians now refer to Davis as one of the most misunderstood men in history, the majority still brand him as the brains of the secession plot.

There is indisputable proof that Davis was a reluctant secessionist who cast his lot with the South because of his basic conviction in the right of each state to run its own affairs. Still, most generally he has been pictured as a hard-headed leader whose bad judgment cost the South any chance it had for victory and whose obstinacy only prolonged a lost cause.

Strangely, the same historians who have forgiven and made apologies for the wartime mistakes of Robert E. Lee and even Abraham Lincoln, the Kentucky-born president of the Union, have been strongest in magnifying the faults of Davis.

Yet remembering that the South was an agrarian nation without the arms, ammunition and industry necessary to keep armies in the field against a mighty industrial foe, is it safe to assume that any man could have done as well as Davis, much less better?

Bearing in mind, too, that Lincoln, with the greater population and resources of the North at his disposal, held grave doubts at times that the Union would survive, could anyone have surpassed Davis in holding together the Confederacy for so long with so little?

Because of the grudging attitude of history toward Davis, the solid contributions he made to the country as a soldier, statesman and cabinet member have been minimized.

For 11 years—from age 16 to 27—he was in Army service. After retiring he returned to soldiering and became one of the heroes of the Mexican War. While representing Mississippi, his adopted state, in the U.S. Senate, he became one of the great American statesmen; as Secretary of War under Franklin Pierce, he was one of the most successful secretaries of all time.

In most respects, Davis personifies the mixed emotions and divided loyalties found throughout the nation, North and South, before and during the Civil War.

On the one hand, he held great respect for the Union; on the other hand, his philosophy of government was based on states' rights, those including secession if sufficiently provoked.

These to-some-conflicting convictions were voiced in a speech he delivered to the Senate in 1850.

"If I have a superstition which governs my mind, it is a superstitious reverence for the Union," he said then.

"But I draw a sharp distinction between nullification and secession. As long as a State remains in the Union, I countenance no violation of federal law constitutionally adopted.

"I maintain, however, the conviction that Mississippi or Massachusetts or any other sovereign State has the right to withdraw from the Federal Union."

So however strong his feelings about the Union, his belief in states' rights was stronger. In the end Davis, the reluctant secessionist, followed Mississippi, his state, out of the Union and into the tragedy that followed. He summed up his logic repeatedly this way:

"If the Declaration of Independence justified the secession of 3,000,000 colonists in 1776, why does it not justify the secession of 5,000,000 Southerners in 1861?"

Davis also viewed the institution of slavery with mixed feelings.

For nearly a decade before the war he warned the South that slavery was on the way out, that machines already had begun to displace human muscles. To that end he urged southern states to industrialize, to become more and more self-sufficient for the health of their economy.

Still, he opposed sudden emancipation of the slaves as northern abolitionists advocated. Davis felt the only hope for improvement in the conditions of the slave lay in the slow process of fitting him for economic competition with whites. Sudden emancipation well might destroy the race, he held.

A favorite pastime of historical writers long has been to draw a comparison between Davis and Lincoln since they were born within eight months and 80 miles of each other in Kentucky. The comparison shows Lincoln retaining a homely, frontier personality, and Davis developing a broad culture and becoming known as a typical southern aristocrat.

In reality, it is a paradox that Davis should have been so typed. By birth and early environment he was probably as much a frontiersman as Lincoln.

Both were born sons of roamers to whom the next stop always loomed as the promised land. But fate gave Davis one break it denied Lincoln—a later-successful older (23 years) brother who took an almost paternal interest in the fifth son and tenth and last child of Samuel and Jane Cook Davis. It was this older brother, Joseph, who became a lawyer and then a wealthy Mississippi planter, and who saw that his younger brother received the education that prepared him for the role he was to play in later years.

Samuel Davis, the father, was a Georgian who fought in the Revolution. His own family was well on its way when he came to Kentucky in 1793 and settled in Mercer County. A short time later he migrated farther west to a 600-acre tract in Christian County at what now is the village of Fairview.

Although his first four boys had been given Biblical names, the fifth son was named for the President that Samuel Davis admired so much. Convinced he would be the last child, the elder Davis added a middle name—"Finis."

The older brother, Joseph, was finishing law study in Hopkinsville and preparing to move to Mississippi when the child was born. Two years later the entire family followed him to Mississippi.

However, that did not break the Kentucky ties of Jefferson Finis Davis. The state of his birth was to pattern much of his life—his education, the friends he made, the first woman he married, the aspirations he held for the Confederacy.

When he was seven Jefferson Davis, with Joseph's help, returned to Kentucky to study at St. Thomas, a boys school run by Dominican friars near Springfield—this despite the fact the family was Baptist.

It is ironic that while Davis, thanks to his then-prominent older brother, was receiving as good an education as was possible in 1815-16, Abraham Lincoln was growing up without benefit of any schooling only 30 miles west in Hardin County.

Davis studied for two years at St. Thomas before going home. But in 1821, he headed back to Kentucky to enter Transylvania University.

At Transylvania, Davis' closest friend was a tall, young man from Mason County, five years older and two classes ahead, who 30 years later was to become third-ranking Confederate general in the war. The friend was Albert Sidney Johnston.

In 1824, Davis received an appointment to West Point. His acceptance of the appointment was prompted by the fact that Johnston had gone there two years earlier.

Kentucky remained foremost in Davis' life once he left West Point and entered the Army. He was sent to fight in the Indian Wars. Popular historical fiction holds that Davis was the officer who swore in as captain of Illinois volunteers a backwoods lawyer who signed simply as "A. Lincoln."

At one post where Davis served, the commander was Zachary Taylor, a Virginian who had settled in Kentucky. Davis met and fell in love with his youngest daughter, Sarah Knox. A year later he resigned from the Army and on July 17, 1835, they were married in the Louisville home of the bride's aunt on what is now Brownsboro Road.

Following the marriage the couple moved to Mississippi. But after only two months Mrs. Davis died of malaria.

Grief-stricken, Davis remained in Mississippi and lost himself in managing the giant plantation of his brother. His entry into politics came in 1843 when he was elected to the state legislature. In 1845, he remarried—this time to Varina Howell.

The Mexican War interrupted his political career, but the interruption made Davis a national figure. He emerged from the war a great hero.

His wartime reputation led to Davis' being appointed to the U.S. Senate. He remained in the Senate until 1859 when he ran for Governor of Mississippi, losing by 1,000 votes.

When Pierce was elected President, Davis was Secretary of War. During those four years he was at his peak, many biographers say. He reformed and enlarged West Point, revamped the Army, had the Rocky Mountains surveyed for the first time, and erected many of the fortifications which later were to stall the Confederate Army.

Once Pierce's term was ended, Davis returned to the Senate and remained there until, after Mississippi followed South Carolina in secession, he resigned in January 1861.

In rapid order six other states seceded, a convention of southern states was held, and Davis was elected President. He was inaugurated February 18, 1861, two weeks before Lincoln. The firing on Sumter followed and the war was on.

During the four bloody years of war, Davis was beset by ever-increasing problems. A hostile cabinet added to his task of keeping the ill-equipped, ill-fed, outnumbered Confederate armies in the field. By late 1863, the failure of European governments to recognize the Confederate nation, plus the economic pressure of the Union blockade, caused Davis to grow pessimistic.

Early in 1865, the Confederate lines guarding Richmond, the capital, began to buckle, forcing Davis and his cabinet to flee farther South. On April 9 Lee surrendered to Grant at Appomattox Courthouse.

Davis held his last cabinet meeting April 11 in an abandoned railroad car at Greensboro, North Carolina. After two days of debate, it was decided to sue for peace.

The next night, however, Lincoln was assassinated. Davis, knowing the South had lost an influential friend at the moment she most needed such a person in Washington, expressed sorrow.

On May 1 President Andrew Johnson issued a proclamation charging Davis with complicity in the death of Lincoln. A reward of $100,000 was offered for his capture.

Davis was taken prisoner at Irwinville, Georgia, on May 10. The story was circulated that he had been seized while trying to escape by dressing in woman's clothing.

What actually happened was dramatic enough. Two troops of cavalry were hot on Davis' trail. Before dawn on May 10 they reached the camp where Davis and his wife—who had joined him three days before—were asleep in a tent. It being dark when he was awakened, Davis picked up what he thought was his raglan coat. The garment actually was his wife's, so nearly like his own as to be mistaken for it. As he left the tent, Mrs. Davis threw a shawl across his shoulders.

The raglan and the shawl, of course, were what gave rise to the rumors that he was trying to escape disguised as a woman.

Davis was removed to Fortress Monroe, Virginia, by boat and spent two years in prison while the government debated whether to try him for treason.

Finally he was released from prison on May 15, 1867, on bail posted by Horace Greeley and others who had been his lifelong opponents.

Davis moved to Canada but soon returned to Mississippi where his once-prosperous plantation lay in ruins.

In his last years, Davis came to Kentucky many times. His final visit was in 1886, to dedicate the Baptist Church which still stands on the site of his birthplace at Fairview.

"Wherever I go, when I come here I feel that this is my own, my native land," he said then.

Davis died in 1889, and with his death the Confederate escapade was officially closed. . . .

A man whose family had followed one tide of emigration moving through Kentucky and had gone north to come under the influence of nonslaveholding people was the victor.

A man whose family went south and came under the influence of the slaveholding cotton planters was the loser.

Who can say what might have been the result if Lincoln had gone south and Davis had gone north? (6/1/58)

THE STORY OF   If all the words written about Daniel Boone
DANIEL BOONE   were laid end to end they undoubtedly would
reach from Pennsylvania, the state of his birth, to Kentucky, the state of his adoption, to Missouri, the state of his death, in an unbroken bridge of glowing romantic phrases.

Perhaps no man of his ilk in all American history has so whetted the imagination of both writer and reader as Boone has done over a period of more than 170 years.

For Boone personifies the frontiersman, the fearless hunter and explorer, who created the mold into which Davy Crockett, Kit Carson, Paul Bunyan and many another real or imagined hero was poured

He was a man whose very weaknesses—aggressive individualism, inability to adjust to a settled community, financial ignorance— have made him greater in stature as the years have paraded past.

As a result, a seemingly endless succession of books, sketches, profiles, volumes, even poems has been inspired by his daring life and times.

The first of the Boone stories was done in 1783 or 1784 by John Filson, Kentucky's first historian. John James Audubon, the naturalist, upon meeting Boone in the early 1800s, was moved to retell his story. His death in 1829 so stirred Lord Byron, the English poet, that he composed his "Eulogy on Col. Boon and Choice of Life."

Almost every American historian since then has added material to the Boone collection. Genealogists have combed his family tree from tap root to top branch. Fiction writers have woven him into novels of the frontier. Movies have glamorized him.

Yet, in spite of all those factual and fictional works, there still are conflicts and blind spots in the Daniel Boone story. Some of the points are important, some trivial, but they illustrate how muddied are a few of the facts directly relating to Boone.

For instance, there are these questions—among others—to which the authorities offer different answers:

When did Daniel Boone actually probe into Kentucky for the first time?

Most historians give the year as 1769. Still, facts exist which indicate that he wintered near Prestonsburg two years before that. And it is possible that he was in Kentucky as early as 1753 without knowing it.

Whom did Boone really marry?

Genealogists and biographers say it was Rebecca Bryan; written records do not substantiate that belief completely.

What size man was Boone?

He generally is pictured as tall, spare, and sinewy; Audubon described him as "approaching the gigantic." In contrast, others described him as being 5 feet 8 or 9 inches tall. The rifle reputedly made for him would fit a man no taller than 5 feet 11.

What was Boone's feeling toward other people?

Some contended that he was kind and friendly and liked company. Others believe he was adverse to most white men and that it may have been he who coined the phrase "damn yankees."

Where, exactly, was Boonesborough, the fort he erected in Kentucky?

It definitely was on the Madison County side of the Kentucky River and most authorities believe it was below the mouth of Otter Creek in what now is the government-owned reservation surrounding Lock and Dam No. 10. However, Boone, in his account of the founding of the fort, did not mention a creek. He said merely it was "at a salt lick, 60 yards from the river on the south side."

And, of course, there is the recurring question: Do the bodies of Boone and his wife really lie in the grave at Frankfort bearing his name?

Many sources in Missouri, where he died, say no; Kentucky authorities say yes, emphatically.

On most points in the Daniel Boone story there is little or no conflict. The experts agree that he possessed an indescribable something that over the years raised him to a pinnacle while his equally brave contemporaries on the Kentucky scene—his own brother Squire, Kenton, McAfee, Harrod, Logan—have sunk into semi-oblivion.

The Boone saga as known to every school child is basically true in its broad outline. Even without embellishment, it has a storybook-like ring.

The only conflict—and it is purely technical—in the early part of the Boone story is the date of his birth in Berks County, Pennsylvania. According to the Julian, or "old style" calendar, it was October 22, 1734. But by the Georgian, or "new style" calendar, which added 11 days to the old-style dates, it was November 2, 1734.

In brief, the well-known highlights go like this:

Boone was one of 11 children born to Squire and Sarah Morgan Boone, both English Quakers. He attended a school taught by his uncle only briefly and didn't exactly set the scholastic woods afire. In fact, his father is supposed to have said: "Let the girls do the spelling; Dan will do the shooting."

From boyhood he acquired the ability to "think Indian," an ability he put to good use later. In 1750 the entire Boone tribe moved to Virginia, then to North Carolina, and in a short time Daniel was exploring the forests that spread across the mountains to the west.

He took part in Braddock's campaign against the French and Indians in 1755, married, and determined to transplant his family to Kentucky, which he had explored as far west as the Falls of the Ohio by 1771.

After being turned back in his first effort to move his and five other families to Kentucky in 1773, during which time one of his sons was killed by Indians, Boone met with the Cherokees and bought land they claimed on the south side of the Kentucky River. Then he undertook to carve a road from the settlements in the Yadkin River Valley in North Carolina through the wilderness to the Kentucky River where he and his party erected a fort they called Boonesborough.

In June 1774, Boone was successful in bringing his family to the fort. "My wife and daughter," he wrote later," being the first white women that stood on the banks of the Kentucky River."

There followed many brushes with the Indians. Boone was captured by Shawnees in 1778. Adopted as the son of Chief Blackfish, he was named Sheltowee, or Big Turtle, and accepted into the tribe. The ceremony consisted of plucking out all his hair except for a scalp lock and washing in a river to remove his "white blood."

He was held for four months before he escaped and traveled 160 miles in four days to warn Boonesborough of an impending raid.

After representing Kentucky's Fayette County in the Virginia legislature in 1781, Boone began to feel the first cramps of civilization in the area he had opened for settlement. And, because of defective titles, he lost his vast holdings in Kentucky.

As he explained it, "Unacquainted with niceties of the law, the few lands I was enabled to locate were, through my own ignorance, swallowed up by better claims."

In 1788, the last of his land—that at Boone's Station near Athens—was wrested from him by a superior title. By then Kentucky no longer was a log-cabin settlement. The rumble for separate statehood was being heard. These changes in his former wilderness paradise plus his land misfortunes made Boone more and more restless.

Disheartened and in dire need, he moved to the mouth of Limestone Creek, the site of present-day Maysville, where river travelers landed in interior Kentucky. There he eked out a bare existence by operating a tavern and by digging ginseng which he carried with pelts to market in Philadelphia.

After a short time he left Kentucky entirely and moved to the Kanawha Valley of what is now West Virginia. Once again he was elected to serve in the Virginia legislature, after which he moved to unsettled Tennessee before returning to Kentucky and Nicholas County in 1795.

He came back to apply for the contract to repair and improve the Wilderness Road, the path through the wilds he had laid out and marked more than 20 years earlier. But he was unable to get the contract.

Boone's affairs went from bad to worse. It perhaps should be pointed out that his condition was not because of a lack of gratitude or sympathy on the part of Kentuckians. A county had been named for him shortly after Kentucky became a state.

Rather, this apparent neglect was due mainly to the fact his true state of affairs was not known.

Anyway, in 1797 or 1799—the date is obscure—Boone moved again, this time to Missouri. There he found things more to his liking. Hunting was good, and neighbors few and far between. He was appointed magistrate by the Spanish crown and held court under a tree that became known as "Boone's Judgment Tree."

He died in Missouri at 86. Mrs. Boone had died in 1818, two years earlier.

Of all the basic facts, perhaps the greatest difference of opinion exists over the year of Boone's first visit to Kentucky. The year generally named is 1769, when he accompanied John Finley through Cumberland Gap and far into the interior. Boone described the journey this way:

"It was the first of May, 1769, that I resigned my domestic happiness of the Yadkin River to wander through the country of Kentucky. . . .

"On the 7th of June . . . we found ourselves on Red River and from the top of an eminence saw with pleasure the beautiful level of Kentucky."

This eminence was the famed Pilot Knob in Powell County which became a landmark later for travelers along the Wilderness Road.

Nowhere does Boone refer to this trip with Finley as being his first into Kentucky. Most authorities agree it was his first venture far into the interior, but many insist he had been in the area previously, possibly without knowing he was.

As early as 1753, Boone definitely had explored along the line between Kentucky and Virginia. And there are good indications that in 1767 he had entered Kentucky down on the headwaters of the Levisa Fork of the Big Sandy River, undoubtedly through the spectacular Breaks of Sandy gorge, and wintered at a salt lick 10 miles west of Prestonsburg. With him then were William Hall and perhaps Squire Boone, his brother.

Until fairly recently there had been little doubt as to Boone's wife. Early historians had said the girl was Rebecca Bryan, daughter of Joseph Bryan, and the wedding date was August 14, 1756.

However, four years ago James T. Adams, president of Big Laurel College in Big Laurel, Virginia, probed in the matter and came up with heretofore unpublished findings that indicate the accepted facts well may be wrong. In scouring through deed books in Lee County, Virginia, Adams came across this set of conflicting facts.

In Book 7 is a deed transferring title of a tract of land from Benjamin Dickenson and wife Elizabeth to Elisha Adams, by which the Dickensons defended against themselves and the heirs of Daniel Boone because of Boone's wife's one-sixth interest in the estate of her deceased brother, David McKinney. According to the deed, Boone's wife was definitely identified as a sister of David McKinney, which would indicate she was not a Bryan as generally supposed.

Further research uncovered an undated letter to John McKinney signed by Daniel Boone in which he saluted "Dear Bro. & Sister" and offered to sell them his share in David McKinney's estate for $60.

Next, Adams dug through old files and brought to light the Boone marriage records of Rowan and Wilkes Counties, North Carolina. These records failed to show Daniel Boone married anybody, but they did show that one James Boone married Rebecca Bryan, daughter of Joseph Bryan, on August 14, 1756, the day the biographers and genealogists have recorded her marriage to Daniel Boone.

Which brings up the perplexing question: Is it possible that Boone's real name was James Daniel Boone and that this fact has evaded the historians for nearly two centuries.

To add further fuel to the fire, Adams found a diary kept by George Soelle, a touring Moravian preacher, which contained this entry:

". . . and next day went to Nathaniel Boone's . . . whose wife is a daughter of Joseph Bryan . . . ."

If this statement is correct, then did Nathaniel Boone (as proven by the diary), James Boone (as proven by marriage records) and Daniel Boone (as the historians always have said) all marry daughters of Joseph Bryan?

Is it possible that three Boones married three daughters of the same man? Or is it possible that Daniel Boone never really married Rebecca Bryan, but someone else named Rebecca, and in some year other than 1756?

That question likely will never be resolved. Nor will the question of whether or not Boone liked and could get along with other people. His own words are somewhat contradictory.

"I never have been able to trust a yankee," he was quoted as having once said, "and I never have been deceived by an Indian."

One biographer dug up this statement:

"I had rather possess a good fowling piece, with two faithful dogs, and traverse the wilderness with one or two friendly Indians in quest of a hoard of buffaloes or deer, than to possess the best township and spend my time in the company of yankees."

It has been pointed out that his great objective appears to have been to live as remote as possible from all except his own family.

As if to refute that idea, however, Boone—and, incidentally, he seems always to have signed his name "Boon"—said at another time:

"Two darling sons and a brother I have lost by savage hands, which also have taken 40 valuable horses and an abundance of cattle. Many dark and sleepless nights I have separated from the cheerful society of friends and good companions."

In numerous descriptions he was pictured as a kind and mild-mannered man who spoke in a soft voice and who made friends easily.

But in no instance has there been a greater degree of difference of opinion than in the matter of where Boone is really buried. To the satisfaction of most historians, he was first buried in Missouri, then removed with the consent of the Missouri legislature and reinterred with great ceremony in Frankfort. Mrs. Boone is also reinterred there.

Despite that, periodic claims have been made that it is not the bones of Boone that lie in Frankfort.

As recently as this year, the St. Charles, Missouri, Chamber of Commerce claimed that it has documentary proof that the body moved from Defiance, Missouri, in 1845 was not that of Boone, but a total stranger. Therefore, the group reasoned, it would be only right if Kentucky allowed the remains of Mrs. Boone to be brought back to Missouri and put beside her husband.

The Kentucky Historical Society scoffed at the claim, as it had done at similar claims earlier.

And so the conflicts go.

While there may be room for honest doubt as to when Boone first saw Kentucky or the name of the girl he really married, there is no room for doubt about the significant role he played in the settlement of the West. Nor is there doubt that he was a remarkable man.

Perhaps he was illiterate, but there is genuine eloquence in the way he described Kentucky in the journal of his 1769 trip.

"Nature here," he wrote, "was a series of wonders and a fund of delight. Here she displayed her ingenuity and industry in a variety of flowers and fruits, beautifully colored. . . . No populous city with all the variety of commerce and stately structures could afford so much pleasure as the beauties of nature found in this country."

If, as some say, Boone was suspicious of other white men, it may be that his experiences justified such suspicions. Or it may be that Boone viewed the rapid influx of settlers into Kentucky with a feeling of dismay. As he himself said in 1783:

"Peace crowns Kentucky's sylvan shade; now the scene is changed."

As the Kentucky scene changed, Boone moved farther away from ever-expanding civilization.

Kentucky became a land of peace. The Indians Boone had found were gone. So were the wild animals he had hunted. Forests had given way to fields. Mansions had sprung up in place of log cabins. The days of the pioneer hazards were over.

And the man who had blazed the trail for the westward march had become an American legend. (5/1/55)

JUST FOURSCORE AND SEVEN YEARS AGO . . . It now being fourscore and seven years since Abraham Lincoln delivered his famous "four score and seven years ago" speech at Gettysburg, we'll probably be hearing an awful lot about the War Between the States before 1950 has been stored away in the mothballs and history books.

All of which will focus attention again on the personalities, the leaders, who took part in that four-year-long struggle, one of the bloodiest and bitterest intranation wars in history.

Although it was a professed neutral state, Kentucky nevertheless provided some of the most colorful and influential leaders, military and political, of the war. The state was split right up the middle, like an overripe Georgia watermelon, in sentiment and, consequently, furnished cannon fodder for both sides.

For instance, the Presidents of both the North and the South, Abraham Lincoln and Jefferson Davis, were natives of this state. And so was the man at whom the first shot of the war was fired, Major Robert H. Anderson of Louisville.

Anderson, later a major general of distinction, was in command of the army garrison at Fort Sumter, South Carolina, when it was fired upon by the Confederates on April 12, 1861. Anderson refused to surrender the fort and his small force held out for two days.

He was set free with full military honors after the surrender came and later took part in many important battles as a general with the Department of the Cumberland.

Kentucky-born general officers were, figuratively speaking, a dime a dozen in both armies. The state furnished at least 16 generals for the Union and nine for the Confederacy.

To show how Kentucky's sentiment was divided during the war and how it furnished men for both sides, at one time before the trouble started three Kentuckians were on the staff at West Point. When war was declared two of the three, Joseph J. Reynolds of Flemingsburg and Ormsby Mitchell of Union County, were major generals with the Union. The third, Simon B. Buckner, was a lieutenant general with the South.

Incidentally, Buckner was one of the truly great figures of his day before, during and after the war. Following his graduation from West Point and his teaching career there, he served as inspector general for the Kentucky Home Guard, a position he resigned in 1861 to take up arms for the South. He was in command at Fort Donelson when that strong point fell and was a federal prisoner of war for six months before being released in a prisoner exchange. After the war he was elected governor in 1887 and in 1896 was Gold Democrat candidate for vice president of the United States.

How quickly the wounds of war can be forgotten is proven perfectly in the case of Buckner and John Palmer, the man who was Gold Democrat choice for President in 1896. Palmer, too, was a Kentuckian, having been born at Eagle Creek. And he, too, had been a general in the war. However, he had fought for the Union.

Like Buckner, Palmer was one of the most prominent figures in national politics after the war. Taking up residence in Illinois, he served, in order, as governor and U.S. senator before the unsuccessful North-South merger to win the Presidency.

Another nationally prominent Kentuckian to take an active military part in the war was John C. Breckinridge of Lexington. A lawyer by profession, he served as a major in the Mexican War and was elected vice president of the United States in 1857. He was a candidate for president against Lincoln in 1860 and received most of the southern electoral votes. After that he served as U.S. senator for a short while before resigning to join the Confederacy as a major general. He fought at Corinth, Stone's Creek and Chattanooga before being made secretary of war for the South in the closing months of the war.

The highest ranking Kentuckian in the war was Albert Sidney Johnston, born at Washington. A West Pointer and a professional soldier, he resigned his commission to join the Confederate cause in 1861 and later became one of the just five full generals before being killed at Shiloh.

John Hunt Morgan, the famous Confederate cavalry leader, generally is thought to have been a Kentuckian. He was, but by adoption not birth. General Morgan, perhaps the most romantic figure of the entire war, was born in Alabama and came to Lexington as a young boy. He was killed in 1864 at Greenville, Tennessee.

Other famous generals from Kentucky who fought for the North included Richard W. Johnson, Francis P. Blair, John Pope, Edward Spriggs, Thomas J. Wood, Joseph J. Reynolds, John A. McClernard, Thomas L. Crittenden, Benjamin G. Brown, Benjamin H. Helm, William Preston, L. H. Rousseau and Speed S. Fry. Those with the Confederacy included Lloyd Tilghman, Charles W. Field, Humphrey Marshall, Gustavus W. Smith and John B. Hood. (2/14/50)

FRIEND TO THE MOUNTAINEER   Those who love trees no doubt break out in a cold sweat at the mere thought of the number of stately pines that have been felled to provide paper on which to write about the Kentucky mountains.

And only a total stranger to the English language could regard as complimentary most of the things that have been written about the hills that thrust their timber-sided slopes up toward the clouds in the eastern extremity of the state.

The mountains have long been a target of misunderstanding and of downright erroneous writing, much of it composed by writers who never were within a telephone call of the heart of Kentucky's truly mountainous section. Consequently, the countless fact-skimpy books, magazine articles and even newspaper stories pieced together by these long-range writers have, in many instances, painted a completely false picture of the hills and of the people who lived for years in semi-isolation behind their rugged ridges.

But not everything written about the mountains has been uncomplimentary; not all the articles have been by persons unfamiliar and unsympathetic with the philosophy and—to some, crude—customs of the mountain people. The writer who perhaps best understood the mountains and their natives and whose work has done much to counter the false impressions created by others was, appropriately, a Kentuckian—John William Fox, Jr.

Fox, whose birth and burial places are at Paris, Kentucky, wrote about the mountains and about the tight-lipped but hospitable people who scratched a bare living from the thin soil of the region with a knowledge that came from having studied both subjects first hand. During the 25 years he was writing his dozen or so best-selling books and 45 short stories, he lived in the mountains and made numerous trips into the remote sections of Leslie, Letcher, Perry, Clay, Bell, Harlan and Pike counties where two ranges of mountains all but cut off residents from the outside world. Often he spent days at a time living at the cabins of persons who later turned up as characters in one or another of his stories.

For instance, one of Fox's most famous characters was "Devil" Judd Tolliver in *The Trail of the Lonesome Pine*. Rather than just being the creature of a fertile imagination, Tolliver was a real person, indeed. His real-life counterpart was "Devil" John Wright, who lived along the Kentucky-Virginia border near the present town of Jenkins, Kentucky.

Wright was a famous figure, supposedly having fought on both sides during the Civil War. Those who knew him claim that his greatest regret was that he didn't quite break even in this life— that he killed 32 men and only sired 31 children. During the time Fox knew him, Wright was serving as a Kentucky peace officer and helping the Consolidation Coal Company buy up land options in Letcher and Pike counties.

In reality, the mountaineers owe Fox a lasting debt of gratitude. He described them in their hill-locked surroundings in an accurate manner. He used the material so abundant in that section and wove it with a master touch into romantic, gripping stories that emphasized over and over again the deep-rooted honesty and self-effacing, naturally hospitable nature of the proud people of the hills. Not once did he sneer at them or make light of their educational backwardness; instead, he brought out their finer, nobler qualities.

Few authors have surpassed Fox in the fine art of description. His word picture of specific areas in such of his books as *The Little Shepherd of Kingdom Come,* one of the first books published in America to sell more than a million copies, and *The Trail of the Lonesome Pine,* being made into a motion picture for the third time, are so clear that even now, some 40 years later, those off-the-beaten-path sections are recognizable.

Up until now, little has been done to remember Fox, the man who pictured the mountains of his native state in a different—favorable —light. Surprisingly, little has been written about the man himself.

47

And except for a bronze plaque mounted on an old millstone at the entrance to the farm where he was born and a plain stone in the Paris cemetery, there are no markers in his memory.

However, in a short time Paris will have a lasting memorial to Fox in the form of a library. It will contain several of his manuscripts written in his own handwriting, the desk at which he worked, some of his correspondence and books as well as other personal items, and these will be housed in Duncan Tavern, the historic old building that stands just behind the Bourbon County Courthouse a block from Paris' main street.

The library will take up one entire room of the stone tavern, built in 1788 and restored by the Kentucky Society, Daughters of the American Revolution, in the late 1930s.

Personal items to go into the library are being furnished by the novelist's sister, Miss Minnie C. Fox, who now lives at Big Stone Gap, Virginia, where the family moved in 1890. The manuscripts and many of the letters will be presented by Scribner's, the publishing house that handled the Fox novels.

If those who spend their writing hours scouring books—and, it often seems, looking under wet stones—for materal on which to base the so-called biographical motion pictures ever run out of prospects, then they could do no worse than to spend a little time checking the life and times of Fox. For his story contains enough of the stock ingredients—romantic background, cloak-and-dagger experiences, lost and regained health, ill-fated romance, death at the height of fame—to satisfy the most exacting movie maker.

To start at the beginning, Fox was born at Stony Point, some seven miles south of Paris, in 1863, the eldest son of John William Fox and his second wife, Minerva Carr Fox. His father, though born in Clark County, Kentucky, was from an old-line Virginia family; his mother was a native of Mayslick, Kentucky.

The elder Fox's first wife was Catherine Hill Rice of Bath County, and she bore him three sons—James W., Sidney A., and Everett B. Two years after she died in 1860, Fox married Miss Carr. To them were born five sons and two daughters, the first being John William Jr.

The author's father was from a schoolteaching family and he gave more than 40 years of his life to the profession. His first school was at Twyman's Branch in 1849 when he was 19 years of age. Later he taught at the old Jefferson Academy near Lullbegrud and in 1857 took over as headmaster at Sharpsburg Academy in Bath County. In 1861, after the death of his first wife, he taught at Mayslick Academy and the next year moved to Stony Point.

During the struggling days of Kentucky's post-Civil War school system, his deep desire to see his neighbors' children educated often outran his meager income, and family funds usually were low.

Miss Nell Buckner of Paris, a long-time friend of the family and with whom Miss Minnie Fox visits each summer, recalls stories of how the elder Fox would take orphans into his home to live while they went to school.

Besides teaching, Fox was a surveyor, serving as Bourbon County surveyor for many years. He also was a botanist and geologist, collecting and exhibiting geological samples. In reality, his enthusiasm for geology, which rubbed off on his son James, indirectly caused John Fox Jr. to go to the mountains in later years for the first time.

James, his older half-brother, was the first teacher of John Fox Jr. Later he completed his early schooling under his father's exacting tutelage and entered Transylvania College in Lexington at the age of 15. While in school there, Fox met James Lane Allen, then Kentucky's most famous contributor in the field of literature. Although many years of age separated the two, there is some evidence that they became fairly fast friends and some say Allen influenced Fox in his later decision to become a writer.

After two years at Transylvania he entered Harvard and, in 1883, was graduated with honors as the youngest member of his class. While at Harvard he rowed with his class crew, won prizes in tumbling, and was an amateur actor.

Fox's first brush with writing came after Harvard when he joined the staff of *The New York Sun,* a job he left in a short time to enter the Columbia School of Law. It took him just two months to learn that law wasn't for him. After that break, he joined *The New York Times* only to be forced by illness to resign some months later. He then returned to Paris to recuperate.

Actually, that illness turned out eventually to be the luckiest break of his entire career, for it was while regaining his health that he was introduced to the mountains, an introduction that in time inspired him to write about the people he met and came to love.

James Fox, an engineer and an early leader in getting at the fabulous coal wealth that is buried under the cloud-capped mountains, was at that time doing some coal exploration along the Kentucky-Tennessee border between Williamsburg and Jellico. He convinced John that the hill country was the ideal place for him to complete his recovery.

In the mountains, Fox did regain his health. There also he

joined with other members of the mining party, mainly young men fresh out of college and working in the untamed section of pure excitement, in organizing a volunteer police force among themselves. Eventually they brought several noted lawbreakers to justice and made life in the area safer. Fox also organized a school and taught in it for a time.

Now cured of his illness, he returned to Paris and taught school there. But the mountains had won his heart. His eyes and his mind, according to those still living who knew him, were constantly turning toward the distant and hazy hills to the east. He made a number of excursions into the mountains, often spending weeks far from civilization. There are several cabins in Letcher and Pike counties in which he supposedly spent time. Anyway, stories he heard and people he met were being stored up for future reference once he blossomed out as an author.

Meanwhile, the Fox family moved from Paris to Big Stone Gap, a few miles across the Virginia border from Harlan County, where they invested heavily in land. James, his father and other sons were certain that a great pass through the mountains would be developed soon and that Big Stone was the most logical place for it to be.

In 1892, two years after the family moved, the first story flowed from the prolific Fox pen. The book was *A Mountain Europa,* which contains some of the most vivid descriptive passages ever written. That was followed in 1895 by *A Cumberland Vendetta,* a story that was inspired by one of his trips over into Harlan County.

Neither of these stories brought real fame to Fox, however. But the same year he completed his second book, he also spent a day and a half writing a story about a little Leslie County creek for which *Harper's* paid just $6.

That story, called "On Hell-fer-Sartin Creek," made Fox famous as a storyteller. It also made the crooked little mountain stream, which flows into the Middle Fork of the Kentucky River a few miles above Bear Branch, a name known all over the nation.

The story, written in the dialect of the mountains, is considered a classic portrayal of the mountaineers' speech. In 1897, the story was published as the title story of the volume.

Then came another interlude in the Fox story, an interlude that took him away from the hills and, after a while, back into the newspaper game. He volunteered as a soldier during the Spanish-American War and was selected as a member of Col. Theodore Roosevelt's famous Rough Riders. But after some time he gave up soldiering and became a war correspondent for *Harper's Weekly.*

After the war Fox returned to the mountains to live and write. In rapid succession he turned out *Bluegrass and Rhododendron, The Little Shepherd of Kingdom Come, Christmas Eve on Lonesome, The Lost Stetson, A Knight of the Cumberlands, The Trail of the Lonesome Pine, The Heart of the Hills,* and some 40 different short stories. His spreading fame kept him constantly in the public eye and for years he went about the country giving dialect readings from his various works.

Perhaps Fox's amazing ability to take actual persons he knew and work them into a romantic story was demonstrated best in *The Trail of the Lonesome Pine.*

Leading characters in the story were real people. There was "Devil" John Wright, who was turned into "Devil" Judd Tolliver. The leading feminine character, the daughter of Devil Judd in the story, was, in reality, a young mountain girl named June Morris. Jack Hale, the hero, was a composite of three persons, one of them being the late Rogers Clark Ballard Thruston, Louisville geologist, metallurgist and historian, who knew Fox intimately.

Fox's marriage, an ill-fated thing, came in 1908 when he wed the celebrated comic opera singer, Fritzi Scheff. They were divorced a short time later and the affair became a sore spot to Fox.

Thruston, in his letter of 1943, also commented on the marriage. He wrote:

"John and Fritzi stopped in Louisville on their bridal trip and were the guests of Mr. and Mrs. J. D. Stewart. Mrs. Stewart was my oldest niece so I saw something of them. We went to the golf links for a round. Before starting, Fritzi said with a petulant tone, 'John has not kissed me for three days.' I was not surprised when I heard of the separation."

The last Fox book was *Erskine Dale,* published in 1919 a short time after he died at Big Stone Gap of pneumonia contracted on a fishing trip after his return from a long stay in Europe. Since he frequently had said that his "heart always will be in Kentucky," his body was returned to Paris and buried near a holly tree on the crest of a low hill in the family plot alongside the body of his father and his half brother James. His mother later was buried there, too. The cemetery custodian says that today, 30 years after Fox's first book appeared, more visitors enter to view his grave than all the others in the beautiful plot on the edge of town.

Several people in Paris remember Fox, some even his father. Perhaps Miss Buckner, the long-time friend of his sister, has the most vivid recollections of him. She recalls having attended dances and other social affairs with him. Her memories give a clear picture of him, a picture that has not been set down in any of the few sketches done on his life.

Miss Buckner remembers him as not a large man, but wiry and with a delightful laugh and a deep love for music.

"He had a good baritone voice," she said, "and he and Judge Clay often gathered at my house and I played the piano while they sang college and folk songs together. John often played the banjo.

"John Fox was socially very attractive. He was handsome and looked older than he actually was. That seemed to please him in the early days since he entered Harvard when he was only 17.

"They say," she laughed, "that he was a very charming speaker, but I always found him a little hard to talk to. Instead of talking, he liked just to sit and listen. I guess that's why he got along so well with the mountain people."

Miss Buckner recalls also that he felt he could write in his own room at Big Stone Gap. He was a careful writer, she says, going over each line time and time again, often reading it aloud to other members of the family to get their impressions and to make certain it conveyed the picture he had in mind.

His room adjoined that of his father, whose advice he valued highly, she remembers.

"He wrote a lot at night," Miss Buckner said, "but any hour of the day or night he would go into his father's room and consult with him. They would discuss the choice of words and phrases for hours at a time."

Miss Buckner explodes the theory that Fox had in mind a particular tree when he wrote *The Trail of the Lonesome Pine*. Although there are pictures in existence that claim to have been of the tree, now deceased, he wrote about, she says they are fakes.

"I have heard his sister as well as his brother, Oliver, say definitely that there was no particular pine tree about which the book was written," she said.

That Fox was popular is proved by the variety of friends he attracted. They ranged all the way from "Devil" John Wright, the mountain bad man, to Thomas Nelson Page, the writer, and to Theodore Roosevelt.

Page, in writing of Fox's death, referred to his "spare, sinewy frame" as well as to his "affliction with the most pathological indecision in particular matters, in which he was chronically vague and unpunctual." But those faults and others were outweighed, Page commented, by his "absolute charm, naturalness and absence of poise as well as a courtesy that endeared him to his intimates."

Some critics have said that the Fox stories are trite, that plots like the one in *The Little Shepherd of Kingdom Come* in which Chad, the mountain orphan, rose from abject poverty to educate himself and eventually learn of his Bluegrass ancestry, are strictly from corn.

But there's little or no rebuttal for success. And success is what the Fox novels have enjoyed—in fact, are still enjoying since *The Little Shepherd* now is being printed in a new edition by Grosset and Dunlap and selling well.

Neither is there any denying of the down-to-earth, heart-tugging simplicity of his stories. His plots are simple, the action broad and easy to follow and believe.

Combined with descriptive passages that left the impression that the reader was standing at the side of his characters in the very heart of the hills, that recipe brought Fox fame that reached all over the world, a fame still alive more than a quarter of a century after his last book was completed. (6/12/49)

KENTUCKY ROGUES   The other day I was reading—in the newspaper, naturally—where some party had made a speech about how over the years so many men prominent in American history have been closely identified with Kentucky.

This speaker cited Daniel Boone, Henry Clay, Dr. Ephraim McDowell, George Rogers Clark, Abraham Lincoln, Jefferson Davis, Zachary Taylor, Fred M. Vinson, Alben W. Barkley, the 100 or more Kentuckians who had been governors of other states and others on the credit side of the ledger.

But history also has a debit side. Not all those who stalk the pages of history were praiseworthy leaders or empire builders.

To that end, it might be pointed out that sizeable array of rascals and rogues likewise have been closely drawn to Kentucky by birth or the course of events.

The rogues gallery would include the likes of Jesse and Frank James, America's most famous outlaws; William Quantrill, Martin Bates and Sue Mundy, Civil War guerrillas; Simon Girty, the renegade white who led Indian attacks; Aaron Burr, twice tried for treason, once in Kentucky; Jack McCall, the murderer of "Wild Bill" Hickok, and the Harpe brothers, ruthless highwaymen of the early 1800s.

Few of these reverse-English heroes were native Kentuckians. But all are identified with this state in some place or another.

Take, for instance, Jesse and Frank James. Only Missouri was more prominent in their checkered careers. Both parents were Kentuckians and their first bank robbery was in this state at Russellville. Two other robberies were staged here—a Columbia bank and the Mammoth Cave stagecoach. On the latter job, Jesse James acquired the watch he was wearing when Bob Ford shot and killed him.

Between the Russellville bank job in 1868 and the death of Jesse James in 1882, the gang was in and out of Kentucky often, usually slipping in to hide. James hideouts are strung from Pike to Pulaski and from Logan to Warren counties. The gang laid low, often for weeks, at the farm of George Hite, an uncle of the James boys, near Adairville.

The James brothers, no doubt, learned some of their cunning from Quantrill, the guerrilla under whom they served in the Civil War. Quantrill started as a Confederate but soon became leader of a swarm of cut-throats who acknowledged neither civil nor military authority.

Quantrill has been called the "bloodiest character in American history" because of his raid on Lawrence, Kansas, when the entire town was burned and 140 persons killed. Shortly afterwards, Quantrill extended his raids into Missouri and eventually into Kentucky.

It was in Kentucky in the spring of 1865 that he met his end when he and part of his band were trapped near Bloomfield. Quantrill was hit in the back by a pistol ball and died later in Louisville.

Another savage guerrilla leader, and a native Kentuckian, was Martin Bates. A 7-foot, 11-inch giant, Bates was a Confederate who turned guerrilla and ravaged the Kentucky mountains. He survived the war and became a circus attraction.

The most unsavory home-grown guerrilla was Marcellus Jerome Clarke, better known as Sue Mundy. Born in Simpson County, he entered the war for the Confederacy. But late in 1863 he formed an outlaw band that became one of the most feared throughout the border states.

Clarke was captured in March 1865, in Meade County. He was tried, found guilty, and hanged in Louisville on Broadway near 18th Street.

Simon Girty, the white renegade, was responsible for much of the bloody Indian warfare in Kentucky between 1780 and 1791. He was born in Pennsylvania and became an Indian interpreter in the Virginia militia before deserting to the British.

As a British agent he planned and led numerous Indian raids on Kentucky settlements, perhaps the best known being on Bryan's Station in August 1782. With 400 Indians and British, Girty led a siege to the stockade. Unable to dent the defense, the Indians withdrew after two days.

Girty masterminded the ambush into which the pioneers were lured at Blue Licks a few days later. There the Indians slaughtered 70 men, one a son of Daniel Boone, as they pressed pursuit of the Bryan's Station attackers.

Aaron Burr was in Kentucky off and on for two years at the time he was plotting to establish an independent republic—with himself at its head—in the Southwest. Discredited politically and condemned in the East after killing Alexander Hamilton in a duel, Burr came to Kentucky in 1805 and began his plot.

President Jefferson ordered an investigation which resulted in Burr's arrest and trial at Frankfort for "high misdemeanor." Defended by Clay, he was acquitted only to be tried again later in Virginia.

Louisville-born Jack McCall was an adventurer and gambler who headed west. In late July 1876, at Deadwood, South Dakota, he lost $500 to J. B. "Wild Bill" Hickok at poker. Two days later McCall sauntered into the same saloon while Hickok was engaged in another game. Standing at Hickok's back, he whipped out his pistol and shot him in the head. He eventually was hanged for the crime.

Perhaps the most unsavory characters drawn to Kentucky were the Harpe brothers—Micajah (Big) Harpe and Wiley (Little) Harpe. They blazed a path of terror the length of the state. They were pursued and Big Harpe was killed near Dixon in 1806. His head was severed from the body and hung from an oak tree as a warning to other outlaws.

Little Harpe escaped and turned up next as one of the river gang operating from Cave-in-Rock, Illinois, just across the Ohio River. He eventually was killed in Mississippi.

Incidentally, the road where Big Harpe was strung from the oak tree is known to this day as Harpe's Head Road. (10/8/59)

MIKE FINK   The other night I was reading a very learned magazine piece in which some college professor was saying that grade schools should devote more time to "semi-legendary figures" in the study of American history.

A knowledge of combination fact-and-fiction characters is necessary, the professor claims, for full understanding of that quirk in the American nature which leads us all to go the truth one better in perpetuating the exploits of heroes.

He says this is the way a nation develops its own brand of folklore, creates a cultural heritage that should be presented to students of history.

He listed Daniel Boone, Davey Crockett, Buffalo Bill Cody, Johnny Appleseed, Jim Bowie, and a dozen or more others as examples of real figures who have reached semi-legendary status, at least.

Now I have no bones to pick with the good professor and his basic idea. Since so many good students think (erroneously) that history is deader than a certain sea, maybe it would be a good idea to jazz up study of the subject along the lines he proposes. The only thing would be to make sure the fact and the fiction were kept separate and not allowed to meld into one big blob of nothing.

However, I take violent exception—well, semi-violent exception —to the professor for not having included Mike Fink on his list of parties who actually lived and breathed, but whose life and times have been flavored and colored until they reach folklore status.

Fink was the braggart hero of the Ohio River keelboaters in the late 1790s and early 1800s. As such, he was more closely associated —in fact and in fiction—with Kentucky than any other state.

As a historical person, not an awful lot is known about Mike Fink. But in the field of legend, he's the focal point of more tall tales than you could shake a keelboater's pole at.

In fact, some five years ago he was a central figure in a series of TV movies made in Kentucky by Walt Disney.

It is certain that Fink was born at Fort Pitt in 1770 and that he became a keelboater on the Ohio. It is also certain that he was a notable marksman—so notable, to be sure, that posters up and down the river announcing shooting matches would read: "The match is for five prizes with Mike Fink excluded."

Next to shooting, the stories go, Fink liked best a good fight with no holds barred.

"I'm the son of lightning, the king of destruction. . . . I'm half horse and half alligator and the rest of me is crooked snags and redhot snapping turtle. . . . I'm death and destruction. . . . There's no one can hide from me, no rock that can kill me," he'd roar and tear into any man brave enough to take up his dare for a fight.

Fink was a great one for frequenting the taverns scattered along the river. He'd gather at the bar and tell stories that should be repeated before no group less hardened than veteran mule skinners. Any man who failed to laugh uproariously at his jokes soon learned the error of his ways.

It was said that the animals came to know the sound of the crack of his deadly rifle and would take to their secret hiding places at the first hint he was about.

Louisville appears prominently in the Fink legend. As a matter of fact, it was here that he was placed on trial after the one time in his wild, rambunctious life that he was arrested.

The details of that arrest make quite some story.

Seems Fink and his crew were polling down the Ohio below Louisville and had gotten tired of the standard menu of sow belly and roast potatoes. He longed for a fresh leg of lamb.

A short distance later, the boat passed a riverside field where lambs were cavorting about. Placing a tin of snuff in his pockets, Fink leaped into the water, swam to the shore, and powdered the faces of several lambs with snuff.

He then found the owner of the lambs and called his attention to the strange behavior of the snuff-powdered animals, which were coughing and leaping high in the air. They were, Fink confided, afflicted with the black murrain and would pollute the whole flock unless killed and thrown into the river.

The distraught owner begged Fink to save the flock by eliminating the contaminated animals. He even offered several gallons of fresh peach brandy as a bonus.

Well, Fink obliged, and for several days his crew ate fresh lamb and washed it down with peach brandy.

Eventually news of the Fink trick reached the farmer and he registered a complaint with the judge in Louisville. When Fink returned to town he was arrested. The sheriff begged that he surrender without the expected fight, and Mike agreed on one condition—that he be allowed to go to court in his keelboat.

"I'm not at home on dry land," he argued.

The sheriff, relieved that the situation had been resolved so easily, agreed, and the 36-foot-long keelboat was mounted on wooden wheels and hitched to a team of oxen. All the boatmen stood in place on the deck, keel poles in hand, and Fink was at the tiller as the oxen pulled them though the streets to court.

Fink and crew sat on a front row in court while a scowling judge presided. Once the trial started, it was apparent that things weren't going too well for the home team.

"To your places, boys," Fink shouted suddenly, leaping to his feet. "We're leaving."

With that, the boatmen jumped out the window and pushed their boat—wheels, oxen and all—back to the river. Before the startled judge could issue an order to stop them, the group was poling rapidly up river.

All of which is why I nominate Mike Fink for inclusion in any list of semi-legendary figures. (10/12/61)

WHEN THE MISSISSIPPI RIVER RAN UPSTREAM   I trust that you gentle readers—and I use the word "readers" optimistically—won't object to my making a pun by stating that this is going to be a piece about the most earth-shaking event ever to hit Kentucky.

For, you see, it's going to be about the great New Madrid earthquake that rocked most of Kentucky off and on for two months late in 1811 and the early weeks of 1812. It was during this period, and as a direct result of the quakes, that Reelfoot Lake, some arms of which extend up into Fulton County, was created.

Actually, the greater part of the continent was rattled by the series of tremors. A total of 86 shocks were felt in Louisville during the weeks that followed the first one. But it was the section lying along the Mississippi River where Kentucky, Tennessee and Missouri touch that the greatest shocks occurred.

There, on February 8, 1812, even the bed of the Mississippi was buckled upward to such an extent that the waters of the river flowed upstream for nearly 24 hours. It was then that a section which once had been a great forest, but which had disappeared into a yawning chasm 20 miles long during an earlier shock, was filled with water, thus creating Reelfoot Lake. The trees of the submerged forest still lift skeleton arms above the surface of the lake, one of America's greatest natural phenomena.

The first shock was felt in New Madrid, a small Missouri town located on the upper side of a wide curve in the Mississippi called Kentucky Bend, on December 16, 1811, at about 3 a.m. There was, according to accounts, a low rumbling noise resembling the distant firing of cannon, after which the earth began to tremble. In a few minutes the moon, which had been shining brightly, was completely hidden by the sulfuric vapor that poured from crevices in the ground.

A short time later the river began to roar as one intense shock caused its current to retrograde for a few minutes. The boiling, foaming water created panic among the residents as they fled to higher ground.

There were light shocks almost daily until January 23, 1812, when one as hard as the first occurred. It was generally quiet after that until February 4 when another severe series started. The earth was in nearly continual agitation, visibly waving like a gentle sea, all day.

Four days later came the most severe shock of all, the one that sent the Mississippi roaring upstream for the most of one whole day.

Here's the way an eyewitness, E. Bryan of New Madrid, described the spectacle in a letter written in 1826, 11 years after the first quake:

"On the 8th (of February) about sunrise a concussion took place which was so much more violent than the others that it was called the 'hard shock.' The earth was transformed into a total darkness and the chickens went back to roost and the cows mooed and the horses pitifully neighed.

"At first," the letter continued, "the Mississippi River seemed to recede from its banks and its waters gathered up like a mountain, leaving for a short period of time many boats, which were passing down the river, on the bottom of the river. The river rose 15 feet perpendicularly, expanding as it were at the same time and the banks were overflowed by the retrograde current. . . .

"In the last hard shock described the earth was horribly lacerated; the surface from time to time covered over of uneven depths by the sand which issued from the fissures that were made in great numbers all over the country, some of which closed up immediately after they had vomited forth their sand and water. In many places, however, there was substance resembling coal thrown up with the sand. It is impossible to say what the depths of the fissures were. The site of New Madrid, Mo., was settled down at least 15 feet. . . . Back from the river the numerous large ponds which covered a large part of the country were totally dried up.

"The most remarkable feature of the entire disturbance . . . was the discovery of a huge lake on the Tennessee side of the Mississippi. . . . 'Tis said that where the lake was formed was a vast forest of fine timber lands and in places only the tops of the trees can be seen. . . .

"Most of those who fled have returned but always become

greatly alarmed by the slightest trembling of the earth. Hardly a week passes but we feel a light shock. One circumstance worthy of mention is: this section was once subject to severe thunder, but for a long time previous to the first shocks there was no thunder and very little since."

And so did an eyewitness describe the most earth-shaking event ever to hit Kentucky. (12/31/49)

CAVE EXPLORATION TRIP RECALLS FLOYD COLLINS SAGA FOR SKEETS MILLER — Like a shadow from out of the inky blackness of the west-central Kentucky caverns which he discovered, the name of William Floyd Collins this morning has found its place back into the newspaper headlines all across the country.

For just after sunup a party of 30 persons, complete with two tons of assorted equipment, pushed beyond the electrically lighted tourist boundary of Crystal Cave. Crystal is the cave that Collins, an unknown cave guide, discovered in 1917 long before he became a national figure when he lost his life in nearby Sand Cave.

The party of speleologists—cave specialists—is out to retrace and study scientifically the lower three levels of Crystal Cave, a route first walked and crawled over by Collins in March of 1922. The cave has some 10 miles of exhibited routes on the upper two levels and unknown mileage of little—or never—explored passages lower down.

But the gaunt shadow of Collins hangs over the expedition for reasons other than just the fact that Crystal Cave—which later was renamed Floyd Collins Crystal Cave—was his greatest discovery.

Besides that, the expedition set out almost exactly 29 years to the day after Collins was officially declared dead in Sand Cave, the narrow, gun-barrel shaped hole in which he was trapped early in 1925 while trying to find a new entrance to Crystal Cave.

More than that, however, one of the five nonspeleological members of the party is William Burke "Skeets" Miller, the newspaper reporter who seven times wormed his way down through the slimy, tight tunnel that was Sand Cave to interview Collins. The only reporter to perform the feat, Miller won the

Pulitzer Prize for reporting in 1925 for himself and his paper, a daily by the name of *The Courier-Journal*.

Miller's prize was the cake icing for what was perhaps one of the most gripping sagas in the history of American journalism. The Floyd Collins story was big news for 17 days. That covered the time he was discovered in his trap until the coroner's jury slid down an improvised shaft and pronounced him dead.

During that period, however, every element for a great newspaper story was present. There was the stark melodrama of a man hopelessly caught far underground in a muddy tomb. There was the suspense of repeated efforts to free him. There was the family huddled at the entrance of the cave. There was the nervy reporter who risked his own life to get the story. There was the veiled insinuation that Collins, Miller and *The Courier-Journal* were combining in one of the greatest hoaxes of all time.

And, in the last stage, there was the classic newspaper double-cross, a practice common in those days of cut-throat reporting.

Incidentally, a young aviator who later made quite a name for himself was the victim in the double-cross—a fellow by the name of Charles A. Lindbergh.

More than 100 newspaper reporters kept their readers informed of the plight of Collins during the 17 days. Most of them lived at the Dixie Hotel in Cave City, six miles away.

"We ate up every old rooster in that part of the country," wryly comments Powell Lee, a *Louisville Times* reporter who covered the story for his paper.

"Skeets" Miller, now night executive officer of the National Broadcasting Company but then fresh out of Louisville Male High School, had been working for *The Courier-Journal* only three months when the Floyd Collins story broke. It came in as a routine news story from a local correspondent on January 30, 1925.

Floyd Collins, a cave explorer, was trapped in a cave near the Edmondson-Barren County line, the correspondent reported. But no one, not even the family, was very excited because he had been trapped many times before, once for 48 hours in Crystal Cave.

The story seemed cold as a witch's kiss Sunday morning when *The Herald,* another Louisville paper, headlined: "Collins Free—Vows Never Again."

But later that day, the news was flashed that instead of being free, Collins was still trapped in the cave, a "foxhole," local folks called it. His brother, Homer, and father, Leonidas, had been down to look for him and had gotten to his side without being able to free him.

That was when "Skeets" Miller entered the picture. After more than just some little pestering, he persuaded Neil Dalton, then *Courier-Journal* city editor, to send him down on the story. After all, he pointed out, he was about the size of a jockey— 110 pounds—and could easily crawl around in tight places.

"O.K.," Dalton finally gave in, "go on down there—but don't you go crawling around in any cave."

Miller arrived on the scene Monday morning. That was February 2. His first contact was with Homer Collins, younger brother of the trapped man. He had just been down in the hole.

"You want a story," he told Miller, "then you go down in that hole and get it yourself."

That challenge was all it took to make him forget the warning of Dalton, the city editor 100 miles away in the Louisville office. Borrowing a pair of overalls from Homer Collins, Miller squeezed past the rock-studded entrance and into the chilly, clammy darkness of Sand Cave.

So began one of the most nerve-tingling adventures of any reporter.

Let "Skeets" Miller pick up the story there and tell in his own words about that first trip to Floyd Collins' side:

"I butted here and there inside the entrance before finding which way the pitch-black passageway led. I had to slide along on my stomach through ooze and slime. The cave was cold and drafty and my teeth began to chatter from the cold and from fear of the black unknown that lay ahead.

"I called out to Collins but there was no answer. Crawling further, I reached a sharp dip and caromed head-first down the incline and against a wet mass. It groaned and moved.

"I pushed back in terror and the mass moved again and groaned weakly. I lay head down on top of the mass and in my fright I imagined that I, too, was trapped.

"The mass was, of course, Floyd Collins. After some minutes I was able to work backwards up the passage and then managed to push my right leg alongside his body. Except for the one leg, I could not get past his shoulders.

"I was able to raise his head and place it on my leg. He had twisted the burlap bags brought in by his brother over his face to protect against the dripping water.

"He spoke incoherently, but was able to tell me that his

left leg was pinned by a large rock into a crack at the floor of the cave. He didn't think the leg was broken.

"I slowly inched my way back out of the hole. Once on the surface I had no intention of going down again."

Miller's first act outside was to telephone back to the paper in Louisville. It was then well up in the morning. He then went to a hotel and fell into a deep sleep. He was awakened by the telephone. It was Dalton, *The Courier-Journal* city editor.

"How are you feeling? Need any help? Do you want to come home?" he was asked in rapid succession.

"No," Miller replied.

"Then," Dalton roared, "why in the world did you give your first person interview with Collins to *The Times?*"

Seems that when Miller had called in over rather faulty circuit connections, *The Courier-Journal* staff had not reported for work. So the call had been given to *The Times'* city desk and A. Y. Aronson, then managing editor, had splashed the story, with eight-column headlines, across page one.

Later that afternoon, still Monday, Miller again went underground with food and a plan for getting Collins free. The idea was to strap a harness across his shoulders and pull him loose. That plan was discarded when Collins protested, "I'd rather lay here than have my foot pulled off—don't do it."

Miller went down a third time on Monday. By now the story was front page news all over the land. The cave site crawled with curious spectators.

On Tuesday, February 3, Miller went down into the cave three times in five hours. Once he took a string of electric lights, which seemed to cheer the trapped man. Soup was fed to him through a rubber tube while Miller held his head on his knee.

That same day, Miller tried another of the many proposed rescue plans. He attempted to raise the rock with a crowbar and then slip a jack under it. Several times it seemed the jack was able to take hold only to slip in the slimy sand and drop the rock back into place.

"Get out and rest, then come back," Collins told him. "Next time it'll work."

By now the rumor mills on the outside were working overtime. Since Miller had been the only reporter to talk to Collins, the story was started that the whole thing was a *Courier-Journal* hoax to sell papers. Chicago papers, which had dozens of men at the scene, hinted that there was nobody in the cave.

Another rumor was that Collins was crawling out of the

cave via another entrance at night, then returning to his place in the morning to keep the publicity gag going. Miller received dozens of crank wires and telephone calls. One from Iowa read: "Correct story I am in a cave. Signed: Floyd Collins."

Collins was fed for the last time early Wednesday, February 4. A short time later another slide formed a barrier in front of him. Miller, with Ernest Maddix, a Central City coal miner, was permitted to go down into the cave again. It was Miller's seventh trip in three days.

"We reached the block," Miller says, "and called to Floyd."

" 'Come on down—I'm free', he called back.

" 'If you're free reach the bottle of milk I have placed in the crevice over your head.'

"There was a silence, then he replied, 'No, I'm not free.' "

That was the last time anybody spoke to Floyd Collins.

The next day, engineers started a shaft down outside the entrance in an effort to reach him. After 12 days there was no hope he was alive.

Meantime, on February 10, to quiet the rumors that persisted, a military probe was started. Miller testified for more than an hour and the verdict was that Collins was indeed trapped in the cave and that there was no hoax involved.

The shaft reached his trap on February 16. He was dead. The next day the coroner's jury identified the body. It was decided to leave the body in the trap. A photographer from a Chicago paper was selected to make pictures and turn them over to the newspaper pool outside for the use of all papers.

The photographer made the trip down, returned, and handed over a holder to the pool. Only trouble was, he turned over a blank holder. The waiting aviator took the blank holder and flew it to Chicago. The aviator's paper lost out.

The aviator was named Lindbergh.

The Collins story didn't end there. In April, the family was given permission to remove the body and bury it near the entrance of Crystal Cave. Still later, it was moved again to the interior of the cave, where it is today.

The Collins family sold Crystal Cave, which it had exhibited since early 1918, in 1927 to Dr. H. B. Thomas for $10,000.

Still, the Floyd Collins story was not ended.

On March 19, 1929, The Courier-Journal ran this headline:

"Reports Body of Collins Stolen." The article read: "Dr. H. B. Thomas, owner of Crystal Cave, today sought aid of officers in three counties in an effort to locate the body of Floyd

Collins which he said was removed last night from the metal and glass casket in which it was on display in the cave."

The following morning, this follow-up story appeared:

"Return Collins' Body To Cavern—The body of Floyd Collins was returned today to a coffin in Crystal Cave. Dr. H. B. Thomas was authorized to return the body to the coffin after it was found in a sack late Tuesday on the bank of the Green River, 400 yards from the cave entrance, where a chain was sawed from the door." (2/14/54)

INTRODUCTION   *The plain and simple logic that most Kentuckians display when they find themselves thrown into unusual circumstances is remarkable. Dad was intrigued by this trait of common sense and its almost frightening ability to deal with a perplexing dilemma in the most uncompromising of terms.*

Many no-nonsense Kentucky philosophers have been reared amidst simple and unadorned surroundings. If it is true that one's response to a situation can be predicted by examining his background and environment, it seems only natural in times requiring split-second thinking and cold, hard logic that the Kentuckian shows his true mettle. Although his words may be logical and hit hard at the problem at hand, an unmistakable trace of humor is often discernible.

Take, for instance, a gentleman in Marshall County who, though not exactly Phi Beta Kappa material, nevertheless managed to save his money to buy his first car. He drove his new possession everywhere he went.

When asked by a curious acquaintance how difficult it was to drive, he simply explained, "They ain't nothin' to drivin' a car. All you do is throw her in high and stay between the telephone poles!"

How can anyone argue with logic like that?

CHAPTER 3

COMMON SENSE

Kentuckians traditionally have taken steps to insure that what a person says and what he does are more or less the same.

Take the case of an Anderson County farmer who J. T. Cox of Lawrenceburg and Frankfort tells about.

A man notorious for his drunken lazy ways stopped at this farmer's place and asked if there was any work he could do. The farmer allowed that there were some loose shingles that he needed to get nailed down on the barn, and he'd even give a bonus of a belt of good bourbon if the job was done right.

"There's the nails," said the farmer motioning to a sack. "Get to it and I'll be back in a while."

Later the farmer returned and found the guy sitting under a tree.

"Did you get all the shingles nailed down?" asked the farmer.

"I done it good," replied the worker. "Where's that bourbon you promised?"

"Why," snorted the farmer detecting a credibility gap of mammoth proportions, "it's over there in the sack of nails."

Some people follow orders to the letter. Such was the fresh-in Navy boot Mrs. Isaac Hardeman of Louisville tells about who was pulling guard duty at Great Lakes Naval Training Center during World War II.

An admiral named Berry had been assigned to the station so hurriedly that he arrived a week before his family could follow suit. The first day his family arrived at the main gate this boot, who had been told not let anyone in without proper identification, was on guard duty.

"But," the admiral's wife butted when he refused to let her in because she failed to have the proper credentials, "we're the Berrys."

"Ma'am," he replied, "I don't care if you're the cat's meow, you ain't goin' through that gate without a pass."

A characteristic of the Kentuckian that has always intrigued me is the way we try to justify in a reasonable manner everything we do.

Often, of course, our reasoning is more than just merely foggy, but, nevertheless, we've figured it all out to the point that it is logical to us, at least.

Consider the case of the chronic gambler (a crap shooter born and bred) in Franklin County whom John Ed McConnell, a Louisville businessman, used to know. This fellow lived near the Forks of the Elkhorn, McConnell's old home ground, and he seldom was without a pair of dice on his person.

He was constantly taking the bones out of the pockets of his bib overalls, fondling them, blowing on them to keep them warm, and he was ready at the least provocation to roll them for the meagerest of stakes.

Once he was asked why this ever-ready attitude and, true to his Kentucky breeding, he had what to him seemed a logical explanation.

"I figure a man ought to shoot craps a little every day," he reasoned. "It just might be that this is his lucky day and he'd never know it."

As I have often said, Kentuckians have a knack for rationalizing almost any situation they find themselves in. Take, for instance, a man who was on the short side that visited Ralph Day of Louisville.

"You've gotten a bit overweight, haven't you?" kidded Day.

"I weigh 225 pounds and the charts say that with that I should be 6'3"," the chunky visitor protested. "I'm just too short, but I'm certainly not overweight."

Sometimes it doesn't take much to sidetrack a perfectly normal conversation and set off on a tangent that surprises all involved. Pete Shaw of Russellville once told me about being in a restaurant in his town one cold drizzly day when a stranger from out of state entered.

"Is this town dry?" he asked the waitress, meaning could he possibly get a drink of something more bracing than mere coffee.

"Heavens, no," she replied innocently, "it's been raining here for the past 48 hours."

Outwood Hospital, once a U.S. government tuberculosis sanitarium near Dawson Springs, now is a mental health facility. Walter Calvert, retired Hopkins County court clerk, was telling a group, including Madisonville lawyer Frederick E. Nichols, of an incident that happened at the hospital.

Seemed an elderly man was being examined for possible admission. A doctor was talking to him in an effort to determine the clarity of the man's thinking.

"My office is out that door and down the hall to the right," the doctor said. "Go down there and see if I'm in my office."

Without showing any surprise, the patient fired off a quick answer.

"There's the phone," he countered, pointing to the doctor's desk. "See for yourself."

Often people are so literal minded that it blinds them. Dave Isenberg of Cave City ran in to just such a person in a drugstore in Bowling Green.

Isenberg ordered several prescriptions whose sum total costing $23.25 was handed to him in a small bag.

"That's a mighty small bag for $23.25 worth of medicine," he said.

"Well," asked the clerk, "would you like me to put it in a bigger bag?"

Some years back Alvin Bunger, who was with the Kentucky Department of Economic Security, told me a story which proves that sometimes the best gems of logic are found in the least likely settings.

He once knew a poor fellow who was from western Kentucky who was a bit weak in the skull. Consequently, the courthouse yard loafers and poolroom cowboys in the little town where he was from were forever kidding him and making him the butt of crude jokes.

Much to the surprise of everyone, the guy married and the next time he came to town the jokesters were waiting for him.

"Hear you married a twin," one slicker leered while four or five others snickered in anticipation of the many doors of humor that would open.

"Yep," the dim-witted man replied.

"Tell us," the tormentor went on, "how do you tell them apart?"

"Why," the groom countered, "her brother's pert near a head taller."

Before the April 3 tornado hit Louisville, an east end resident had stopped at a watering place on Brownsboro Road for several poppers before going home to dinner.

As he climbed into his car to drive home, the twister hit with blinding fury. His car was picked up and literally blown against an apartment house on the opposite side of the street.

When the guy regained his senses, he was shocked to see that the building into which his car had been blown was completely demolished.

"How," he mumbled dazedly, "will I ever explain this to my insurance company?"

One who was a master of the verbal reprimand was Carlisle Oldham, once the judge of Ohio County. Like his son, John, who is athletic director at Western Kentucky University, he had a good command of the mother tongue and could talk most authoritatively when the occasion arose.

Judge Oldham was particularly sharp with offenders who were frequent visitors to his court.

On one occasion, Dorothy Gentry of Hartford recalled a year or two back, a man who'd been there in front of the judge before was brought in on a charge of public drunkenness.

"Are you guilty or not?" asked the judge sternly.

"Yes, sir, I believe that I am," the man answered, "and I'd like to waive the hearing."

"What do you mean you'd like to waive the hearing?" the judge countered.

"I mean, Judge, sir," he said in a trembling voice, "that I don't want to hear no more about it from you, Judge, sir."

A Kentuckian will sometimes dig deep for evidence to support either his pessimistic or his optimistic attitude of the moment. As proof of the latter, consider the elderly lady in eastern Kentucky who was involved in a story told by William B. Hazelrigg when he was commissioner of highways.

Several years ago, his story went, a party of engineers surveying the line between Martin and Johnson counties discovered an error. It turned out that the small chunk of land that this little old lady lived on was actually in Johnson County and not Martin County as she had always thought.

The surveyor called on her and explained the fact that her home was actually in Johnson County.

"I'm sure glad to hear that," she said, brimming with optimism. "These last few winters in Martin County have been somethin' fierce."

There used to live in Elizabethtown two elderly ladies who, when the winter breezes began to blow, would get in their car and head for Florida. Since both ladies were terrible drivers, friends were continually amazed how they made it down and back in one piece. So someone asked them how they did it.

"There is nothing to it at all," one of the ladies explained. "We just get astraddle of the little white line in the highway and stay there!"

Every time I'm tempted to gripe about the weather, I remember
a conversation Roy Tooms, a London lawyer, had with an
aged woman who had been sick. When he remarked that the
weather had been pretty miserable lately, she replied with great
feeling: "I don't care how bad the weather gets, just as long
as I'm here to see it!"

Since the crunch came, I've heard learned economists,
geologists, industrialists and even a president take turns at
explaining the energy crisis, how it came about, and how to solve it.

But none explained the cause or cure nearly as well as a
man in Bath County who hadn't heard of the energy crisis until
just recently.

You see this man wasn't much on pursuing news through the
newspaper or the television. Still he had his quota of native
intelligence.

Shortly before Christmas he was in the general store of Ralph
Crouch in Bethel. There he joined the crowd around the potbelly
stove in the back of the store. The conversation turned to
the energy problem.

"Ralph," he interrupted, after listening for a few minutes,
"what's all this about an energy crisis?"

Crouch tried his best to explain the situation in terms that the
man could understand. He told about the lack of gasoline
and how so many stoves, refrigerators and freezers caused a
lack of electrical power.

"You know, Ralph," the man said after pondering the matter
for some time, "it just seems a lot people got above their raisin'."

It is getting harder and harder to wriggle out of jury duty. Some
years back 11th District Judge George Bertram was asked to
release a man from service because he couldn't hear out of
one ear.

In denying the appeal the judge referred to a precedent set
by the late Judge W. H. Spragens.

"You don't need but one good ear," Judge Spragens ruled when
hit with the similar request. "This is a grand jury, and it
will be hearing only one side of the case."

Down in Marshall County, my old home grounds, they tell about a
farmer, not exactly the sharpest mind around, who was
plowing his field one day when a traveling evangelist passed
by in his horse-drawn buggy.

"Brother, are you lost?" the evangelist queried.

"Naw," came the reply. "I been plowing this here field for 40
years and I always found my way home."

Sometimes adults follow the example of children and go
right to the heart of the matter.

One of the shortest and most explicit explanations on record
must have been submitted by a semi-educated coroner in
an eastern Kentucky county some years ago after a driver had
drowned when his car plunged into a river.

His report read: "Car went into river and staid there."

It seems that a few years back a revival was held at a rural church
in LaRue County. During the course of the meeting the preacher
had been encouraging the listeners to rise and give verbal
testimony to various points he had covered in his messages.

This particular night the sermon had been on love and
brotherhood and how one of the great human shortcomings was
the stubborn refusal of many people to forgive others for
wrongs, real or imagined, committed against them.

In groping around for a strong climax that might bring on
some testifying from the floor, the preacher spotted on the
first row an old man who supposedly didn't have an enemy in the
world.

"Here, friend, is what I'm talking about," he orated, pointing
to the old gent. "Here's a man who is nearing the four
score and ten mark in years and who is living proof of the sermon

I have just preached. He is beloved by all and doesn't have an enemy in the world. Brother, please tell us how you've accomplished this."

The old man struggled to his feet.

"Preacher," he said, a slighty evil grin on his face, "it was simple—I just outlived every one of them devils."

No matter how many graduate schools a professional man or woman has gone through, at some time or other he will be confronted by a situation not covered in the textbooks.

Usually such a situation will arise without warning when there isn't time to check out the crisis and so the person just has to rely on extinct and common sense and hope for the best.

James C. Baughman, pastor of the Middletown Christian Church, tells about a Kentucky minister who discovered the truth of that statement the hard way while performing a wedding.

The minister had gotten safely through the opening part of the service and was moving confidently into the home stretch.

"If there be anyone here who objects to this marriage, let him speak now or forever hold his peace," he intoned.

"I object!" came the unexpected response from a man seated in the back of the church.

"Why do you object?" the somewhat startled minister asked.

"Because she promised to marry me."

The rookie parson paused and the seminary lessons on marriage quickly flashed through his mind. Recalling nothing that would cover this situation, he had to act on his own.

"Well," he declared in a quavering voice, "objection overruled."

I'll lay odds that every coach who has agonized through a poor season has felt his team had invented new ways to lose ball games.

But when it comes to originality, I doubt that many coaches could top the way Dave Lawrence, now dean of students at the University of Louisville, once lost a track meet.

He lost a track meet because one of his runners believed that regardless, when you see a traffic light turn red you stop.

The year was 1935 and Lawrence was teaching at Sulphur High School in Henry County. When county fair time arrived it was decided that a track meet among the county schools would be an added attraction. The last event was a modified cross-country run, where the runners began in Eminence and ended up at the fairgrounds in New Castle, the county seat.

Lawrence's Sulphur team was close enough in the standings that a win in the cross-country event would assure them of victory. And, since his ace was a long-legged boy who could run all day without drawing a deep breath, he felt the trophy was in his grasp.

In fact, the Sulphur runner was running in first ahead by a good 150 yards and drawing away as the pack moved into New Castle. However, as he galloped into New Castle toward the town's only stoplight opposite the courthouse, the light changed from green to red.

The Sulphur runner came to a screeching halt, but the other runners continued without a pause. They dashed past him while he was waiting for the light to change. By the time it was green again he had settled into a comfortable last in the field.

So Sulphur lost the race and the meet by the length of one traffic light.

Years ago when automobiles were still a novelty and roads were little more than passable, Roy Huder Sr. quotes Bowling Green CPA Earle Duff as recalling an enterprising farmer who spent most of his time pulling cars out of an especially troublesome mudhole in the road near Woodbury.

One day a motorist asked him what he did when he wasn't extracting cars from the mudhole.

"Why," he answered simply, "I haul water and put it in this mudhole."

Much of the mountainous eastern quarter of Kentucky was settled originally by British Highlanders, and at one time the scholars contended that the purest Elizabethan English was spoken in our Highland section.

But, like all gray mares, time ain't what it used to be. While many mountain-area people still speak with a distinctive twang, few have retained much of the accent and the phrasing of their ancestors.

A supposedly true story I heard several years ago points out this fact.

It seems that a high ranking British naval officer attached to the British Royal Navy staff in Washington had been wanting to visit the mountainous section of Kentucky for quite some time. So it was arranged for him to come to the state. One of the towns he visited was Hindman, the county seat of Knott County. Being properly brass, he wore his Royal Navy uniform, complete with the frills and trim.

During his brief stop in Hindman he got into a conversation with several of the men gathered around the courthouse in the center of town.

"What are you, German or something?" asked one man after looking closely at the uniform.

"No," came the reply, "I'm British."

"I knowed you was some kind of furiner," the native said. "I could tell by the funny way you speak English."

A man came into a Central City lumberyard, reports Larry Stone, and ordered a goodly supply of two-by-fours.

"How long do you want 'em?" asked the lumberyard owner.

"Well, I'm buildin' a house so I want 'em for a long time," he replied.

Since he retired several years ago and settled in Louisville after 40 years of school teaching in Indiana and Illinois, Fred J. Tuttle has been memorizing the Bible. To those who ask why, he has a standard, schoolteacher type answer.

"I," he says, "am cramming for the final exam."

Few people have ever gotten a more unusual answer to a
question than did James Cheatham of Louisville when he stopped
at a restaurant for lunch just off Kentucky's Mountain Parkway.

"How far is it to Salyersville?" he asked the waitress who
was working his table.

"I never heard of it," she answered, "but it sounds like it's a
long way off."

Since the sky is so full of the things today, it is hard to believe
that it hasn't been too many years ago that airplanes were a
positive novelty. Moreover, on the belief that if the Good Lord
had intended man to fly He'd have given us wings, many in
those days regarded going up in a plane as the equivalent of
suicide.

Slim Pickins, the Greensburg gossip, tells about a plane
landing in his town during those bygone days. The pilot
of the plane asked an old gent who came over to inspect the
machine if he'd like to go up.

"I don't know," the man mused. "How much do you pay?"

Kentucky political partisans never pass up an opportunity to
dig at one another even if they are related. Sharon Keeling of
Mackville tells a story which proves the point.

Her grandfather, the late J. C. Jenkins of Willisburg, was a
staunch Republican while his son-in-law was an ardent Democrat.
One night a thief broke into the meathouse and stole four of
the five hams stored there.

"It had to be a Republican who stole those hams," Mr.
Jenkins said to Perkins the next day.

"How do you know it was a Republican?" Perkins wondered.

"Because," the GOPer told him, "if it had been a Democrat,
he'd have taken all eight hams."

It was during the days of the "open range" law that cattle
were free to roam and graze wherever they found grass, even
along the right-of-way of the Tennessee Central Railroad
which served that area. Sometimes cattle feeding too near the
tracks would be hit by locomotives, recalled Harold Smith
of Tompkinsville, whereupon the owner usually would sue the
railroad.

Well, one farmer had taken the railroad to court after his
prize cow had come out second best in a run-in with a train.
His lawyer was trying to make a point of the fact that the
locomotive's engineer couldn't see very well.

"Now just admit it," the lawyer led on the witness, "your eyes
aren't too good are they?"

"Yes, they are," protested the railroad man hotly.

"Tell this jury how far you can see," cooed the lawyer.

"Well," spat the train jockey, "I kin see the moon—how
far is that?"

Years ago Stanley Evans operated McMillan's Ferry, the only
means residents of the Turkey Neck Bend section of Monroe
County had of getting across the Cumberland River to
Tompkinsville, the county seat.

Since the ferry was powered by a set of oars that Evans manned,
the crossing wasn't exactly made with blinding speed. In fact,
customers often complained about the slowness.

For the gripers Evans had a stock answer: "If you're in such
a hurry, you ought to a-come yesterday."

Ray Abner, Louisville, is reminded of an incident that was
related to him by a retired engineer on the Eastern Division of the
L&N Railroad in the days long before the diesel engines replaced
steam locomotives.

This day the engineer had stopped his freight train to
take on water at Blackey in Letcher County. While he was waiting
for this to be done, a boy about 15 years old and with eyes as
big as cantaloupes from seeing his first train appeared on the tracks.

Noting the boy's interest, the engineer asked if he would

like to come aboard for a closer look. He would, and he spent the next several minutes examining the fire box, the various levers and gauges.

The thing, however, that really caught his eye was the lubricator glass, and he stood gazing in open-mouthed wonder as he watched the drops of oil bubble from the bottom to the top of the glass.

"Well, sir," he finally said, "I've seen me a lot things, but that's the first danged time ever I seed a drap drap up."

Years ago, says Dennis Beams of Campbellsville, a couple of farm boys from out in the country were making a run on the free ice water provided at a town soda fountain.

After the boys had been in for water a fifth time, the proprietor got the wearies from so much non-profit patronage. So the next time the boys came in he gave them carbonated water in place of the genuine stuff.

"Let's go," one of the boys said after taking a big swig, "I never did like town water, nohow."

There are various ways to determine how far under the weather a person is, including the method used in an incident related by Emma McDonald of Fountain Run.

An elderly man in the area suddenly took ill and his daughter, with whom he lived, sent her children to the nearest neighbor's house to report the latest developments.

"How sick is he?" the neighbor asked one of the kids.

"Oh, he's awful sick," came the answer. "He's done quit cussin'."

Although I wouldn't know myself, it is said that one seldom gets anything, including sudden wealth, without paying for it in some manner.

I remember some years ago when west central Green County was the setting for one of the most dramatic oil strikes in the country. Wells producing up to 300 barrels a day were brought in at extremely shallow depths.

Almost before anyone realized it, speculators and wildcatters from everywhere had descended upon the county and once productive farmland was scarred beyond recognition by bulldozers, drilling rigs, pumps and storage tanks.

But some landowners who had struck it rich were somewhat hesitant about their new-found blessing.

"How are the wells on your place doing?" I recall asking an old man as he sat rocking on the broad front porch of his farmhouse near the village of Pierce and watching drillers at work in a nearby field.

"They've brought in four already and they're makin' better'n 100 barrels a day," he replied.

"What are you going to do with all that money?" I kidded him.

"I know exactly what I'm goin' to do," the farmer answered almost bitterly as he gazed at his scarred farmland. "I'm gonna buy me a farm that ain't got no oil on it."

In addition to giving the event on-the-spot coverage, our newspaper provided still another service when the Ladies' State Amateur Golf Tournament was played in Hopkinsville a few years back.

When a shortage of caddies developed, 14 *Courier-Journal* carriers were commandeered into service as bag toters during the four days the ladies chased par.

Mrs. Ann Finch, our district manager in Hopkinsville, arranged to make the carriers available and Fleming Thornton, the high school football coach who acted as caddy master, held training sessions to acquaint the boys with their new duties. Everything went well except for the one boy who misunderstood instructions and almost missed the final day.

This kid, only 12 and the youngest of the carriers, served as a spotter the first two days of the tournament and as a caddy on the third.

On the fourth day, with the match play field reduced drastically, a separate handicap tournament was scheduled for those ladies who had been eliminated.

When the 12-year-old didn't seem ready to report for duty that morning, his mother wondered why.

"Oh," he explained, "they're having a tournament just for crippled people today."

"What in the world do you mean?" his mother pressed.

"You know," he said "a handicap tournament."

I am in awe of those persons who are farsighted enough to look around corners that loom ahead and cover their tracks almost before they are made. One such person was a lady who came into an antique and import shop in St. Matthews.

"Do you have any items imported from England?" the woman asked.

"Yes, indeed," the proprietor assured her. "Is there anything you have in mind especially?"

"Well, I'm looking for some sort of small gift items that have 'Made in England' stamped on them," replied the customer. "You see," she said, "I'm going to England in a couple of weeks and there are several friends that I'd like to get gifts for.

"However, I don't want to be bothered bringing small gifts back with me, so I thought I'd buy them gifts here and have them gift wrapped and ready to give to my friends when I return."

Long ago I learned never to make fun of or feel superior to those who reputedly were behind the door when the raw ingredients for IQ were passed out. Compared to many of us, some of those unfortunates are positive geniuses.

Consider, for instance, the 45-year-old man in western Kentucky who wasn't considered very bright. Because of his shortcomings, he was more or less adopted by his sister and her husband and lived in luxury in their home.

"People say I ain't very smart," he told some of the courthouse loafers one day, "but you ain't never seen me workin', have you?"

When his breakfast was brought to him on his 95th birthday, the Rt. Rev. Herbert Hillenmeyer also received a group of nuns singing happy birthday.

"Let me remind you," he said in thanking them, "that 95 years ago this day I was on a milk diet."

One of the many visitors that day casually asked him to what he attributes his longevity.

"I attribute it," he said calmly, "to the fact that I was born in 1878."

Arm a person with a questionnaire to be filled out and there's just no way in the world to anticipate the answers he (or she) will give to relatively simple, even run-of-the-mill queries.

For instance, Edward Mueller of New Albany once told me about the disarmingly honest answer written on one space on the form submitted by a man applying for employment at the place where he worked.

Question: "Why did you leave your last job?"

Answer: "Done all the work."

And, along the same lines, there's an incident Earl Day of Whitesburg told me about some years ago.

Seems a crew of relief laborers was working on a road repair project in Johnson County when one of the machines disturbed a swarm of bees.

First aid was administered and shortly afterwards the efficient foreman of the crew came to the worker and asked him to fill out an accident report.

All the questions listed on the report required only a simple "yes" or "no" answer except the last one, which read, "How could the accident have been avoided?"

That caused the worker to cogitate deeply for some time. Then, after wetting his stubby pencil, he laboriously wrote:

"The bees could of been going forward instead of backing up."

Thinking back to the April 3 tornado, William D. Barkley of Louisville figures a classic understatement was indulged in by one victim of the twister who was asked by a TV newsman what he thought when it hit.

"Well," the interviewee mused, "when I heard the wind a-blowin' and I saw my neighbor's house go a-flyin' by, I knew somethin' was wrong."

Years ago when he lived in McHenry in Ohio County, Boz Eaden of Beaver Dam recalls the excitement caused when the first airplane came over the coal mining community. A crowd gathered to gawk.

"I'd sure hate to be up there in that thing," said one observer.

"Well," added another, "I'd sure hate to be up there and not in that thing."

One particular day a phlegmatic farmer from the Tennessee River bottoms was driving along a dusty country road in a one-horse buggy on his way to Birmingham, a small community now under Kentucky Lake, when a man in a balloon came drifting over just above the tree tops.

The aerialist was performing at the fair in Paducah, but wind currents had carried him far afield and he was lost.

"Ahoy, down there!" he shouted to the buggy driver. "Can you tell me where I am?"

"I know where you're at," the localite replied, barely glancing upwards. "You're hangin' out of the sky in a little basket. Giddup, Susie!"

We hear a lot these days about how bright the younger generation is, but strictly as a matter of defense, let me point out that their parents—my generation—didn't exactly ride in on a load of pumpkins.

What I mean is that while the kids may be as alert as high-IQ owls, they don't always outclass their elders in one-to-one confrontations of raw wits. In fact, there usually are instances where age overcomes youth.

Ralph Day of Louisville provides a for-instance that took place in a Kentucky high school.

It was a spring day a month before graduation, and four girls, all seniors, decided to goof off. So they got into a car and spent the morning driving in the country.

They arrived at school in the early afternoon and immediately met one of their teachers who asked them where they'd been.

"We started to school this morning in my car and we had a flat tire," one of the girls volunteered, "and we just got here."

"That's reasonable," replied the teacher. "But I gave an important surprise exam in my class this morning. If you'll come to my room I'll let you take it now."

The four laggards went to the teacher's classroom.

"I want the four of you to take seats in opposite corners of the room," instructed the teacher. "I'm not going to give you the full exam. Instead, I'm going to ask you just one question and your whole grade for the semester will be based on it.

"The one question is: Which tire on the car was flat?"

Ralph Carlisle provides an example of how tight-lipped many Kentuckians are. A stranger stopped at a crossroads store and noticed a dog dozing next to a tobacco chewer.

"Your dog bite?" he asked the man.

"Wouldn't have me no dog that bit," came the laconic reply.

With that the stranger stopped to pat the beast on the head only to about have his hand snapped off.

"I thought you said your dog doesn't bite," he complained.

"My dog don't," the tobacco chewer replied, barely looking up. "But that ain't my dog."

Olive Hill grocer Lloyd Stamper tells about a man who never had any dealing with a bank but who finally decided to deposit his money. He was given a deposit book and a stack of checks which, being inexperienced in such matters, he began to write quite freely.

Soon he'd used up all the money and the bank called to tell him he was overdrawn.

"I can't understand that," he said. "I got lots of checks left."

As an example of how strongly a gambler can feel about his own particular lucky piece, there's the story told by George Trotter, the Lebanon editor, about a guy who plays poker there every Saturday night.

One Sunday morning after a session with the cards, he accidentally dropped a poker chip into the collection plate when it was passed to him at church.

After church he went to the vestryman in a frantic tizzy.

"When the collection plate was passed," he explained, "I dropped in a poker chip unintentionally. It was the lucky chip I always keep with me and I sure want it back."

After digging around in the change in the collection plate, the errant chip was retrieved.

"Man, alive," the relieved poker player sighed, "I'm sure glad to get back that lucky chip. Here's a half dollar instead."

"Oh, no, you don't," replied the vestryman. "I know what kind of poker you play. That's a blue chip and it'll cost you $5.00."

Years ago when Paducah was still served by some passenger trains, the depot was located several miles southwest of town. One day a salesman from New York pranced into the Palmer House, announced himself, and said he wanted a room.

It became obvious immediately that being far from the bright lights of Broadway, this gentleman considered himself in Hicksville, USA. Everything he saw in Paducah he disliked.

"Why it cost me $1.50 to get from the train station," he fumed in conclusion, "to the hotel. Why would they ever build a train depot so far from town?"

"Well, sir," replied the clerk who had taken about as much abuse as he could stand, "I guess they just wanted to put the station close to the railroad."

William Lightfoot of Madisonville tells of an incident that took place on the Henderson Division of the L&N Railroad years back. This day the freight train had stopped at Earlington to take on water.

It so happened that a rookie fireman, whose duty included filling the water tank, was working his very first run. He climbed on top of the tender behind the locomotive and lowered the spout from the water tower. When the tank was full and he lifted the spout back to its resting place on the tower, he slipped and fell into the tank of eight-foot deep water.

Needless to say he began to tread water to keep from drowning. The engineer heard the commotion and saw the fireman thrashing in the tank.

"All you have to do, son, is put the water in the tank," he grinned. "You don't have to tromp it down."

An incident took place some 15 to 20 years ago and it had to do with a Russell County family's first experience with the marvel we call the television.

This family lived in a remote hollow of the county served by the REA power lines. Despite the fact that all the families up and down the gravel road on which they lived owned a television set, the head of this family staunchly refused to buy one. Finally, after much coaxing, the father broke down and a big console model was delivered and placed in a prominent corner of the living room.

The family gathered around and tuned in WHAS-TV, the only station that they could pick up in their locale. At first the picture was crystal clear but, due to some atmospheric conditions, the picture began to get fuzzy. The man leaped to his feet.

"Bertha," he called to his wife who had gone to the kitchen, "we better get ready to kill the hogs—they's the worst snowstorm you ever seen between here and Louisville!"

An example of the kind of day-to-day humor one finds in small towns is exemplified in a conversation Fritz Lord, Louisville, overheard in eastern Kentucky some years back between the local funeral director, a right portly soul, and a doctor.

"If you don't lose some weight," the M.D. said, "you'll be going to one of your own funerals one of these days."

"Doc," came the reply, "I've been in this business all my life and I've buried just as many thin ones as fat ones."

Food for thought was contained in a "house" ad that appeared in Tom Gish's *The Mountain Eagle,* Whitesburg's paper. It read in part:

"By one measure, *The Mountain Eagle* may be the biggest newspaper in the country.

"The widely circulated *New York Times* sells about one million papers in an eight million population town. That's one sale for every eight people. *The Mountain Eagle* sells about 5,000 papers in an 1,100 population town. That's more than four and a half *Eagles* for everybody in Whitesburg. Obviously, *The New York Times,* to be as big as *The Mountain Eagle,* would have to sell 34 million newspapers daily.

"The conclusion is easy. If you want to reach Letcher County, or an eastern Kentucky audience, place your ad in *The Eagle.*"

I've known a few people in my time who seemed to be lost balls in the high weeds who wound up able to buy and sell a room full of Phi Beta Kappas.

Such a man attended Morehead Normal School long before it became a state college and then a state university. The poor soul appeared to be almost uneducable and he was only able to get through on the charity of classmates who helped him with exams and teachers who graded him leniently.

Years passed and the 25th reunion of his class was held. Those in attendance were shocked beyond belief when he drove up in a block-long car driven by a liveried chauffeur. Since everything about him hinted of great affluence, he was asked when the smarts had set in which made him so successfuul.

"Aw, it ain't no great secret," he explained modestly. "All I done was to develop a little gadget I could make for $1 and sell for $5 and I've been satisfied with just a four per cent profit."

INTRODUCTION   *If Kentuckians have a common denominator, it is, according to my father, their sense of humor. Whether they are tellers of tall tales or objects of practical jokes, Kentuckians will always display an adroit ability to transform the most commonplace events into humorous and lighthearted experiences.*

Some of the Commonwealth's famous—as well as the not-so-famous—sons repeatedly have shown themselves to be true experts in the art of forcing a laugh from their fellow man.

Once former Governor Bert Combs was explaining what went through his mind when the audience stands to applaud a speaker at the end of a talk.

"When people stand up," he pointed out, "I worry because I'm afraid they're going to walk out and leave me with all those dirty dishes to clean up!"

Or take the old man who was stopped by a Kentucky state policeman for erratic driving. When the officer asked for his driver's license the old gent explained that this was the first time he had ever been stopped.

"You don't have a license?" the efficient trooper asked.

"Nope," the old timer responded, "never needed one 'til now."

The Kentuckian can and does show that a true sense of humor has no economic or education restrictions.

CHAPTER 4

KENTUCKY NOTABLES AND FORGETTABLES

Besides needing some referees who will assess technical fouls on home teams for their misconduct, basketball could use a few more George Conleys.

Some years ago Conley, who lives in Ashland, was refereeing a game where one fan was giving him an especially hard time. Finally Conley whistled the game to a halt and walked over to the startled fan.

"Here," he said handing the whistle to the loudmouth. "You know so much more about basketball than I do, you call the game!"

If there is one point to be drawn from this story it is this: No matter how detailed the disguise that one assumes, it seldom will fool an observer who has good eyes and an elephant-like memory.

Some 50 or so years ago Mr. Louis Merenbloom operated a large department store in Corbin. Being a person who personally served each customer in his store, he prided himself on knowing what each person bought.

After World War I when the Ku Klux Klan was making loud noises all over Kentucky, the hooded society held a march in Corbin. Although he was distressed about it, Mr. Merenbloom gathered with the other townspeople along the sidewalks to watch the group parade through town.

Since the sheets covered them from their heads down to their ankles, the identity of each passer-by was concealed from everyone. Everyone, that is, except Mr. Merenbloom.

"Hello, Bill . . . Hello, Sam . . . Hi there, Tom . . ." he called out as they marched by.

The one thing that the marchers couldn't hide was the shoes they wore. And since almost all of them had bought their shoes at Merenbloom's store, their identity was not a complete secret.

U.S. Marshall W. B. "Big Six" Henderson was in the office of the Clinton County court clerk in Albany when there entered an elderly gent whose brother, son and grandson had all been arrested for moonshining during Henderson's days as a federal agent. Learning Henderson was a fed the old man had one question for him.

"You ever know that 'Big Six' Henderson?" the old gent asked.

"Yes," came Henderson's reply. "I know him real well."

"He," the old boy spat, "shore was a mean *%#&*, wasn't he?"

Next to a Marine from Texas or a person who does crossword puzzles with a fountain pen, I guess the most confident person I have ever heard of has to be this fellow from Leslie County who appeared in a story I was told some years back by Bill Moss of Russellville.

An insurance adjuster was sent to Leslie County to investigate a matter involving the company he represented.

It so happened that the man he had to see lived far up a remote hollow. It also happened that this gentleman he was to see was not exactly hospitable in his reception of strangers, especially insurance snoops.

Since the adjuster had never been in the mountains before, and the only information he had was derived from exaggerated stories he had heard in the outlands about quick-shooting feudists, he stopped in Hyden, the county seat, to hire a guide to show him where he needed to go.

The guide was a big raw-boned fellow who was reputed to know the area like the back of his hand.

They started out over the backroads and the guide never said a word. The adjuster grew more and more restless as they drove along.

"Think we'll have any trouble?" he asked uneasily after a while.

"Buddy," the big guide drawled glancing across at him, "you're with all the trouble in this county right now!"

For several years Cawood Ledford, the gifted WHAS sportscaster, has recreated highlights of the running of some of the more memorable Derby races. These broadcasts are aired on the radio during the ten days before the race itself.

Some years ago the 1966 race was replayed on the air the afternoon of the renewal that year. Just as it came on a lady rushed into a store on Bardstown Road.

"Is it time for the Derby yet?" she asked excitedly.

"Just a minute," the store owner told her as Ledford came on with his narration.

"And the winner," Ledford concluded with the track noise dubbed in, "is Kauai King."

"He did it, he did it," the woman shrieked dancing up and down. "I knew he could do it again."

During his days as a state senator, Martin Duffy, Louisville, has heard numerous bills debated before that august body. And he's heard many and varied explanations offered by lawmakers as they attempt to cover their tracks after taking a stand one way or another on the various proposals brought up that might get them into trouble back home with the voters.

For instance, he recalls asking a senator how he intended to vote on a measure that had stirred up a great deal of debate.

"I haven't decided yet how I'm going to vote," came the answer, "but when I do you can be sure I'm going to be quite bitter."

One of Kentucky's real All-American success stories is Clyde Reed, who started from scratch and developed one of the state's largest crushed stone operations near Kentucky Lake. The hours

Reed worked to become successful is pointed up in a conversation he had with Damon Surgenor of Louisville.

Surgenor was commenting on the hours worked by a man who ran a nearby asphalt plant.

"He sure is a hard worker," Surgenor said. "He comes in at 6 a.m. and stays until 6 or 7 p.m. every night."

"I know," Reed replied casually. "I see him when he comes to work in the morning and I see him when he leaves at night."

Henry Watterson, who was editor of our newspaper for 50 years and who lived to be 80, once revealed his personal rules for longevity, and it's amazing how closely they parallel those set down by baseball great Satchel Paige: "Know how to relax; never work when you can play; never walk when you can ride; never sit down when you can lie down."

Combine these recipes and you ought to outlast the hills. That is if you don't get picked up for vagrancy first.

Jack Haury, Louisville, tells about an unnerving, practical joke he saw acted out some years ago.

He was working in Atlanta and shared desk space with a group of engineers. Hangers for coats and hats dotted the wall of the room.

One of the gentlemen was extremely meticulous and almost prissy about his dress habits. When he came to work one day wearing a new hat, the others unveiled the joke which had the poor guy as frustrated as a puppy trying to go off in opposite directions with two little boys.

The jokers bought two other hats exactly like Mr. Proper's new topper—one a quarter size smaller, the other a quarter size larger. They started switching hats on him. One day they'd leave him a hat that fit, the next day one that perched on top of his head, and the third day one that came down over his ears.

Before they let him in on the joke, the man who had thought his head was shrinking from day to day had made an appointment to see a brain specialist.

After Anthony Fowler died a few years ago, a flood of stories were circulated around Elizabethtown, his hometown, in which he was involved during the years he made the rounds in the business district selling *The Courier-Journal* and *The Louisville Times*.

One story concerns a brash Big City stranger who happened to be in an office when Fowler came in with his papers.

"I'll give you a quarter apiece for all the papers you have if you can change this bill," the stranger sneered producing a $100 bill.

"Well, now," replied Fowler quietly digging into his pocket, "I believe that I can do it."

And, much to his embarrassment, the slicker found himself the overstocked owner of an armful of newspapers.

Since I never question the lie . . . er, the facts supplied to me by either golfers or fishermen, you might say that I am a trusting soul.

So trusting, in fact, that I never thought to ask Ed Ferguson of Louisville how he happened to hear this story from the principals involved.

The story involved a Catholic priest who Ferguson describes as a golf fanatic, the kind who would go to any extreme, brave any weather to get in a round.

It had been a hard winter and the snow had kept the priest away from golf for several weeks. Then came weather reports that the next Sunday would be a beautiful day.

Unfortunately, the priest was scheduled for early Mass that Sunday, but his desire to play golf led him to take an extreme measure as he called one of his assistants on the phone.

"I've come up with laryngitis," he whispered hoarsely over the phone. "Can you fill in for me at Mass tomorrow?"

Figuring to get the jump on the other golfers, the priest was at the golf course before sunrise. As he was standing on the first tee waiting for that first glimpse of sun, there was stirring in heaven and St. Peter turned to the Good Lord.

"What are you going to do about that?" St. Peter asked.

"Watch," came the reply as the priest hit his first drive.

The ball screamed off the first tee and high into the sky, hit on the edge of the green, and rolled into the cup.

"And just who," the Good Lord said, "is he going to tell about that?"

The central figure in this story depicting how some people take everything literally is an uncle of Dr. A. D. Albright's wife. The relative, affectionately called "Uncle Dee," once was a magistrate in McMinn County, east Tennessee.

Not only was Uncle Dee a devout Baptist, he was also a literalist of the first order. When he performed a marriage, an official duty which he reveled in doing, he had it in his mind that he was an agent of the Lord.

Late one evening a man and a woman came to him to be married. He joyfully went through the ceremony but later, in going through his records, he was shocked to find that the license the man and woman had presented him was issued in another county. And according to Tennessee law, the marriage was null.

Uncle Dee was deeply troubled by his oversight and he moved to correct the mistake. He began canvassing hotels and motels in the surrounding towns trying to locate the unknowing young couple. The next morning he found the inn where the couple had registered and spent the night.

He went to their hotel room and began rapping on their door. Eventually he was able to rouse them and explained the problem.

There was a moment of silence.

"Your honor," the yet-to-be-bride said, "if it's all the same to you, let's just call the whole thing off."

Completely bewildered, Uncle Dee needed some time for his response which he made as he was leaving.

"What man has joined," he intoned, "God has put asunder."

An incident former Governor Bert Combs recalls involved a man in the mountains of eastern Kentucky who wouldn't attach his name to just any old piece of paper. The man's name was "Root Digger" Hall and he lived near the village of Auxier in Floyd County. His name came from the fact that he made a great deal of his living from digging ginseng and other medicinal roots that grow wild in the woods.

One day Root Digger was walking down a spur railroad track near his home when he rounded a bend and came eyeball to eyeball with a slow-moving coal train. Before he could leap out of the way the train had nudged him off the track and into the ditch.

Fortunately Root Digger was not hurt, but the railroad, not wanting the matter to linger on and maybe see the thing go to court later, decided to send a representative to see Root Digger and present him with a small sum for his lumps.

"The railroad wants to settle this matter quickly," the adjuster said, "and if you'll just sign this paper everything can be taken care of right now."

"I ain't gonna sign no paper," Root Digger answered. "If I done any damage to that train, I'll pay for it, but I ain't gonna sign no paper!"

During World War II Hubert Kessinger of Louisville worked with a manpower census crew in the eastern Kentucky mountains. One day they stopped at a cabin up a remote hollow in Perry County.

An old man was sitting on the front porch chewing tobacco. At his side was a rifle.

"Do you shoot people often?" one of the crew members asked by way of starting a conversation.

"Naw," drawled the man matter-of-factly, "jist once."

Everyone, I suppose, receives letters that might be termed spite mail. These letters are so hot that they ought to be written on asbestos paper and delivered by the mailman equipped with tongs.

John Dromo, the former University of Louisville basketball coach, remembers one he received simply addressed to "Dromo, the poor dumb coach."

"I didn't mind being called poor and dumb," Dromo confessed. "The thing that bothered me was the post office knew where to deliver it."

There is a character who reputedly lived in Franklin County named Truthful Dawkins. There have been many and sundry stories that have been credited to this tall tale teller.

One such story concerned a gentleman named Lee Bibb Smith, a fine guy with only one great fault. He was an addicted poker player. And he never missed his chance to do his thing, much to the displeasure of his wife, who just happened to be an avid churchgoer.

Finally, tiring of the constant bugging and threatening to leave him, Smith promised to give up poker and join the church. He agreed to be baptized the following Sunday.

However, the Saturday night before his baptism he decided to have a final poker fling and he got involved in a game that lasted all night. It was 10 o'clock the next morning before he realized that he was almost late for his own baptism. Quickly realizing the lateness of the hour he pocketed the cards he had drawn and hurried to the creek where the service was to be held.

Everyone in the community was there when he arrived. Being late he just rushed into the creek where the preacher was waiting.

When the preacher plunged him under water the cards in his pocket came floating up—a 10, a jack, a queen, a king and an ace, all spades.

"He's lost, he's lost," his wife moaned upon seeing the cards rise to the surface. "The devil is goin' to get him for sure."

"Ma'am," consoled a man standing next to her, "if he loses with that hand, the devil ought to get him."

It seems that I am forever hearing about things that others say and do and admiring them for their imagination and cleverness.

For instance, there is the Lexington man who filled out his income tax forms properly and sent them in on time. The only thing he didn't do was to sign the form. This he did intentionally.

"If I've got to guess how much I make," he reasoned, "let them guess my name."

Shortly after World War II, the teams of the late Ed Diddle, head coach of Western Kentucky University, began making regular trips to play in New York City at Madison Square Garden.

On one such trip Bob Gillespie, a member of the Western squad, called Mr. Diddle's attention to a matter that had crossed his mind.

The entire Western team was housed on the same floor of a New York hotel near the Garden. Noting that the elevator was too

Joe Creason with staff photographer Thomas V. Miller Jr., who often accompanied him on his stories, in Leslie County. *(Photo by Nancy Boyle, 1953)*

Joe Creason on assignment. *(Photo by Cort Best, 1954)*

At his desk in the Sunday department of *The Courier-Journal & Times.*
(Photo by Gean Baron, 1961)

With Jimmy Stewart, Debbie Reynolds, and Walter Brennan while filming "How the West Was Won" in Kentucky in 1963. *(Photographer unknown/ Courtesy of Mrs. Joe Creason)*

At *The Courier-Journal* and *The Louisville Times* information booth at the Kentucky State Fair. *(Photo by Charles Fentress, 1965)*

The Courier-Journal
THE LOUISVILLE TIMES

JOE CREASON

TROLLER
CHAIRS

THE LOUISVILLE

WAR ENDS

London, May 7 (AP)—The war against Germany, the greatest in h
ditional surrender of the once-mighty Wehrmacht. The surrender t
made at General Eisenhower's headquarters at Reims, France, but off

Joe Creason, then president of the Kentucky Tennis Patrons Foundation, with Spain's Manuel Santana and Arthur Ashe after an exhibition match in Louisville in 1968. *(Photographer unknown/Courtesy of Mrs. Joe Creason)*

U.S. Senator John Sherman Cooper and Joe Creason at the 1973 Festival of American Folklife on Kentucky folk traditions and culture in Washington, D.C. *(Photographer unknown/Courtesy of Mrs. Joe Creason)*

Joe Creason

HE FIGURED right off that the space made available for him wasn't part of the room-with-bath economy plan, but at first Carl J. Richert of Louisville didn't realize how plush the accommodations would be that he was forced into using recently at the Waldorf Astoria Hotel in New York.

Richert, a vice president of Louisville's First National Bank, was to be in New York on business for a week. He'd wired ahead to the ~~Waldorf~~ and had gotten confirmation ~~...~~ st for a single room.

~~...~~ rrived, he was told ~~...~~ nd nothing was ~~...~~ onfirmation, he ~~...~~ planned to ig-

~~...~~ red to get ~~...~~ hority and,

~~...~~ ogized, "the ~~...~~ be reserved for ~~...~~ n to another gues ~~...~~ s to give you temp ~~...~~ for the night and ~~...~~ your room to-

Richert agreed to the change somewhat reluctantly, but then almost collapsed when he was ushered to the "temporary space." For it turned out to be 35-H, the so-called President Nixon Suite.

The suite in which he roughed the nigh[t] had six rooms, including a drawing room which alone was large enough to contain, among other fixtures, 26 chairs and four full-size sofas. Incidentally, the suite rents for $500 a night, compared with the $38-per room he was paying for.

"Since it would be some trouble fo[r] you," Richert graciously proposed to th[e] clerk after ~~...~~ his quarters, " don't min ~~...~~ eek."

"Oh, w ~~...~~ ou out," th[e] clerk gr ~~...~~ n, who jus[t] owns th ~~...~~ d tomorro[w] night in ~~...~~

Joe Creason presenting a Kentucky coffee tree to Lieutenant Governor
and Mrs. Julian Carroll at the old Governor's Mansion in Frankfort in 1974.
(Photographer unknown/Courtesy of Mrs. Joe Creason)

small for the entire team to ride on at once, Gillespie posed a ticklish question.

"Coach, this elevator is awful small," he pointed out. "If the hotel catches fire, how are all of us gonna get out of here?"

Mr. Diddle didn't have an immediate answer but it was obvious that he was working on one. For as soon as the entire team was settled in its rooms the coach had the student manager gather the whole team in the hallway for an important announcement.

"Boys," he spoke to them in his lispy voice, "just in case this place catches fire, I want the regulars to take the elevator and the scrubs to take the stairs."

Sometime back, reports Herb Meehan of the Associated Press Louisville office, a woman was stopped by a policeman in a southeastern Kentucky county seat town. He asked to see her driver's license.

"It says here you are supposed to wear glasses," the officer said after noting that she was not wearing any.

"But I have contacts," the woman replied.

"Lady," the officer rebutted, "I don't care who you know—you still got to wear glasses."

More than 40 years ago Louisville attorney Bemis Lawrence taught school in a little one-room schoolhouse in the then isolated Turkey Neck Bend section of Monroe County.

The unusual experiences he had were enough to fill a Harvard Five-Foot Shelf.

At that time the state didn't have the policy of providing books for the students. Whatever the students read the parents had to provide. Since the Great Depression was in full swing, the parents of one big raw-boned boy refused to buy the lad a geography book to read. It was the father's contention that there was nothing that the boy could learn from the geography primer.

In an effort to shake the old man from his refusal to buy the book, Lawrence asked the boy to stay after school one day. After the other kids had left he pulled out a geography book and turned to a picture of the Pacific Ocean.

"That's one of the oceans," Lawrence said. "The world is two-thirds water. Just think of everything you can learn from this book. Now you go home and tell your father what I have just said."

The next morning the boy reported back to the teacher.

"Pap said that if the world is two-thirds water," the boy said, "what I ought to learn ain't geography, but how to swim."

Just mention fixing horse races and you'll get Tip Hubbard of Bowling Green to tell you about a man who entered a bookmaking joint and announced that he wanted to put $500 down on one of the hay burners in a three-horse race. Later he came back twice more to put an additional $500 on the same horse.

"Friend," the bookmaker said, "I can't take any more of your money because I'm the owner of the horse you're betting on and he can't run a lick."

"Then that race is going to be one of the slowest ones on record," the bettor confessed, "because I own the other two horses."

In its day the late lamented Kitty League was one of the most amazing circuits in all of professional baseball. Not only did it send more players to the major leagues than any other Class D loop, but it was also noted for the unusual incidents that took place.

There was the instance of the umpire calling a pitch a ball for a most unusual reason.

It was the ninth inning and the team from Hopkinsville was ahead 8-0. Then things started going awry for the team. Two easy flies were dropped and then a walk, a hit and three more errors followed.

Finally with two out, two strikes on the batter and the bases loaded, manager Frank Scalzie called for time to go talk to his pitcher, the late Bobby Foster of Central City.

In the discussion Scalzie instructed Foster to throw the first pitch high and inside and maybe catch the batter napping. Foster agreed and sent the ball right over the middle of the plate for a perfect strike that would have ended the game.

Only the umpire called it a ball.

"Well," the umpire confessed to the irate Scalzie, "I heard you tell the pitcher to throw the next pitch high and inside and I just figured Foster would obey you."

One summer when John Maguire was nine he went on a trip up into the mountains with his father. They took the L & N line as far as possible, then rented horses to ride. This particular day they had ridden into the rugged Hell-for-Certain Creek area in search of the home of a Mr. Franklin.

As they rounded a bend in the creek bed they came upon a young boy seated on a stump beside a path with a rifle between his legs.

"Sonny," the elder Maguire asked, "does that path lead up to Mr. Franklin's house?"

"Naw," the boy said, "it leads up to Pappy's still, but it don't lead down!"

Sometimes it is true that he who laughs last, laughs longest.

Take the case of the timid driver in a story I heard.

This driver had pulled into a truck stop along a busy highway to get something to eat. About the same time three guys with skull and crossbones on the back of their leather jackets came varooming up on their motorcycles.

The wheel goons came into the place and after giving it a quick inspection took seats at the same table as the lone truck driver. After they'd moved in, one of the motorcyclists took the trucker's bread and butter, another took his steak, while the third helped himself to the man's coffee.

The driver never said a word, and after a minute or two he quietly got up, paid his check and went outside to his rig.

"That ain't much of a man," one of the motorcyclist's sneered.

"No, and he ain't much of a truck driver either," the waitress replied looking out the window. "He just ran over three motorcycles out there in the parking lot."

Years ago an old gent who had lived his entire life in Anderson County on a farm at the end of a dirt road was induced to ride a truck all the way to Louisville, a good sixty miles away.

When he returned the boys down at the general store were waiting for him.

"What were you thinking when you got that far away from home?" one asked him.

"I'll tell you," he replied in an awed tone. "I was thinkin' if the world is as big on the other side of Louisville as it is on this side, it shore is a whopper!"

Golf can drive even the most mild-mannered person to the point where he loses his self-control.

Take the golfer Edwin Markham of Louisville used to play with every Thursday before the partner moved away. The outings were pleasant until this friend flubbed a shot and then he'd slam his club to the ground and erupt into language that is restricted to XX-rated movies.

When his golf partner moved out of town Markham didn't play with him for several years until he came back for a visit. Then the two of them got together for a game like in the good old days.

The first thing he told Markham was that he'd finally learned to control his temper. No longer did a bad shot send him into cussing a blue streak.

"Nope, I don't cuss anymore," he repeated. "Now when I miss a shot I just spit, and where I spit the grass doesn't grow any more."

Because I am not the type to be able to come up with a quick retort until some time after the fact, I could never dream up the practical joke that Buddy Lepping of Louisville describes as having been played on an acquaintance of his.

Early one evening the victim received a phone call.

"This is the phone company," an efficient voice said. "We have $86 worth of long distance calls charged to your number. Have you made these calls?"

"I can assure you I have not," the voice at home pleaded.

"We thought not," the caller reassured him. "We think the

person using your number has tried to place another call and will
try again soon. We're going to try and trap him and we need your
help."

"You've got it, you've got it," he assured the caller.

"Good," the telephone caller said. "When we call back do
exactly as we say and do it quickly."

A minute or two later the phone rang and the voice on the other
end shouted: "Tear your phone out of the wall."

It was only after he had done so that the man discovered that
he was the victim of a practical joke.

One character I recall from my early days in Benton was a fellow
who was noted for two things: he was Marshall County's premier
watermelon grower and he also was the best or worst (pick your
own adjective) free-style cusser in western Kentucky.

Benton's business section is located on top of a hill. On this
particular day the farmer was driving his wagon into town with a
load of ripe watermelons to sell on the street. Near the top of the
hill the tailgate of the wagon suddenly pulled loose and the entire
load of watermelons spilled out. Those that weren't smashed on
the spot rolled down the hill.

A large crowd gathered immediately, expecting the farmer to
peel the paint off the nearby buildings with his cussing. However,
all he did for several minutes was to survey the mess without
saying a word.

"You know," he said to no one in particular, just shaking his
head, "I just ain't got the words to do this one justice."

Henry Jones of Winchester told for years this story about two
fellow citizens, whose identity will not be revealed for obvious
reasons, who were on a fishing expedition. It being unseasonably
cold for that time of year, they took a bottle of moonshine whiskey
along for medicinal purposes. As the day went on they continued
to doctor themselves by nipping from the jar.

Came late that afternoon, however, and neither man had caught
a fish. Then in a flash of inspiration one of the men took the

biggest minnow he could find in the bait bucket, tied his line around it, poured some of the moonshine down its gullet and dropped the thing in the water.

Almost immediately there was a great commotion in the water. He reeled in his line and found the minnow holding a 4½-pound bass.

"Don't you know," the fisherman later told Jones, removing any doubt as to the truth of the story, "for all his exertion, that poor minnow was wringing wet with sweat!"

Bert Combs enjoys telling a story on himself that took place while he was governor. He spoke at a meeting one day and did what he felt was an impressive job.

Later as he was passing through the crowd he came upon an eight-year-old boy who didn't seem to be too impressed.

"Son, do you know who I am?" the governor asked.

"Naw," the kid replied.

"Do you know who the governor is?" Combs went on.

"My Pap," the boy snapped, "says we ain't got one!"

The apparent lack of adequate track equipment at many high schools in the state was underscored in a story related to me by Phil Eskew, the Indiana High School Athletic Association commissioner.

Seems that this Indiana high school was trying track for the first time. And one boy wasn't overly impressed by the fact that he would be competing against a lot of other young men who had him beat when it came to meet experience.

When the 440-yard dash was called, all the runners with the exception of the boy representing the novice school pulled out starting blocks or dug toe holes for a fast start.

"Don't you intend to use starting blocks or dig yourself a toe hold to help you get a better start?" Eskew asked the boy.

"No, sir," came the reply confidently. "I don't intend to be around here that long."

Shakespeare had Jacques, a character in *As You Like It,* deliver a long dissertation on the seven ages of man. Former Sen. John Sherman Cooper contends the ages are three: youth, middle age and my, aren't you looking well.

Shortly before his death, Dr. David Lawrence of Jamestown, whose practice took him into Bugwood, told me of a conversation he had with an elderly man regarding the old days. It had been some time since the section had had a preacher. Although several had tried, they were always intimidated by a group of young toughs and they eventually left.

"Then," Lawrence was told, "this big preacher nobody had ever laid eyes on before came into the area and said he was goin' to hold a revival. The first night the church house was packed, mostly because everyone wanted to see the rowdies run him off.

" 'I been sent here by the Lord to preach,' " he said first thing when he took the pulpit, " ' and damned if I ain't gonna do what I say.'

"With that he reached into his pocket and pulled out two of the longest pistols you ever did see and laid them on the pulpit.

"And you know," the old man said, "that preacher held a right good revival that night."

Jesse Wilkerson, Caneyville, spends his days making elaborate inlaid walking sticks for friends and reminiscing with anyone who stops by. He's a veritable encyclopedia of information and stories about his region.

"I was born over near Falls of Rough," he said, "and I can recall when Caneyville here was a collection point for lumber and ties and about the roughest place on the whole Illinois Central Railroad.

"They used to tell about a drunk man stopping a passenger train near Paducah.

" 'Where do you want to go?' the conductor asked.

" 'I want to go to hell,' the man smarted off.

" 'Well, then,' said the conductor, 'I'll put you off in Caneyville.' "

Julian Carroll has undertaken a strenuous schedule since taking over the position of lieutenant governor of Kentucky. At times it seems as though he needs a day that is 32 hours in length instead of the regulation 24 to get everything done.

In fact, he's found it necessary to make a schedule sheet for the next day with the time when he's supposed to do everything.

Somewhere In Kentucky there is some man who openly marvels at the detailed nature of this list and the great lengths the Lieutenant Governor will go to remind himself of different things.

You see, when Carroll moved into the lieutenant governor's office in December of 1971 he brought along a desk clock that was presented to him some time ago. The clock has an alarm attachment which because of continued use over the years has the habit of going off at different times without being set.

One day this gentleman was visiting Carroll and the Lieutenant Governor was describing his busy agenda and the time schedule which he draws up daily.

Suddenly the alarm clock went off and at the same time the telephone intercom began to ring.

"Excuse me," Carroll quipped, "but I see it's time to answer the phone."

Since Abraham Lincoln was born in this Commonwealth, it is customary for us in the word game to dust off a Lincoln story from time to time and dredge from it a great lesson that is applicable to today's times.

However, one Lincoln story I have heard has no built-in moral. In fact, the only thing it proves is that he was a mighty agile man with his wits.

It is strictly coincidental that the other man in the story, Peter Cartwright, the early Methodist minister who pursued the devil across the Kentucky frontier before he, like Lincoln, moved to Illinois, was also a Kentuckian.

In Illinois Cartwright, a gifted speaker, was elected to the state legislature and in 1846 took on Lincoln, then beginning his political career, for election to the Congress. As was the custom then, the candidates debated face to face at different gatherings around the district. Often Cartwright's orations resembled hellfire and brimstone sermons.

"I wish all those who intend to go to heaven would please stand up," he orated in one little village.

Every person in the audience stood up except Lincoln.

"Now I wish all those who intend to go to hell would please stand," he continued.

Not a person budged.

"I see, Brother Lincoln, that you didn't stand up either time," Cartwright thundered. "Where do you intend to go?"

"Brother Cartwright," Lincoln replied in an unruffled voice, "I intend to go to Congress, if you please."

I often think of sports and when I do I am reminded of the story once told by Pee Wee Reese, the former Brooklyn-Los Angeles Dodgers baseball player.

After managing the Brooklyn team, the late Charley Dressen suffered from a case of the sour grapes. In the middle of the 1955 season, although the Dodgers were running away with the pennant, Dressen predicted its sunny days were numbered.

"The veterans haven't got it any more," he said. "Robinson, Furillo, and Reese can't hit good pitching any longer."

"Dressen is crazy," Reese answered indignantly. "I never could hit good pitching."

The crossroads store is the traditional gathering point for farmers in the slack-work season. In winter they huddle around a potbellied stove inside and during the summer they sit out front in the shade and tell stories and swap tales in which the first teller doesn't have a chance.

The biggest fish ever caught and the greatest crops ever grown have been revealed in give-and-take conversations at the crossroads store.

One such incident occurred at the store in Grab in Green County years ago. It was mid-summer and the farmers were discussing this, that and other things.

"I never could eat enough watermelon," one man said eyeing a pile of melons on the store porch.

"I'll bet you can't eat that 40-pounder there," one man dared.

"Give me an hour to decide if I can or not," the first man stated.

The delay was granted and he of the great appetite disappeared. An hour later he returned.

"I'll bet you I can eat that melon," he said.

"Why'd you need that time to decide?" he was asked.

"Well," came the reasonable answer, "I had a melon at home about that size and I went home and tested myself by eating it."

Whether the moonshine whiskey story told by David Bishop of Louisville really happened or not, having some acquaintance with the product I know it might have. Anyway, these three veteran moonswiggers met regularly to do some sipping.

The ritual was always the same. All hands would bring a gallon of white lightning. When each had consumed three-quarters of his stock, one would leave. Then the others would have to guess who had left.

An instance cited by Willie Dawahare, the merchant and former mayor of Hazard, gives evidence to the fact that man cannot live by promises alone. For years Dawahare and Jim Caudill, who once coached football at Hazard High School, had been friends.

Because of their close relationship, whenever Dawahare would go on a trip and the need to fly became necessary, he would always take out $75-100,000 worth of flight insurance and make Willie Caudill, the son of his close friend, the beneficiary.

Almost always he'd have some hair-raising story to tell about how Caudill almost collected on the insurance policy.

After one particular close call in New York, Dawahare told Caudill, "You almost cashed in on that insurance this time."

"Willie," Caudill replied, "all I've ever been getting from you for three or four years now is promises, promises, promises!"

From all I've heard they just don't make men anymore like George Morgan, who years ago was the entire staff of a popular hotel he operated in Providence.

He was, to say the least, a bit unorthodox in his philosophy of hotel management.

To illustrate, a persnickety guest once insisted on being awakened on time so he could make a train at 4 a.m. the next morning.

Since there wasn't an alarm clock available, Morgan somewhat reluctantly agreed to stay up and see that the man made his train.

A heavy rain was falling when Morgan's loud rapping on the door awakened the man from a deep sleep. But when the man heard the rain on the roof he climbed back into bed.

"I don't think I'll go today," he said. "It's too bad outside."

"That's what you think," Morgan said pulling the covers off the bed. "I stayed up all night to wake you and believe me, brother, you're going to make that train."

For even the guy who thinks his name is a household word he will sooner or later run into someone to whom he's as much an unknown as the farmer who raises all the beans that some of us never amount to a hill of.

Let me cite an illustration of what I mean.

Monticello, the county seat of Wayne County, currently is basking in the warm glow of civic pride that comes from having two native sons—U.S. Senator Walter D. Huddleston and Ed Hancock, state attorney general—who hold political positions of great importance.

Both men are modest about their prominence and that's good in view of the incident that took place shortly after Huddleston was elected to his first term in the Senate.

A big parade was arranged in Monticello in honor of Huddleston and Hancock. The two men rode together in a convertible with Hancock's father, Festus, seated between them on the back seat.

As the parade slowly wound through Monticello an old man from over in the Cumberland River region turned to Proctor Rankin, who stood next to him on the sidewalk.

"Can you tell me," he asked, "who are them fellers ridin' with Festus Hancock in that car?"

An old farmer who Bemis Lawrence of Louisville knew when he was teaching school in the Turkey Neck Bend section of Monroe County exemplifies the good fortune of being able to record his name in one bold and uncomplicated stroke of the pen.

Lawrence had just gotten out of Western Kentucky State Teachers College (now Western Kentucky State University) and had landed a teaching position in what was then one of the most remote sections of south central Kentucky. He remembers Uncle Hick, the patriarch of the section, as being a natively intelligent man who had no formal education. As a matter of fact, he could neither read nor write his own name.

One day in the mid-1930s, when the government tobacco allotment program was just getting started, the rural mail carrier showed up at Uncle Hick's house with a letter outlining the acreage he would be allowed to grow. Since the letter was registered, it required that Uncle Hick sign for it upon delivery.

"Just sign your name here," the postman said, pointing to a small "x" he had drawn on the proper line of registry.

"Ain't no need to do that," Uncle Hick replied. "Somebody's already writ my name."

During her career in teaching, Elsie Kennedy of the University of Kentucky College of Education has accumulated a wealth of real life stories. While she was art supervisor for Clark County schools, she recalls a letter sent to a fourth-grade teacher.

"Dear Mrs. Howard," the letter went, "if you will excuse my son to go to the bathroom at 3 p.m. each day the bus ride home will be more pleasant for all concerned."

All of us tend to be super critical of things that we don't understand. Take the man in Pineville who had been on the dole for years and had come to expect his welfare check to be at the post office on a certain day without fail.

However, once the check didn't arrive on the right day. When it hadn't arrived after five days, he demanded to see Postmaster Guy Hoskins.

"Now listen here, Guy Hoskins," he ranted, "if you don't do somethin' about gettin' that check of mine, I'm gonna transfer my business to Corbin!"

Ed and Bob Nolan, brothers who grew up in Harlan before becoming doctors and settling in Louisville, recall a preacher who often delivered sermons that were more emotional than logical and who was a regular over a radio station in their home town years ago. Although he'd start out with a Bible text, by the time he was near the end of his sermon he'd have worked himself up into an emotional frenzy.

One Sunday he was preaching on how much he hated the devil, which was considerable, you may be sure. He became more and more wrought up until finally his voice was a hoarse, run-for-your-life-the-dam-is-burst croak.

"And when I see that old devil," he gasped, "I'm gonna kick him and hit him and scratch him."

"And when I lose my strength," he went on, "I'm gonna bite him, and when I lose my teeth, I'm gonna gum the hell out of him."

The telephone was rare in the Butler County area of the Green River country. A farmer, who never had seen a phone, had come from the north side of the river to peddle fresh strawberries in Logansport and had stopped the first man he saw outside the general store to ask if he'd like to buy some of his fruit.

"I don't know," the man said, "I'll have to ask my wife."

With that the man went to the wall phone in the store, rang it and spoke to his wife. The peddler watched with interest from outside the store.

"My wife says she's already got strawberries," the man reported.

"Let me tell you somethin'," the peddler replied emphatically. "I may be dumb and I may be from the north side of the river, but if you think you can make believe your wife is in that little box on the wall there, you're crazy as hell."

There was an old farmer in Marion County some years ago who was constantly fretting about something. It was either too wet or too dry, too cold or too hot; the pesticides were too strong or too weak; prices were too low on products he sold or too high on items he bought.

In short, everything, especially the elements, was always conspiring against him.

Then one year all the pieces fell perfectly into place and he came up with a bumper yield in all his crops.

"You sure can't complain about the elements being against you this year," a neighbor was saying to him after inspecting his bountiful harvest.

"I guess not," the pessimist conceded grudgingly, "but all this growing sure does take a lot out of the soil."

I have to laugh when I remember the case of the hard-bitten old mountain feudist who had spurned religious matters until he retired to his deathbed and the preacher was summoned to prepare him for the voyage into the mysterious beyond. After much haggling, he convinced the feudist the first thing he had to do was forgive members of the family with which his tribe had been warring for more than 50 years.

"Wal, I guess I forgive 'em," he said reluctantly. "But if I git well, none of this counts."

It was the late Depression years and Sarah Blanding was dean of women at the University of Kentucky. One night Dr. Frank McVey, then president of the school, and his wife hosted a dinner at Maxwell Place, the president's home. Because of the distinguished group of guests to be entertained, Mrs. McVey called on Miss Blanding to help with the menu. What would go best with the filet mignon she planned to serve, Mrs. McVey wondered?

Filets always should be smothered in mushrooms, Miss Blanding advised. When Mrs. McVey pointed out she'd already overspent her food allowance, Miss Blanding volunteered to pick enough mushrooms that grew wild at the UK farm to serve the meal.

Although she had great faith in Miss Blanding's ability to distinguish mushrooms from toadstools, Mrs. McVey, nevertheless, had the Maxwell Place cook prepare some ahead of time and these were fed to Boy, the family dog. When Boy seemed to survive, she concluded they were safe for her guests.

The guests were complimentary of the delicious mushrooms. However, as dessert was being served, Alfred, the Maxwell Place butler, slipped into the room.

"Miss Francis," he whispered to Mrs. McVey, "Boy just passed away."

Quietly excusing herself so as to not excite the guests, Mrs. McVey rushed to the phone and called Dr. John Chambers, who was in charge of UK health services.

Mrs. McVey explained to the doctor about the apparent mix-up with the mushrooms and the toadstools and how the family dog had died after eating several of them. And she added that her guests had eaten some from the same batch.

In a few minutes Dr. Chambers, along with six other doctors armed with stomach pumps, appeared, and it was explained to the diners that inadvertently they had been fed toadstools.

Each diner submitted to the stomach pump. Later, as the last of the visitors departed, wan but well, Alfred made a further report on the demise of Boy.

"Miss Francis," he said, "that car that hit Boy didn't even stop!"

Paul Pace of Hardinsburg once told me about the case of a man his father, the late Judge R. O. Pace, had talked into making the race for magistrate in a Muhlenberg County district. One day the man came to Judge Pace and announced that he was dropping out of the race.

"My opponents are making it hard on me by calling me every name in the book," the candidate confessed.

"You can't let it worry you that they are calling you bad names," the judge comforted him.

"I know," the man replied, "but it looks as though they're about to prove 'em!"

INTRODUCTION   Kentucky's name conjures up a variety of
images: a Bluegrass horse farm with past and future Derby winners
frolicking within its white-fenced confines; the smooth and
distinctive taste of bourbon whiskey; the smell of golden burley
tobacco maturing in unpainted barns.

But in the late fall and throughout the winter, Kentucky is
synonymous with only one thing: basketball.

From the mountains of eastern Kentucky to the inner city
of Louisville to the flatlands of the Purchase, future basketball
stars can be seen practicing their dribbling and sharpening their
shooting eyes on courts that are often little more than bare places
of ground with barrel hoops for baskets. These young men dream
of the day when they might don the uniform of one of the
state's universities and lead the school to victory.

On just about every weathered barn, garage door, and alley
telephone pole, basketball goals are erected by parents who, like
their children, dream of athletic success. For the adults, however,
the dreams are often of the past rather than of the future.

For in Kentucky basketball is more than a pastime, a nice way to
spend a few hours on a winter evening. It is a way of life, a
melodrama played out on a 95 x 50-foot stage with the cast being
drawn from the players, coaches and fans.

The stories dealing with Kentucky's long and illustrious love
affair with basketball are many, and Dad was lured by the charm
of them all. The ones that follow attempt to catch that magic
which every Kentuckian has come to recognize as "hoop hysteria."

CHAPTER 5

HOOP HOOPLA

TINY, BASKETBALL-MAD MOUNTAIN COMMUNITY KEEPS ITS DATE WITH DESTINY Up here where the scenery is filled with high hills and every barn door is decorated with a basketball goal, folks at the moment are living on a large technicolor cloud.

For this pinpoint-size Knott County community finally has kept a date with destiny after a generation of waiting.

A week ago, Carr Creek won the 1956 Kentucky high school basketball championship.

And the folks who live along Carr, Betty Troublesome, Yellow, Irishman and the other creeks that rise far up the mountain hollows of south Knott County couldn't be prouder if the entire area had been selected to be pickled and put on display in the Smithsonian Institute.

In winning the championship at Lexington, Carr Creek picked up where it left off 28 years ago.

Until 1928, when it exploded all over the basketball scene, it was nothing but a remote, unknown mountain settlement school.

That year the creekers, who played in cutoff overalls and on a dirt court, came out of their hills to win the Kentucky Class B title and push Ashland to four overtimes before losing the championship.

Later, they were the sensations of the national tournament in Chicago in winning three games.

This year the team went all the way, and Carr Creek bounced squarely back into the glory of the headlines.

Which, no doubt, set many persons to thinking along this line:

"What is Carr Creek? How big it is? How does one get there? What are the boys like who won the championship?"

Well, Carr Creek is a school, a creek and a community. They all bear the name of a pioneer settler in the coal-rich area.

Carr Creek Grade and Consolidated High School perches halfway up the side of a steep hill that rises above the creek on the east side. The total enrollment is 497, half in the upper four grades.

The lower grades are housed in two frame buildings that date back to 1920, the year Carr Creek Community Center, which founded the school, came into existence. The high school occupies a two story, native stone building with an attached concrete block gymnasium. The grades will be gone from the hillside next year; a consolidated school is to be built at Cody, three miles south.

Carr Creek is the smallest community in population ever to win the Kentucky high school basketball championship. Lying inside the two road markers that read "Carr Creek" are 20 houses, J. D. Amburgey's grocery and the Post Office. These buildings are scattered along the road—Kentucky 160—and up the hill by the school.

Carr Creek is 12 miles south of Hindman, the county seat, and 22 miles due east of Hazard. It is out of reach of telephones and railroads.

When Morton Combs, the principal and coach, came here, in 1938, there wasn't even a road over the mountain to Hindman.

The boys who brought the title here are anything but pampered athletes. All 10 squad members are the sons of coal miners. They know well what it is to work hard. All have a regular schedule of daily home chores, from milking the family cow to chopping firewood.

None live within walking distance of school. They catch the school buses that crawl up the hollows within the 10-mile radius from which Carr Creek claims students.

Jim Calhoun, sophomore guard, catches the bus that taps the Yellow Creek area at 6:15 a.m. John Mullins, a reserve, leaves his home near the head of Irishman Creek at 5 a.m. and walks two miles down a path to catch the bus at Amburgey.

The bus delivers students only as far as the bridge over the creek. Some walk up the rutted, winding road to school; others take a steep short-cut up the hill.

Buses used to go to the top. But three years ago, in coming down with a load of children, the steering mechanism failed on a curve and a bus plunged some 200 feet down the hill. Fortunately, no one was seriously hurt. Since then, no buses go up the hill.

Every boy who goes to school here dreams of someday playing on the basketball team. Goals of sorts—barrel hoops, bottomless buckets and the like—are nailed over every barn door. Summer or winter, rain or shine, boys of all ages dribble lopsided balls over

114

the cow tracks and fire shot after shot at the goals.

The mountain itself is one of many examples of how mountain people have banded together to help themselves in education.

Until 1920 there was no school near Carr Creek. Then a group of residents from the various hollows organized the Carr Creek Community Center. Circulars asking for donations for a school were mailed out.

The Daughters of the American Revolution and the War of 1812 took an interest.

A one-room school with 26 students opened that fall. Later, as donations came in, other buildings and quarters for boarding students were erected. No student able to pay was accepted as a boarder.

Boarding students were kept until 1946. By then, better roads and buses made such unnecessary.

In time, about half the school property was deeded to the county.

The high school building is spotlessly clean and shows the pride the entire community takes in it. The inside walls were painted this year by students. All the county contributed for the gym was $5,000. The men of the area built it. They also built the immaculate lunchroom and the home economics room.

Educators throughout Kentucky know the high standards of the Carr Creek High School. It offers a long list of subjects including physics, typing, shorthand and bookkeeping. Fifty per cent of its graduates—three times over the state average—go on to college. This year, four of the five regulars on the Pikeville College basketball team are Carr Creek products.

Coach Combs, an unruffled native of Hazard, believes that teams win games by their own efforts. But he doesn't discount some outside aid his Indians may have had getting their title.

He tells how, before a regional tournament game expected to be tough, he walked into the dressing room and found his nine-year-old son, Glen, and the team manager over in the corner.

They were devoutly reading the Bible and praying. (3/25/56)

HEY DIDDLE, DIDDLE!   Undoubtedly, the best-known citizen of Bowling Green, Kentucky, is a big drawling individual who, from December to late March, performs basketball magic from behind a towel, bath size.

That introduction, of course, fits only one man—Edgar Allen Diddle, a hoop Houdini whose full title reads athletic director and head basketball coach at Western State Teachers College.

Most coaches find a towel, bath size, a convenient bit of equipment for after a game; but during a game, it's nothing more than an added hazard to their masterminding. But not Ed Diddle. He's never without a towel on the sidelines. Over the years, a towel has become his personal trademark as distinctive as was the pregame prayers of "Uncle" Charley Moran's football teams at Centre College in the days—1917 through 1920—when Diddle was the first-string blocking back.

During a heated game Diddle uses his towel as a necessary prop in one of the finest one-man shows since John Barrymore came of age. When a beautiful play clicks for two points, he's likely to heave the towel to the rafters or beat the floor with it in jubilation. In moments of depression, when it seems dark for Western, he may try to ram the entire towel into his mouth, or bury his head and weep like a spanked baby. Even in less dramatic situations, he'll twist it like a rope in his hands or wave it around his head like a whip.

Actually the towel waving act isn't a show, but a means of letting off steam. And such a safety valve is probably a good thing, because at times it seems he's about ready to blow a gasket.

It all started years ago when, as now, in moments of excitement, the palms of Diddle's hands would perspire. He began using a towel to wipe his palms, and it developed into a nervous habit that now has become almost a part of him.

But whatever the reason, since coming to Bowling Green in 1921, Diddle has waved Western from the basketball cellar up the ladder to a point right alongside the best in the country. His record, excluding games of this season, is 401 wins against 129 losses. He has won the Kentucky Intercollegiate Athletic Conference title so many times it has become monotonous—12 times in the last 16 years, to be exact. In addition, Western has picked up nine Southern Intercollegiate Athletic Association trophies over the same span. It finished a very close second in the Madison Square Garden National Tournament in 1942 and went to the quarterfinals of the same meet the next year. Last year the Hilltoppers won 25 of 29 games and were rated fifth in the land by many experts. This year's team, according to Diddle, should be one of his best.

As might be guessed from the towel-tossing explanation, Diddle represents one of man's nearest approaches to perpetual motion. He plays each game as hard as do any of his players. Every time a player comes out of the game Diddle meets him on the sideline to shake his hand while at the same time, maybe, giving him a ringing lecture on what he did wrong.

He has a habit of getting his tongue twisted during exciting moments, and that has led to telling of innumerable stories about him. He's likely to get his tongue all wrapped up and coin a new word or phrase.

Take the time, a few years back, when Diddle was having trouble with "Red" McCrocklin, his star center, in practice.

"The trouble with you," he sputtered, waving his arm wildly, "is that you're too inde-damn-pendent!"

Not long ago, Diddle made a swing over into Indiana and brought back a long, tall center named Oran McKinney from Lynnville. Shortly afterwards he and Ted Hornback, his more-than-able assistant, were watching McKinney, who is on this year's team, rip the net in practice with shots from either hand.

"He's really an ambidextrous player," Hornback mused.

Later Diddle was near the bursting point with excitement as he described McKinney to some friends.

"That big center from Indiana," he bubbled, "sure is an amphibious player—he can lay 'em in with either hand!"

Diddle was one of the first coaches to develop the pivot play, having struck upon the idea in the late 1920s. A player named "Curly" Ellis was on the shooting end of the Diddle-dreamed play. It got so Curly could scorch the net on just about every play.

"Coach," a spectator said one day at practice, "Curly can hit a million from that spot."

"A million," screeched Diddle as his enthusiasm clove hitched his tongue. "My gosh, he could hit a thousand!"

Some years ago Western was playing in Madison Square Garden, and the game was closer than your next breath. Guard "Tip" Downing was bringing the ball down the floor and had reached the center circle when he decided to shoot. As the ball left Downing's hand, Diddle rose with a scream of rage.

"If you ever do that again," he roared, "I'll kill . . . Did you ever see such a shot?"

The brakeman's shout came as the ball slipped cleanly through the hoop. Diddle heaved his towel nearly to the ceiling, doubled over with joy and whooped:

"Whoo-o-o-yee! That's my boy!"

Another time Diddle was giving McCrocklin, an all-time Western great, a going-over. Seems McCrocklin persisted in driving for the basket by circling around from the side instead of coming straight down the middle. Finally Diddle, boiling mad, called him aside.

"Know anything about physics?"

"A little," McCrocklin confessed.

"Then," Diddle ranted, "what's the straightest point between two lines?"

Once, another player was giving him trouble. Diddle called him into his office for a showdown. Those outside could hear much loud talking and desk-pounding. After about an hour Diddle and the player emerged. Both were moist-eyed.

"Ted," Diddle said to Hornback when the player had gone, "we reached an understanding. Why, before I finished with him, I had tears as big as my cheek running down his fingers!"

But don't let those stories give you a distorted picture of Diddle. He may fall slightly under the spell of a heated game and come up with an entirely new vocabulary, but he is regarded as one of the South's sharpest students of basketball.

By nature Diddle is easy-going and extremely likeable. He speaks in a drawling voice and can tell one story after another as long as he has an audience, which he usually has. Even though he's a strict disciplinarian, the players swear by him. As a matter of fact, that discipline is a part of his basketball philosophy.

"I feel responsible for the boys on my squad," he says. "If their dads feel safe in sending their sons to me, I feel obligated to improve them morally as well as physically. If I fail to do that then basketball isn't worthwhile."

"I insist that my players stay in condition for two reasons. First, it isn't fair to have them play if they can't stand the fast pace; and, second, they can't win unless they are in condition. And when they don't win, that's striking right at my means of making a living."

Diddle is a practicing amateur psychologist and the boys in his squad are the subjects on whom he practices. He studies every member of his squad in great detail—their temperament, likes and dislikes, home environment. This, he says, enables him to know their nature and consequently be better able to handle them.

Once a week, on Mondays, Diddle calls all his players together. At that meeting, just about everything is discussed. If a player needs a haircut, Diddle calls it to his attention. If one has indulged in a little too much horseplay, on or off the campus, that is brought out. If one has done something outstanding, he's congratulated. Ed has been right busy congratulating this year's squad because a majority are outstanding students, four being in the 1947-48 collegiate "Who's Who."

Although a New York writer once quoted Diddle as saying he had no system, but just "played by ear," that isn't true at all. Western teams are well coached, and they reflect the long hours Diddle and Hornback devote to fundamentals.

After studying the members of a particular year's squad, Diddle sets standards of play he expects the boys to meet. Either they measure up to that level or they are dropped from the squad.

Over the years some of the finest players to perform on southern courts have measured up to the Diddle standard. Although he's reluctant to list the greatest players to come under his wing since he came to Western, he will talk at length about such stars as W. B. Owens, president of the Kentucky High School Athletic Association; Pap Glenn, present Male High School coach; Harry Hardin, coach at Fairdale; Carlisle Towery, who many experts call one of the greatest professional players of all time; Peck Hickman, University of Louisville coach; Harry Saddler, McCrocklin, Max Reed and various other players.

A training table is maintained for the basketballers and Diddle insists that they consume the proper diet.

"If the boys want to drink," says Diddle, "let them drink water, or milk, maybe."

Once he became so flustered and upset upon finding two empty pop bottles in a player's locker that he shouted:

"The next time I find a locker in your pop bottle, you'll be off the team!"

Practically all Western players come from within 150 miles of Bowling Green. The many Western graduates who are coaching throughout Kentucky form a fine underground system of spotting prospects. Once Diddle gets a hot tip, he and Hornback make a trip to see the boy in action. If he has the three Diddle "musts"— is tall, has big hands and feet, and is able to shoot—they follow his progress through the county newspapers. That way, they make a final appeal to enter Western only to those they reason can fit into Hilltopper basketball plans.

And speaking of boys with size, some years ago Diddle and Kelly Thompson, now assistant to the Western president, were talking with Bruce Dudley, then sports editor of *The Courier-Journal*. Diddle's son, Ed Jr., was kicking a football outside.

"That's my boy, Bruce," Diddle said proudly. "And you know, he's about as big as I was when I was his size."

Ed Jr. has about kept pace with the old man, and now has the three musts—he's 6 feet 2 inches tall, wears a size 12 shoe, can shoot, and has hands the size of overgrown country hams.

Incidentally, he is a member of this year's Western squad.

Those who know Diddle best say you never can tell about him, that he is as unpredictable as the weather and given to doing the unexpected. Some years ago Western had taken a licking from Murray at Murray and Diddle was thoroughly disgusted. After the game he hunted out Hornback and announced that, instead of returning to Bowling Green with the team, they were off for Chattanooga to look over a red-hot high school player.

Well, they struck off for Tennessee. Diddle soon fell asleep and didn't stir a muscle for four or five hours. Then suddenly, as they passed through a small town, he jerked erect and said:

"Ted, let's stop here and eat. If I don't get some sleep soon I'm going to starve to death."

Diddle hailed originally from the thriving center of Gradyville, Adair County. He entered Centre in 1915, but left in 1917 to join the Navy. In 1919 he returned, captained the basketball team, played on the football team that met Harvard in 1920, and met the girl who later became Mrs. Diddle.

In the fall of 1921 he was hired to coach basketball at Greenville High School and did well enough to attract the attention of the late Dr. H. H. Cherry, then Western president. Dr. Cherry offered him $150 a month to come to Western, but Greenville upped the ante to $250. However, Diddle decided to take the bigger job, even though it cost him money.

At first he coached football, basketball, baseball and track. He gave up football to "Swede" Anderson in 1926, and track just sort of petered out. But he has stuck with basketball and baseball. Hornback, a former Western great, joined him in 1939, and now also is head of the physical education department.

Last year Western avenged all but one of its four losses in later games, beating the University of Louisville, Bowling Green of Ohio and Eastern Kentucky. Only a 57-46 loss to Georgetown University of Washington, D.C., remained unavenged. However, the Toppers meet that team this year at home next Friday night.

"We intend to pay Georgetown back for that loss with interest—compound interest!" Diddle vows.

Either they'll do just that or Diddle probably will wave his good right arm off just below the elbow. (12/28/47)

ARE SMALL SCHOOLS LOSING   There are those among us
THEIR BASKETBALL GRIP?   who will argue until the cows
come home, or later, that basketball is near-ideal for the likes of
Kentucky; that it's the one sport in which—since only a few
players are needed—the smallest high school can compete more or
less evenly with its largest neighbor.

And there are several David and Goliath incidents over the 32
years of Kentucky state high school tournaments to add some
weight to their arguments.

Now maybe I'm just being like the nervous alarm clock—all
alarmed over nothing—but I wonder if nowadays the small high
school, one with, say, 40 boys enrolled, can compete evenly with
the school that has 100 or even 300 boys, as some do. As a matter
of fact, it seems to me that superiority in numbers is beginning to
be felt in basketball just as it has been felt already in other
sports, particularly football.

Look over the sixteen teams that will compete here this week for
the Kentucky championship. With the possible exceptions—Bush
and Hindman—there isn't a really small school numbered among
them. What's more, neither Bush, with about 165 in high school, or
Hindman, with about 200, honestly could be called small.

But otherwise, the largest schools in the state are represented.
There's Louisville Male, which has an all-boy enrollment greater
than a couple of colleges in this state. And there's Paducah
Tilghman, Owensboro, Central City, Clark County, Newport,
Corbin, Lexington Lafayette, Maysville, Pikesville—
all with more than 300 students.

Even the middle-ground group, which includes only Dawson
Springs, Tompkinsville, Campbellsville and Fairdale, all have
more than 200 students.

To continue along the same line of thinking, go down the list of
tournament winners for the past six or seven years, since the
change became noticeable. Except for 1948 when Brewers, with
only 26 boys in high school, carried off the trophy, the meet has
been pretty well dominated by the large schools.

Once you reason through the thing, you can understand why the
upper hand in basketball, like in other sports before it, is swinging
toward the big schools, those with large groups of boys from whom
to pick the 15 or 20 players needed. After all, it stands to reason
that the more boys there are to choose from, the better the chances
of turning up with the 10 required to win a state title. The odds
of uncovering those 10 players from among just 30 or 40 boys in a
high school probably would look like the National Debt to One.

There was a time when there was little or no enrollment distinction between high schools in football playing. In those dear, dead days, any school that could drum up 20 candidates for the team could play football and often knock themselves off a giant. But times change and today most coaches feel they need 20 boys trying out for center alone. In other words, a superiority in numbers has been built up. You can about count on the thumbs of your right hand the big boys who are now kayoed by some small school rival.

That same thing, it seems to me, is developing in basketball. The day may be coming when, for tournament purposes, the high schools will have to be divided into two groups—those of under 150 students and those with over that total, or some such arbitrary figure. Otherwise the little guys may fade out of the picture entirely.

Of course the time when the little schools no longer can hope against the big city school in basketball probably will be much slower coming than it was in football. But many of the larger schools just now—in the past five to ten years—are taking their basketball seriously. For the first time they are attaching some importance to the game. Basketball now is a big money sport, one that draws in more fans than most gyms can hold, and only winners make money. So the big fellows are interested in winning.

Personally, I'm sorry to see that trend developing. I hope I'm all wet, as I have been once or twice before, in assuming that there is a trend underway. There was something heartwarming and wholesome in such small schools as Corinth, Midway, Sharpe, Heath, Hazel Green, Brewers and the like, many of which didn't have indoor gyms, taking home the big prize. To me, it was a sort of reaffirmation of the philosophy that the little fellow really does have a chance, after all.

Come on you Bush and Hindman! (3/15/50)

TALL TALES (BUT TRUE) OF BASKETBALL IN KENTUCKY   To underscore how politics has become a way of life in the land of bluegrass and racehorses, Kentuckians for years have learned that ancient poem which ends "... And politics—the damnedest in Kentucky."

Change "politics" to "basketball" and you'd have a fair start at describing another unusual facet of life in the Commonwealth.

Even more so perhaps than politics, Kentucky takes its basketball very seriously, indeed.

How popular the game is in this state can be seen in the crowds it draws. Louisville's spacious Freedom Hall was jammed last week with fans at the National Collegiate Athletic Association finals. And it'll be packed again this week for the Kentucky State High School Basketball Tournament.

Popularity is one thing, predictability another. And here's what really puts the bounce in Kentucky's brand of basketball. Ever since the days half a century ago when games were played on outdoor courts before a handful of spectators, the unexpected is what Kentuckians have come to expect when two teams square off in basketball.

Item: The 1958-59 Oil Springs High team won two tournaments in the same night. Due to a slip in scheduling, Coach Rusty Yates entered his team in two tournaments in one week and the boys advanced to the finals of both. In the championship round, Coach Yates divided up his squad and sent half the boys off in different directions. He kept in touch with both games by telephone. So when team "A" started having trouble in its game at Prestonsburg, he quickly dispatched reinforcements from Team "B," which was winning easily in its meet 22 miles away at Salyersville. The shock troops pulled out that game 68-60, while the boys who stayed behind won their tournament 78-50.

Item: Two years ago Millersburg Military Institute defeated St. Patrick's of Maysville in a game that has to rank among the longest start-and-stop contests ever played. The game went through nine overtime periods, and required nearly four hours before MMI eked out a 106-105 win. After each of the three-minute overtimes, the gym clock, which started only at the 8-minute mark, had to run 5 minutes before the teams could have at each other again.

Item: The 1966-67 Graham team was being badly mauled in one game. The opposition ran its score to 98 points early in the fourth quarter, but the Grahamites were determined no team would score a hundred on them. So, on the ensuing throw-in, a Graham player took careful aim and banked the ball into the other team's basket, thus preventing the tormentors from having the satisfaction of hitting the century mark on their own.

Item: Some may have wondered what the Graham team would do as an encore to the deliberate basket scored for the opposition. They weren't long in finding out. Later that same season the team went into a game against Central City trailing 1-0 before the opening toss. Central City scored on a technical foul called before the game started because the numbers on the Graham players' uniforms didn't match the numbers given the official scorer.

Another team that once started a game behind 1-0 was Kavanaugh School in 1930. In that case, however, things worked out so that later—a regulation game and seven overtimes later—the Kavanaugh coach, Earle D. Jones, was hailed as a great strategist.

Kavanaugh had drawn powerful cross-town rival Lawrenceburg High in the district tournament at Frankfort. But Jones was confused about the starting time and was tardy in getting his boys to the scene of the battle. A technical foul which Lawrenceburg scored on was awarded, and Kavanaugh started the game in the hole with the score 1-0.

The regulation game ended tied 20-20. After Kavanaugh won by 28-21 in the seventh overtime, disappointed Lawrenceburg rooters accused Jones of pulling a fast one by intentionally bringing his boys in late, thus upsetting their team emotionally. Kavanaugh supporters, in turn, hailed it as the smartest bit of strategy they'd ever seen.

"So you see," Jones said many times later in discussing the heroics of that game, "the difference between a smart coach and a goat is just a few points."

That Kavanaugh team went on to win its way to the state championship tournament in Lexington. When the team played its first game there, its Number 1 rooter was Mrs. Rhoda Kavanaugh, founder of the famed (now closed) prep school.

By then Mrs. Kavanaugh, who sometimes helped coach, already was something of a basketball legend. At most games she would position herself under the basket armed with a long umbrella. When one of her boys did poorly, she wasn't above flailing him smartly with the umbrella whenever he came within reach.

One of the referees calling Kavanaugh's first game in the tournament that year was Frank Lane, later a major-league baseball executive. Lane's trademark was that when a player made a foul, he'd pop him on the hind side to emphasize to the scorer who made the infraction. Early in the contest Lane detected a Kavanaugh boy fouling and reacted with a resounding whack to his flank. The spectators were silent, but suddenly the gym rang with the sound of Mrs. Kavanaugh's high-pitched voice from high in the stands: "You big bully," she screamed, "don't you ever dare to hit that boy again!"

Referees, it seems, always are having their troubles. Last year during a game at Berea one of the officials suddenly called time out and went rushing from the playing floor to the dressing room. He returned a few minutes later wearing a different pair of pants and a ripe tomato blush. Zipper trouble, you know.

Speaking of pants, the Carr Creek team that captured the imagination of state tournament fans in 1928 didn't have any— game pants, that is—until they'd advanced to the regional meet. The Creekers played at home on an outside dirt court and wore overalls. Only after the boys reached the regional tourney at Richmond did they have uniforms—and borrowed at that.

It was common gossip that the Carr Creek team was so short of basketballs that the boys practiced by shooting pumpkins at barrel hoops nailed over barn doors.

Lack of proper attire once was common at many schools. Dr. David Lawrence, now dean of students at the University of Louisville, recalls that when he coached at Sulphur High in the early 1930s the school had no budget for shoes or even socks for the players. One day his star player reported he wouldn't be able to practice that afternoon.

"Because," the boy explained, "I wore my Sunday socks today."

Most teams today are resplendent in brilliant uniforms that would make Jacob's coat of many colors seem drab in contrast. Gyms, too, have come a long way since the days when many schools simply pushed desks to one side of a study hall, hung goals to the wall at either end, and pressed whatever space there was available into service as a playing floor. It wasn't much, but at least that took the teams indoors and away from the outside courts that usually were a sea of mud during the winter months.

An idea of what playing conditions were like in such makeshift gyms was pointed up in an incident that took place some 45 years ago at a school that shall remain forever nameless.

This school played its home games in a second-floor study hall where the only lights were several kerosene lanterns hung from the ceiling. One night the brightest lanterns were hung over the goal at which the home team warmed up before the game. Although his team hardly could see the wall at its end of the floor, the visiting coach didn't complain because the bright lanterns would be over their goal during the second half.

However, when the teams returned to the floor to resume the game, someone had switched lanterns and the bright light still was over the home team's goal!

There are several reasons which explain why basketball has become such a way of life in Kentucky. For one thing, the game is easy to understand and is played at a time when, before TV, there was very little in the way of entertainment in most small communities.

Moreover, the cost of outfitting a team is nominal and, more than in any other sport, a school with a small enrollment has a chance of defeating rivals many times larger.

When Brewers won the state title in 1948 and wound up the season with a 54-0 record, there were only 21 boys in the high school and 16 of them were involved in basketball.

The last year that University High, the University of Kentucky training school, had a team was in 1965. The school then had 30 students in the senior class. Of the 30, twelve boys were on the team and six girls were cheerleaders.

Cheerleaders are an integral and colorful part of any school's basketball program, and the girls train for their duties as diligently as do any of the players they urge on to deeds of derring.

A few years ago, during a time-out in a tense game, a Fulton cheerleader removed one of her contact lenses and placed it on her tongue to wet before replacing it in her eye. Just then the game resumed. An exciting play developed and she swallowed the lens.

Kentucky fans, young and old alike, respond to the excitement of a hard game. Like the Lexington man who was unveiling a brand new set of false teeth at a game. At one point, with the going a bit sticky for the home team, he opened his mouth and emitted a mighty roar of encouragement. The outburst loosened the lower plate and the new store-bought choppers sailed down into the spectators seated several rows below him.

Communities, especially in rural areas, take great pride in winning teams, and players become local heroes. Although Corinth had been runner-up in the state tournament in 1929, it was given little chance of getting out of its own district and back to the championship round the next year because of the powerful Walton team just down the road.

However, Corinth defeated Walton and went on to take the state trophy. A few days later a sign was erected at the city limits reading: "Corinth: Home of State Basketball Champions."

A sign was also erected a short distance away at the Walton city limits. It read: "Walton: Please Do Not Discuss Basketball In This Town."

On a per capita basis, few communities have backed a team more completely than did Cuba in 1952. When its team reached the state tournament that year, it was reported 99 of the 100 residents of the tiny Graves County village were in the stands. The one person missing had stayed behind to milk the community cows.

Just mention basketball and partisan fans get worked up even when they don't know all the facts. Like the two fellows, neither one a likely Phi Beta Kappa candidate, who were discussing the situation after their favorite team, Monticello, had drawn a bye in a tournament.

"I see where we drawed Bye," one man said. "Where in the world is Bye at?"

"I'm not sure," the other replied, "but ain't that that little place down there this side of Science Hill?"

Kentucky colleges haven't been without their odd and unusual basketball happenings. Ellis Johnson, now at Marshall University, was good for at least one unexpected happening per game when he coached at Morehead.

One year in the early 1950s, powerful Western Kentucky defeated Johnson's team at Morehead, with Bob Lavoy, Western's fine center, alone scoring nearly as many points as the entire Morehead team. When the schools met in a rematch at Bowling Green, Johnson unveiled one of his most flamboyant acts.

After the teams had warmed up, and before the opening center jump, Johnson and his manager marched out on the floor. Johnson carried a tape measure and the manager had a note pad and pencil.

Johnson, deliberately acting out every step while the Western team and fans sat bewildered, measured the width of the floor, and the manager noted the dimensions on his pad. Then he measured the height from foul line to the end line and the circumference of the center circle. This done, he carefully scanned the figures entered on the pad.

"I guess," he called out after holding up his hands for silence, "the difference really must be Lavoy."

Although a so-called state tournament was held as early as 1916, it wasn't until 1918 that the Kentucky State High School Athletic Association made it an official function. Lexington won the first tournament by nosing out Somerset 16-15.

Incidentally, a guard on the Somerset team was a skinny young fellow by the name of John Sherman Cooper.

Whatever happened to him? He became a United States senator. But then that's politics—and basketball—in Kentucky. (3/23/69)

INTRODUCTION   When it comes to down-home, dyed-in-the-wool humor, the famous husband-and-wife team of George Burns and Gracie Allen is difficult to top.

In Kentucky, however, there are many married couples who have displayed a knack for telling funny stories that would make the old radio team turn green with envy.

The humorous inter-play between mates might take the form of out-and-out dialogue between the two parties. Or possibly it will involve the husband talking about his wife, or maybe the wife telling a tale about her mate. But you can believe that no matter how it is told, the story will have a humorous twist to it.

One of my dad's favorite husband-and-wife stories concerned the central Kentucky wife who received a phone call from her local banker pointing out what he regarded as an oversight on her part.

"Your account is overdrawn," the banker regretted telling her.

"No, my account isn't overdrawn," the woman corrected him. "It's underdeposited by my husband."

Or take the comment that a Louisville wife made about the impending retirement of her husband.

"As far as his retirement is concerned," the wife said, "there'll be twice as much husband and half as much money."

If your funny bone can stand it, the following pages contain some of the best husband-and-wife humor you'll ever want to find.

128

CHAPTER 6

Husbands and Wives

There's more ways than one to skin a cat. And Mrs. C. W. Holton provides a classic example in the case of an old farmer who made several visits a week to his safe deposit box in his bank.

It was assumed he was salting away cash, but when it was opened after his death, it was found to contain only several fifths of bourbon.

Seems his wife wouldn't let him drink at home, so. . . .

It was Bob Prater, a friend in Salyersville, who told me about a friend who was needling his wife after she weighed herself.

"See," he said, "I told you that you're too fat."

"I am not," she snapped. "I'm just six inches too short."

When he was a boy in Tompkinsville, Bemis Lawrence, Louisville, remembers two friends who, after moving away, returned for a visit and met each other on the street after 25 years.

"How's life treating you?" one asked.

"Not so good," the other replied. "I've been married twice and I had bad luck with both wives."

"What happened?"

"Well," came the reply, "my first wife left me but the second one didn't."

While dining in a restaurant in Florida last winter, Mr. and Mrs. Fred Scheler of Louisville were attended by a talkative waitress who confessed to being 60 years old.

"Yep," she added, "I'm too young for Medicare and too old for men to care."

Ben Edelen Sr. of Louisville called me to say that his wife Mary lost her credit card for a major department store six months ago, but he hasn't reported it to the proper authorities. After all, he says, the person who found the card is charging less than when his wife had the card.

I wouldn't want to trade places with the guy in Central City who was quoted by Larry Stone: "It's terrible to grow old alone. My wife hasn't had a birthday in 15 years."

If a remark attributed to him by Jim Morrissey of Louisville is true, then Eugene Unrich got his marriage off to a shaky start via a remark he made to his wife Margie shortly after they'd taken the I-do's.

"We're out of ice cubes," Margie supposedly informed him.

"How come?" he asked, ducking. "Did you forget the recipe?"

R. W. Garrison, who now is with the Kentucky Department of Fish and Wildlife Resources in Frankfort, tells of an interesting telephone conversation he had a few years back with a woman who was hardly an encyclopedia of information on squirrels and their ways. At the time, Garrison was district supervisor for the department in the Louisville area, and a few days before, our paper had carried a story about how, because of a mass food shortage, hungry squirrels were migrating into Kentucky from Tennessee.

Evidently this woman interpreted the migration as a sort of sudden mass movement whereby every squirrel in Tennessee climbed aboard a chartered bus and headed north.

"I read about the squirrel migration into Kentucky," she said to Garrison. "My husband works during the week. I'm sure he'll want to go hunting on the weekend. Can you tell me where the squirrels will be on Saturday?"

Not knowing what to tell her, Garrison called Harry Towles, then public relations director for the department and a fast man with logically illogical answers. His reply apparently was just what she wanted to hear because she hung up pleased.

"The squirrels left Russell Springs this afternoon and are expected in Lawrenceburg Saturday morning," he said. "But your husband will be wasting his time hunting the four-lane highways since the squirrels are traveling the back roads."

In these days when quick divorces and even quicker remarriages are commonplace, it sometimes seems to me that one needs to keep updated constantly in order to know who is tied to whom at the moment.

As in the case of a Louisville man I won't identify because his name isn't really important to the story.

Anyway, his wife was in the hospital for surgery recently and the wives of some of the men in the office where he works—and who know him only casually—heard about it and decided to visit her and cheer her up with a get-well-soon potted plant.

However, when they arrived at the hospital she had already checked out. So the women looked up her address in the phone directory and drove to the house. After considerable doorbell ringing and no response, they left the plant on the front porch with a note attached.

Three or four days later the husband called on the gift givers.

"Thank you very much for the gift," he said, "and I hope you'll excuse my delay in thanking you.

"But," he added, "I've just recently gotten a divorce and remarried and you left the plant at the home of my first wife."

When he was campaigning for governor six years ago, Louie Nunn
was making the rounds of stores in a west Kentucky county seat.

In a 10-cent store, he came upon an old man standing at a
counter trying on eyeglasses. He'd put on one pair, squint through
them, then put them aside and test another pair.

"It's hard getting the right glasses that way, isn't it?"
Nunn said to the man.

"Yep," he replied, "especially when you're gettin' 'em for
your wife!"

On Ash Wednesday, reports Mrs. S. Hays Walker of Springfield, a
man and his wife, both good Catholics, went into a restaurant
in a small town in southeastern Kentucky.

"Do you have anything for Lent?" the wife asked the waitress
as she glanced at her husband.

"I don't know," the waitress mused. "What would
Mr. Lent like?"

The way it can be in retirement was pointed up by Dr. Harry
Sparks in a comment he made while serving as master of
ceremonies at the inaugural luncheon for Dr. Constantine Curris,
who succeeded him as president of Murray State University. Dr.
Sparks was commenting on the busy life he had been leading
since he retired as head of the school.

"I used to work for the Board of Regents and they met every
three months," he said. "Now I work for Lois Sparks and she
meets every morning."

The wife of a friend was supposed to meet him downtown, but
she was tardy. However, she had a reasonable excuse.

"The traffic was terrible," she alibied. "A police car was in
front of me the whole way."

University of Kentucky basketball fans are noted for being the most avid of the avid, but Mrs. G. W. Major, Louisville, tells about one who stands out from all the rest like a sore thumb in a red bandage.

The fan is a husband of a friend who, upon returning home last week, found him listening to the UK-Tennessee game on the radio. He was dressed in his pajamas and, to show his true color, a neatly knotted blue necktie!

Walt Gorin of Greensburg figures things were put in the proper perspective recently when he was leaning over the rail at the Louisville riverfront Belvedere, staring at the muddy Ohio River far below. His wife, standing at his side, seemed uneasy.

"Be careful, you might fall in," she worried. "You've got the car keys."

There are countless old sayings that start "I would rather be. . . ." For instance, "I would rather be safe than sorry," "I would rather be right than president," etc.

To the list, add one that Maurice Resch of Louisville says his wife coined for him after he had kidded her about talking so much.

"I," she said, "would rather be wrong than silent."

In conversations I've had with persons who have hit the 100 mark in age, one thing stands out: They've been sustained by a keen sense of humor. An added example of that was pointed up in an interview Elizabeth Spalding of Bardstown had with a woman who was celebrating her 100th birthday.

A widow since her husband, Sam, had died 30 years before, she made this observation:

"I guess Sam's wondering what's happened to me. He probably thinks I've passed on and gone to that other place!"

I've always figured that rural Kentuckians are unique because of the way they treasure a good hunting dog, a prize cow or a work animal far above mere silver and gold.

But after hearing about an incident Richard Howard was witness to in Alabama, I've about decided that folks out in plowed-ground sections are pretty much alike regardless of where they live.

Howard, who came from the hills of eastern Kentucky, was doing graduate work at the University of Alabama and he described the incident to Norman Allen, editor of *The Floyd County Times* in Prestonsburg.

Howard was in a drugstore in Tuscaloosa when a woman entered. It was apparent from her dress and her speech that she had grown up in the cotton fields.

Seems both her husband and the family mule were under the weather and the local doctor and the veterinarian had each given her a prescription which they said could be filled at this particular drugstore.

"One of these is fer my husband and the other's fer my mule," she reminded the druggist as she handed him the prescriptions.

He retired to a back room and in a few minutes reappeared with two bottles in his hand.

"Did you mark them real good?" the woman asked seriously as she took the bottles. "I shore wouldn't want to give the mule the wrong medicine."

This is a weight conscious age that we live in. Various methods are used to keep the weight down and the figure up. Among these is bicycle riding.

A Louisville woman I heard about used this mode as her weight losing shortcut. She was standing in front of a friend of mine in the supermarket check-out line when a woman she'd obviously known some time walked up to her.

"Hello, skinny," the second woman said. "You've lost a lot of weight. How did you get so trim?"

"Riding a bicycle," came the reply.

"My goodness," marveled the questioner. "How long did you ride?"

"Oh, about ten minutes."

Noting the perplexed look that explanation drew, the bike rider went on to supply fuller details of how she'd won—temporarily, at least—her personal battle of the bulge.

"I had been riding this bicycle about ten minutes," she said, "when the brakes suddenly failed. I went flying across Cherokee Parkway, I was hit by a car, and I spent about two months in a cast!"

Being a male chauvinist, I've always felt that women should be as placid and slow to anger as men, a feeling pointed up in a conversation Carl Denton, a Hindman native, recalls hearing one day between two elderly gents outside the Knott County Courthouse.

One man was confessing that he'd had to leave home early that morning because his wife was fussing at him for having broken her best jelly dish.

"I don't know why she got so worked up," he said seriously. "Why, she's wore out two of my best axes choppin' firewood and I ain't ever opened my mouth to her!"

First director of the University of Kentucky Community College at Cumberland in Harlan County was Dr. Edsel Goodbey, who used to tell about a man from the area who took up golf at the age of 77 and became a willing slave to par. His wife, a spry woman who likewise was devoted to active hobbies, was asked if she intended to become a golfer too.

"Law, no, honey," she said, "I wouldn't even know how to hold a caddy!"

A Louisville friend tells about an acquaintance who was on a motor trip with his wife when they had one of those little disagreements which create a frigid condition known as "Not Speaking." As they drove along, they passed a jackass in a field beside the road.

"Relative of yours?" the husband asked, breaking the silence.
"Yes," sweetly replied the wife. "By marriage!"

Since I've heard it several times lately, apparently this story is making the rounds:

This guy's wife gave birth to twins, a boy and a girl, and his brother, who wasn't exactly a mental giant, begged to be allowed to pick names for the children. Reluctantly the father agreed.

"What did he name the little girl?" his wife asked later.

"Denise."

"That's not bad," she sighed with relief. "What did he name the boy?"

"Well," the husband replied, "he named him de nephew!"

For more than 50 years the late W. S. Castleberry was a Baptist preacher in the Purchase section of Kentucky. Needless to say, his experiences—sad, funny and a mixture of both—would have filled the Harvard Five-Foot Shelf.

One serio-comic incident he used to tell about was a funeral for an elderly woman conducted at Lynn Grove in Calloway County. Before the service he stood with the husband beside the casket.

"You know," said the tearful husband, "I'd just as soon give up the best cow I ever had as her."

He was joking, but former Gov. A. B. Chandler offered me an interesting explanation for his vigor and sturdiness at age 74. When he and Mrs. Chandler were married, they agreed that any time there was an argument between them, he would go outdoors until things cooled off.

"It's bound to be good for anyone's health," he grinned, "to spend more than 40 years in the open air."

Ironic, bizarre and bitter-sweet humorous stories relative to the April 3 tornado keep coming in.

On the afternoon that the twister hit, Mr. and Mrs. Hugh Reynolds were on the back pasture of their Henry County farm trying to bring their horses in to be fed. Seeing the tornado coming, they fell into a ditch and when they arose they found the storm had leveled their house, milk house, three barns, chicken house and corn crib. Feed was scattered everywhere.

Almost in a daze, Reynolds saw a feed bucket and asked his wife to help him pick up some of the grain.

"But that bucket is cracked and doesn't have a handle any longer," she said.

"Well," he sighed as he gazed at the wreckage, "nothing's perfect."

Thinking about the Democratic convention reminds me of an incident the late Alben Barkley used to tell about that place years ago when the party met in Chicago. His hotel was jammed with delegates and one night the elevator he was taking to the lobby was so packed that at one floor a woman was able to squeeze aboard but her husband didn't make it.

"My husband, my husband," she pleaded, tugging at the operator's sleeve as the door closed in his face.

"Calm yourself, lady," the operator soothed, "this ain't the Titanic."

Some people are so saturated with pure unadulterated frugality that they'd walk through ground glass in their bare feet to get anything labeled as a bargain, whether or not they really need the popular sale item.

One woman who was that way is the main figure in a story told by Joe Pete, Benton's memory bank of odd and curious occurrences.

This woman—and I knew her well because Benton still happens to be the only place in Kentucky where I was born—was noted for her birddog-like instinct of sniffing out reputed bargains. You can imagine the tizzy of excitement some years ago when a store over the state line in Tennessee advertised a super, colossal, unprecedented, never-again sale of odd lots of women's shoes at a mere 75 cents a pair.

Thus she was prominent in the throng of women on hand when the store opened the next morning, snatching and grabbing shoes like they might never be made again. In fact, she bought 15 or 20 pairs.

After returning home, she could hardly wait to tell friends about the rare shoe bargains she'd pulled off.

"And you know," she said breathlessly, "one pair very near fit me."

Like most small communities, a little town in southern Indiana has its own town drunk. He's a carpenter and, they say, no nicer guy ever stepped into shoe leather. It's just that he has a problem with whiskey. When he gets bombed, the police or acquaintances simply haul him home and turn him over to his wife.

For years his long-suffering wife had put up with this routine without noticeable complaint. But finally she reached the breaking point. When he came in barely able to navigate, he found she had locked the doors and windows and refused to let him in the house.

He sat for some time on the front steps, pondering what his next move would be. Suddenly he arose and reeled to the carpentry shop at the back of the house and armed himself with a hammer and nails. Then he proceeded to nail shut all the windows and doors.

"If I can't come in," he shouted to his wife, "you ain't comin' out!"

Because my ankles bear the imprint of tooth marks from the many times I have put one or more of my feet into my mouth, I have great compassion for a woman, another who is inclined to talk when silence would be more golden, involved in a story told by Dr. Troy Eslinger, president of Lees College in Jackson.

This soul's bout with foot-in-mouth disease broke out when she was visiting the baby department of a Lexington hospital to take a peek at her sister's newly born daughter. As she stared through the nursery window, her gaze wandered to the baby in ad adjacent bassinet.

"My goodness," she mused aloud to the woman standing next to her, "doesn't that baby there have the biggest feet you ever saw?"

"And why shouldn't she?" the woman snapped. "Look at my feet. I'm her grandmother!"

The first woman was terribly embarrassed, but somehow made her escape. That night, however, she returned with a friend to show her the new niece.

"The awfulest thing happened to me this afternoon," she told the friend as they watched the babies. "I was looking at that baby over there and I happened to mention to the woman next to me what big feet it had. You can imagine how I felt when the woman turned out to be the grandmother.

"But," she continued, "the poor thing does have big feet, doesn't it?"

"And why shouldn't she?" spoke up a man standing beside her. "Look at my feet—I'm her father."

Harold Robertson of Sharpsburg, an uncle of my wife, has been married for 50 years, and he explains how it's worked out in simple term. "I always regarded marriage as a 50-50 proposition," he says. "She's had her way for 50 years, now I'll have my way for the second fifty."

INTRODUCTION   The Kentuckian enjoys the unique ability to
come up with just the right comment at just the right time. This
oratory, which usually ends on a humorous note, may take the form
of either a word invented on the spot or merely the use of a
phrase that "hits the nail on the head" and leaves no need for
further discussion.

One person who possessed this tendency for selecting a
distinctive phrase was the late Ed Diddle, the famed basketball
coach at Western Kentucky State Teachers College (now Western
Kentucky University).

Although the phraseology that Diddle devised was somewhat
different, to say the least, because of the context in which his
spur-of-the-moment terms were used, their meanings left nothing
to the imagination.

One such instance that Dad wrote about had Diddle and several
other coaches comparing the amount of adhesive tape used by their
respective teams. As they talked Diddle became more and more
excited.

"I'll tell you one thing," he finally sputtered, "we may not have
the best playing team, but we have the usingest tape team in
America."

Another Diddle tale concerns Fred Sawyer, the seven-foot center
who played for the University of Louisville in the late 1950s and
early 1960s. Diddle was in awe of the opposing giant.

"That Sawyer is the biggest man I ever saw," he conceded.
"Why, he must be six feet 13 or 14, at least!"

The phrasing may be somewhat rough, but there was never any
doubt about the point Diddle was trying to make.

CHAPTER 7

EXPLORATORY ORATORY

A man who often found his tongue more twisted than an eastern Kentucky mountain road, says Jack Miller of Jamestown, was judge of Russell County years ago. The judge, an ancient gent with a long, white beard that he stroked incessantly, was mighty impressed with multi-syllable, jawbreaker-type words, most of which he either used incorrectly or mispronounced miserably.

During his term in office, Miller continues, several cases of smallpox were reported on Jabez Ridge in the remote eastern corner of the county. Fearing an epidemic, a large delegation of residents from the area came to the judge's office to see if he planned to take any steps to ease the crisis.

"You're mighty right I'm a-gonna do somethin' about it," he replied leaning back in his chair and stroking his beard furiously.

"First, I'm goin' out there and I'm a-gonna canteen every man, woman and child on that ridge. After that I'm a-gonna have every last one of them assassinated by the health department for smallpox.

"And you ask if I'm a-gonna do anything!"

H. A. Hansen of Louisville hired a carpenter to install some indoor shutters at his home.

"How long have you been carpentering?" asked Hansen one day.

"I reckon," the man replied as he rummaged around in his toolbox looking for a hammer, "about 25 years carpenterin' and 15 years looking' for my tools."

Charley Aaron, the Russell Springs oil distributor, fisherman and storyteller, once was recalling a heavy sleet that fell one winter while he was attending a rural school in Russell County. Next morning a big, raw-boned boy was late for school and his excuse was that it was so slick he'd take one step forward and then slide back two.

"I never would have gotten here," he confessed, "if I hadn't turned around and started home."

After there had been a rash of long commencement speeches at area schools, Mayor Luska Twyman said just the right thing in starting his talk to the graduates at the Glasgow School for Practical Nurses.

"Ladies and gentlemen," Squire William W. Vaughn quotes him as saying, "my speech will be like the skirts young women wear today—short enough to be interesting, but long enough to cover the subject."

Louisvillian Wilson Hatcher, who has been involved in radio and television for many years, tells about the poor soul who was the entire morning staff on a 1,000-watt radio station in Kentucky the day in 1966 when Hendrick Voerwoerd, prime minister of South Africa, was assassinated.

After he had introduced the last Western recording to play before the first newscast of the day, he rushed to the teletype machine, ripped off a sheet of copy and dashed back to the microphone.

"In the top of the news this morning," he began reading cold, "is this bulletin from South Africa: Prime Minister...."

His voice trailed off as he hit the name, but quickly he regained his composure.

"The prime minister of South Africa has been assassinated," he continued. "We are withholding his name until the next of kin has been notified."

The father of the bride is often the forgotten figure in most marriages. However, George Wilson was to make sure that he did not go unnoticed when his daughter, Debbie, was married a few years ago.

He had cards printed that read: "I am the Father of the Bride. . . . Nobody's paying much attention to me today. But I can assure you that I am getting my share of attention, for the banks and several business firms are watching me very closely."

Frank Lovell, a long time Louisville friend, tells about dining at a restaurant out in the state and having his eye drawn to the rainbow trout offered on the menu. But he was concerned about how long it might take to have it prepared.

"Does the rainbow trout have any delay?" he asked the waitress.

"No, sir," she replied. "Just almondine sauce."

All the impressive but meaningless words which are discussed reminds me of a political orator who was making the rounds through western Kentucky some years back. At one stop he'd been droning on for an hour when a late arrival appeared.

"What's he talkin' about?" the late arrival asked.

"I don't know," was the reply. "He ain't said yet."

Most stories have only one ending or punch line, but, just to show you that bargains still are available where you least expect to find them, this offering comes with two punch lines.

The doubleheader originated with Jerry Howell of Jackson.

It concerns a preacher who was walking past an alley with a young man who had come to him for counsel, when in the back doorway of a building they saw a group kneeling not in prayer but in shooting craps. The preacher was appalled.

"Go back there in that alley and break up that crap game," the preacher commanded his companion.

The guy left and didn't return for two hours.

"Why did it take you so long to break up that game?" the preacher wondered.

"Well," the man confessed supplying the first punch line of the story, "I only started out with a quarter and it takes a while to break up a game when you don't start with any more than that."

"My goodness," the preacher gasped, "you shouldn't be gambling, too."

"Preacher," the game buster retorted, throwing in the second punch line in the process, "what I was doin' wasn't gambling—I was usin' my own dice."

One of my favorite preacher stories concerns the pastor at a small church in south central Kentucky.

Late one November, when the church members were dragging out the big iron kettles to boil the water, sharpening their butcher knives and checking the sausage grinders, the preacher had a momentous announcement to make to the flock.

"Brothers and sisters," he said from the pulpit the next Sunday, "I've been preaching to this congregation for five years. You don't pay me much, but every year at hog-killing time you all send the pig feet and shank bones to the preacher in place of money.

"Now I feel I ought to warn you that if I'm going to stay on as your preacher, I'm gonna have to start eating a little bit higher up on the hog!"

Jamestown attorney Jack Miller is convinced that you never can tell what a man will say when he's under oath in court. To prove the point, he tells about a defendant in a case who was short a witness to his cause for character reference the day his trial was called.

"Then make a statement of what this witness might have said if he were here," the judge instructed. "What would he have sworn to if he'd been on the stand."

"Why, judge," the defendant said in a burst of candor, "he'd of swore to whatever I'd paid him to say. He's such a big liar that for a dollar he'd swear hell was an icehouse."

Some shrewd pundit once observed that a candidate for political office needs three hats: one for throwing in the ring, one for talking through, and one for pulling rabbits out of.

About the only thing that points up is the extreme caution the majority of those who bid for office traditionally exercise in stands they take on critical issues. In short, most hopefuls carefully weigh whether votes gained will more than offset votes lost before they commit themselves on iffy matters.

But that isn't something new. In fact, a former Confederate Army soldier who ran for the state legislature from Warren County shortly before the turn of the century could have given any of the current crop of politicians a lesson in broken field running.

At that time the hottest issue was whether or not a strict law should be enacted to protect livestock herds, particularly sheep, from wandering dogs. Sheep people were all for a severe law; dog lovers opposed it. And since it was hard to determine which group had the most votes, the old Confederate tried to straddle the issue.

However, one day at a speaking of all the candidates he was cornered.

"How do you stand on the dog law?" he was asked.

"I'm in favor of a dog law," he said half-heartedly.

"What kind of a dog law?" the questioner pressed.

"I favor a law," the candidate orated loudly, "that will protect the sheep and not hurt the dogs!"

Next to alligator wrestling or being the one who checks gasoline tanks by dropping lighted matches into them, I think the profession I would least like to pursue is that of a basketball referee.

Although it has been said I have the hide of an elephant, I don't think it's thick enough to withstand the hoots and boos and hisses and uncomplimentary remarks directed at every act performed by a referee.

For no matter what he does, a referee is certain to offend half the players, one coach, and most of the fans, who just naturally suspect any referee is a charter member of Ali Baba's band of 40 thieves.

Sometimes the abuse doesn't end when the final second of a game has ticked away. To show what I mean let me relate to you a story.

A few years ago David McAnelly and Nathaniel Buis of Liberty officiated a game at Pine Knot. They drove over in the same car and on the way home after the game stopped to pick up a youthful hitchhiker.

"Where you been?" McAnelly asked.

"To the basketball game," came the reply.

"Who won?"

"They did—the referees beat us."

"Pretty bad, were they?" McAnelly pressed.

"The big one was fairly good," almost spat the boy, "but the little one wasn't worth a damn."

McAnelly was the little one.

Kentuckians express themselves differently. Fred Burkhard, the Liberty editor, tells of the answer he received from a 75-year-old man when he asked him the inevitable question, "How are you feelin'?"

"I'll tell you," the old boy replied, "there are people in the graveyard who feel better than I do."

The late Charles Whittle of Brownsville was one of the best storytellers that I ever encountered.

Not only did he have a few choice yarns at hand, he could spin them with an innate sense of timing and drama. Strangely, almost without exception the stories he told were set in Edmondson County, a section that obviously has known more than its fair share of unusual characters.

One story he enjoyed to tell concerned the first case that Pleas Sanders, who became a successful attorney, undertook after he began practicing law in Brownsville many years ago. He had hung out his shingle, but clients weren't exactly knocking down his door until he was appointed by Circuit Judge Porter Sims to represent a mentally incompetent man in a trial for pauper benefits.

At one point in the trial, following a long barrage of fruitless questions aimed at revealing the poor man's mental capacity, if any, the judge suggested that a reasonable test would be to see if he could count money. Sanders, however, ignored the suggestion and continued asking questions.

After a few minutes, the judge repeated the suggestion. Again it was ignored.

"Mr. Sanders," Judge Sims interrupted him, "why don't you do as I suggested and see if the man can count money?"

"Judge, you embarrass me," Sanders replied. "I've started the practice of law and this happens to be my first case and, to tell you the truth, I don't have the necessary laboratory equipment to conduct the experiment you suggest!"

R. B. Campbell has come into contact with a lot of people in McKee and Hyden, where he owns drugstores. He has become something of a student of speech patterns, colloquial expressions, pronunciations and such.

A few years ago, he recalls, two men, both around 70 years old, met on the street outside his Hyden store. One man spoke to the other, calling him by name, but the second old-timer couldn't come up with a name.

"You know," he admitted finally, "your face shore is similar, but I can't quite organize you."

One year a man in the market for a horse attended the trade day at Franklin. In looking over the stock, he fell into the verbal web spun by the owner of one big, raw-boned hayburner. The horse, the trader vowed, was seven years old.

The man bought the nag and took it home. However, it soon became apparent that, among other shortcomings, the horse had weathered a considerably greater number of years than just the seven previously quoted to him. At the next trade day he again met up with the man who had sold him the horse.

"That horse you sold me was a lot older than you thought he was," he fussed. "You don't know a thing about horses."

"He may have been older than I said he was," the trader rebutted, greatly offended, "but he warn't a bit older than I knowed he was!"

Leon Wesley, a Methodist minister in Whitesburg, stopped by a garage to inquire about a new automobile. His questions were relayed to the shop foreman in the rear of the building.

"How many miles to the gallon?" a salesman called to the foreman.

"Thirty," he shouted back.

"It's the preacher."

"Sixteen."

Now that politicians have gotten gun shy and have gone to reading carefully worded speeches for the benefit of the TV audience, lawyers in court are the last of the free-style extemporaneous orators in our society today.

A successful lawyer must know how and when to resort to rage, pathos, humor, charm, folksiness and assorted other emotions in order to do the best he can for his client. Moreover, he must know instinctively whether to drive straight to the point or beat around the bush with legalese.

One who followed the direct route but who could, when need be, also take the long road, was the prosecutor in an eastern Kentucky county a few years back. One of his first cases after he had taken office was to press charges against a citizen who was accused of being drunk in public.

Once the case started, the prosecutor took off after the accused with the vigor of a man killing snakes.

"Your honor," the defense attorney cut in during one outburst, "could you please have my worthy opponent use another word besides 'drunk' in referring to the charges against my client?"

"I'll be glad to," the prosecutor replied sweetly. "Judge, I might say this man was soused, oiled, sotted, boiled, pickled, canned, tight, high, stinko, soaked, intoxicated, lit, inebriated, looped, three sheets to the wind, on a bender, wall-eyed, loaded, carrying a load, in his cups, saucer-eyed, full or wobbly-kneed.

"But the truth of the matter is," he roared, "he was just plain drunk!"

As a boy Dr. Kelly Thompson, the retired president of Western Kentucky University, was party to an unusual event when he worked as cashier in the hotel dining room in Lebanon, his hometown.

One morning a traveling salesman came down for breakfast and, after studying the menu, was ready to order.

"I'll have the country ham, biscuits and grits, but I want you to eliminate the eggs," he told the waiter.

The waiter disappeared, then reappeared with an important announcement.

"I'm sorry, sir," he told the diner, "the cook says he can fry, boil or scramble them eggs, but he don't know how to 'liminate 'em.''

Certain crops are indigenous to various parts of Kentucky, but no section really has a monopoly on the kind of product Buck Brady, Hodgenville, heard about in Wolfe County. Brady, who is with the Department of Highways, was inspecting the Mountain Parkway and he struck up a conversation with a localite who stopped to ask what he was doing.

"What do you raise up here?" Brady asked.

"Oh," the man mused, "we raise a little tobacco and a lot of hell."

Sometimes two persons can be conversing in English and never understand each other.

Some time ago Mark Kennedy, a young Louisvillian who attends Morehead State University, and a friend had a minor automoblie accident near Taylorsville. Two men happened by the scene and after the car had been pulled out of the ditch, the talk turned to a puppy one of the locals had with him.

"I found this pup up the road one night," the man said.

"Abandoned?" Kennedy asked.

"Naw," came the solemn reply, "mostly beagle, I think."

It's ironic how little things sometimes can shape a man's life, and J. H. Sanders, one of the truly unusual men I've ever met and who died in 1973 in Greenville at the age of 91, proved the point.

It took a blunt remark by a woman in Arizona around the turn of the century to make him realize that teaching school in Kentucky was to be his lot in life.

"Back then," he told me several years ago, "I used to think I could have been a musician. But one time in Arizona I was asked to sing 'My Old Kentucky Home' at a meeting and, after finishing, I noticed the song had brought tears to the eyes of one lady.

" 'I presume,' I said to her, 'you're crying because you're a Kentuckian.' "

" 'No,' she replied, 'I'm crying because I'm a musician.' "

"Brother," a country preacher asked the farmer, "are you a Christian?"

"Naw," replied the rather dim-witted man, "the Christians live in a big white house right on down the road a piece."

"You don't understand," the preacher pressed. "Are you lost?"

"Naw, I lived here on this place all my life."

"You still don't understand," continued the evangelist. "What I mean is, are you ready for the Judgment Day?"

"I don't know. When is it?"

"Nobody knows," the preacher intoned. "It might be today or it might be tomorrow."

"Soon as you find out, let me know," requested the farmer seriously. "My wife is apt as not to want to go both days."

Bert Combs, who as governor of Kentucky associated closely with former President Harry S. Truman on many occasions, agrees in full with appraisals that our 33rd president was both blunt and outspoken in his speech and his actions.

While he was governor, Combs remembers, Mr. Truman came to Kentucky to participate in a Democratic Party fund raising dinner. As the two men walked on stage, the band struck up the National Anthem. Although the flag was displayed to their right, Mr. Truman stood at stiff attention and looked straight forward instead of turning to face the banner.

"Mr. President," Combs whispered to him, thinking he didn't see the flag, "the flag is over here to your right."

"Hell, I know where it is," he whispered back. "You're supposed to stand at attention and look straight ahead. That's the rule—I know, I wrote it!"

Paul Westpheling, a long time friend who publishes the *Fulton County News,* recently had a conversation in a restaurant in Fulton which taught him something about how even a word as positive as the adverb "out" sometimes isn't entirely sufficient.

"Hey," a waitress announced, "we're out of chocolate syrup."

"Are we plumb out?" another waitress asked.

That set him to wondering how one could be out, but not plumb out of something. The explanation is simple.

"When we're out of something here at the counter, we may still have some in the back," he was told. "If we can't find any in the back either, we're plumb out and we better order some more quick!"

It seems that years ago John Craig was the number one barber in Albany, and his most regular customer was "Uncle" Jim Vincent, the operator of a water powered grist mill on the edge of town.

Since Uncle Jim was such a faithful patron—in early every morning, Monday through Friday, for a shave—Craig agreed to mow his whiskers for only five cents per session. This special-rate agreement continued for years and years, through good times and bad, without interruption.

But one day, after he'd finished the shave, Craig kept a dime instead of the customary nickel out of the quarter that Uncle Jim handed him.

"I thought you agreed to charge me just a nickel for a shave," he objected after counting his change and found it somewhat shorted.

"I did," Craig replied, getting quick to the heart of the matter, "but when I agreed to do that, I didn't know you were going to live forever!"

I recall hearing a preacher who started his sermon by telling about a fellow parson from the county seat who was visiting a rural church where a big dinner on the ground was being held.

When he passed down the line of tables loaded with tempting goodies, he noticed that the peach cobbler prepared by one of the women hadn't been touched. To ease her embarrassment, he asked for a helping. Later, noting that his had been the only portion served from her offering, he asked for seconds and thirds. Finally, he'd consumed the entire cobbler.

Unfortunately, he became violently sick from his over-indulging and he barely had recovered when he met the woman who had made the cobbler on the street a week or so later.

"Why," she greeted him happily, "you're the same man who ate all my cobbler at the church dinner."

"No, ma'am," he corrected her, his stomach churning at the memory, "I'm not the same man, and I doubt I'll ever be again."

A high-powered evangelist was imported to conduct a revival meeting at a rural church near Bee Springs more than 50 years ago. The whole community was aroused by the fervor of the evangelist, including the old man—more noted for his thrift than for his churchgoing—who had seated himself on the front row every night, singing the hymns louder than anyone else and amen-ing all over the place.

When the meeting was in its last week, a group of younger brethren of the church fared forth to collect money to pay the evangelist. The first stop was at the house of the thrifty old man.

"Before that preacher came here," he said to the visitors, "I'd been hungerin' for some good preaching.

"Yes, men," he continued, "that preacher has made me realize how good the Lord has been to me, how He saw fit to make me the smartest man in Edmonson County, how He gave me the best farm for miles around, how He gave me neighbors who love and respect me."

"Then I guess you'll want to make a substantial contribution to help in this great work," one of the visitors said.

The old gent stared at the speaker for several seconds in silence.

"Boys, I'll tell you," he said finally. "I'm gettin' to be an old man and you fellers are all young. I imagine I'll be seeing the Lord before any of you do, so I just think I'll hand Him my donation in person."

Charles E. Woodcock, once bishop of the Episcopal Church Diocese of Kentucky, reminded me of a story of an aged crossroads minister.

The story had Bishop Woodcock as the principal and happened in the early 1930s during a late afternoon vesper service he was conducting at Christ Church Cathedral.

Just as the Bishop stepped into the pulpit, a drunk came staggering into church from off Second Street and reeled down the aisle to a front row seat. There he literally collapsed and fell asleep immediately.

However, in a few minutes he who had partaken well if not too wisely awoke with a start. He raised his head, rubbed his eyes, and saw Bishop Woodcock still in the pulpit.

"How long you been preaching?" the drunk asked in a thick tongue as he tried to climb to his feet.

"Sir," the Bishop replied, somewhat taken aback and not understanding fully the question, "I have been preaching for 15 years."

"Well," retorted the still addled drunk collapsing once again on the seat and closing his eyes, "I've taken it this long—I can wait 'til you get through."

After the April 3 tornado had done its damage, a vast array of bizarre, ironic and downright funny experiences have been recalled.

For instance, our church, Second Presbyterian, serves a section of the eastern suburbs where the twister left a path of destruction. On the first Sunday after the storm Dr. Glenn Dorris, the minister, was standing at the front door when a member entered the church.

"You know," the man said looking from the front steps over an area where not one house was undamaged, "it's safer living next to a liquor store than it is next to Second Presbyterian Church."

"Maybe," Dorris agreed, "but you forget we're in the life insurance, not the home insurance business!"

In talking with hunters I find that all of that species are not expert marksmen.

Bemis Lawrence, a Louisville attorney, tells about the guy who was goose hunting when a big honker came winging overhead. He fired both shells in his gun, but the goose kept going.

"Gentlemen, you are seeing a miracle," he said solemnly to his companions. "You are witnessing a dead goose flying."

Discretion often is indeed the better part of valor, and a story told by Don Seabrook of New Albany proves the fact clearly.

Seabrook's story concerns a legendary preacher named Brother Patterson and an incident that arose when he was called to minister a small church in the mountains near Elizabethon, Tennessee, years ago.

For some time the church had been terrorized by a local tough who loaded up on moonshine, had disrupted services repeatedly, and even had run off a preacher or two. In his first sermon, Brother Patterson denounced the bully by name, calling him a brute and a moral coward.

By chance the two met the next day and the tough announced that he was going to beat up on the preacher something awful. Well, Brother Patterson allowed, that seemed a fair enough proposition, but first he'd like a few minutes for a short prayer.

"O Lord," he began, falling to his knees, "Thou knowest that when I was forced to kill Bill Cummins and John Brown and Jerry Smith and Levi Bottles I did it in self-defense.

"Thou knowest, O Lord, that when I cut the heart out of young Slinger and strewed the ground with the brains of Paddy Miles, it was forced upon me and I did it with great agony of soul.

"And now, O Lord," he went on, "I am forced to put in his coffin this poor, miserable wretch who has attacked me today. Have mercy on his soul and take care of his widow and orphans when he is gone."

Brother Patterson then arose, took a long knife from his pocket, and began to whet it on his shoe sole as he sang in a loud voice:

"Hark, from the tomb a doleful sound, mine ears attend the cry!"

When he looked around the tough had disappeared. Brother Patterson never was troubled again.

Robert Martin, president of Eastern Kentucky State University, tells about a man, his faithful dog at his heels, who entered a bank where the president had consistently refused to loan him money.

As soon as the dog was inside, he bit a customer on the ankle, ran into the president's office and nipped him, then bit another customer on the way out.

The irate bank president demanded to know why the dog was on such a rampage.

"I don't know why he bit that first man," the owner grinned evilly. "But I know why he'd bite you and I guess he bit that last man on the way out to get the taste of you out of his mouth."

A trial was being held in Circuit Court in Somerset years ago, relates S. H. Rice of Irvine, and the key witness on the stand was a fidgety little woman who'd never been in court before.

The case was hard fought and every question asked her was objected to by opposing counsel. The poor woman was nearing utter confusion, a state reached when, after one question, the judge hammered his gavel.

"Don't answer that!" he said to her sternly.

The exasperated woman wheeled and pointed her finger at the judge.

"Old man," she almost spat, "I'd like to know what you've got to do with all this!"

A man that Marion banker Neil Guess tells about came as close as anyone I've ever heard of in expressing total and complete awe by using words you wouldn't commonly think of.

Years ago, Guess says, telephones in Tolu, his hometown, served only the local community. Then one so-called long distance phone was installed and they were able to communicate with parties far away.

One day his father was making a call to Birdsville, all of 15 miles down the Ohio River in neighboring Livingston County. An old man was standing nearby watching him.

"What's that box you're a-talkin' into?" he asked.

"That's a long distance telephone and I'm talking to Birdsville," he was told.

"My goodness," the old man gasped digging deep for words to express the awe he felt, "the man that made that thing could make a possum!"

INTRODUCTION   The articles in this chapter are different in tone and subject matter from other stories and columns in this collection. In the following five selections, my father moved away from his usual mode of writing. He did not adhere to his basic news format of reporting on an interesting event or a third party; instead, he related personal stories and anecdotes to the reader.

These personal remembrances are sometimes light, at other times nostalgic. But always they are entertaining and captivating.

Dad was not above making himself the butt of a joke. In fact, many of the stories might not have been as humorous or as dynamic if the party involved had been someone other than Creason.

These light reflections deal with everyday misfortunes which might befall anyone. They may bring back thoughts on subjects that are quite close to us all. Many of these situations might indeed be shared by others who once were caught in similar circumstances. But it was Joe Creason who put his feelings down on paper for everyone to enjoy.

So, if you laugh at these stories about Joe Creason, remember that you may very well be laughing at yourself.

CHAPTER 8

T ALL CREASON TALES

THANKSGIVING: Thanksgiving days past in my small Kentucky
HOW IT WAS   town still stand out clearly in my mind
despite the passing of a lot of years.

The day always seemed to dawn clear and cold. Long before
sunup I'd be out in the frost-crusted fields with my brother Jack, or
John and Hardy Lovett, checking the box-shaped varmint traps
we'd set for rabbit, raccoon, opossum and other small game. We
never caught anything, but we were always hopeful.

Roasting the several turkeys needed to feed our family—all the
Creasons, Crosses and Dotsons who would gather, some having
come from other states—started early in the morning. As the
morning wore on, the younger children congregated in the kitchen
to drool at wafting, tempting smells and the pumpkin and mince
pies brought up from the cellar where they had been cooling.

Thanksgiving was the one day in the year when children didn't
have to wait for "second table." An early table was spread for the
small fry and they'd get a head start gnawing on giant turkey
drumsticks.

Finally, the turkeys, the oyster dressing, giblet gravy, mashed
potatoes, cranberry sauce, sweet potatoes with marshmallow
topping, hot rolls and all the other trimmings would be ready on
the big center table. The adults, and those of us who had graduated
from the children's table in the kitchen, would be seated and an
appropriate, if brief, prayer would be offered.

"BlessthisgatheringandforwhatweareabouttoreceivemaytheLord
makeustrulythankful.Amen. Will you have light or dark meat?"

A country-style Thanksgiving dinner—and in the country,
"dinner" was the midday meal—wasn't something to be hurried
through. It was for savoring, dawdling over, enjoying to the fullest.

Then, after dinner, while the women cleared the table and

washed dishes, the men gathered in the big living room. They'd puff on pipes filled with pungent, sweet-smelling, home-cured tobacco, and talk about politics and farming. Some of the greatest crops ever grown were produced during the after-Thanksgiving dinner conversation.

That was Thanksgiving past.

Now, even in the country, the day is geared to our fast, sophisticated times.

With fewer city dwellers having rural roots, the flow of relatives back to the farm isn't so great as in other days. Those who do make the pilgrimage back home travel at 70-mile-per-hour speeds over interstate and toll roads and generally arrive only a few minutes before dinner.

And the Thanksgiving dinner—even it has changed. Turkey no longer is a rarity and the main course likely will be roast beef or ham. Moreover, the meal probably will be served buffet style. Everybody will rush through it, the dishes will be stacked hurriedly in the dishwasher, and those who haven't drifted off will gather in the living room.

But not to talk. To watch TV.

Aside from the eternal truth that times just naturally do change, there are several reasons which might explain why Thanksgiving is different today in city, small town or country.

For one thing, it's basically a New England invention—although proof does exist that the first Thanksgiving was held at Berkeley Plantation in Virginia—and the influence of that section of the nation has diminished as the country has grown. New England poets like Hawthorne and Lowell and Longfellow who wrote so sentimentally about the day no longer are so influential as they were once.

Another reason for the decline of Thanksgiving might have been the switching of the traditional date. The day was observed on the last Thursday in November from 1863, when Lincoln made it a national holiday, until 1939, when, in an effort to provide a longer interval between Thanksgiving and Christmas for the benefit of merchants, it was moved up a week. This created confusion for three years, with some states observing the old date, some the new, and a few both.

A third reason for Thanksgiving having lost some of its former glory well may be the loss of status of the turkey.

Turkey once was the sacred symbol of Thanksgiving, a somewhat rare delicacy reserved almost exclusively for that day. Today it's so relatively cheap in price that it has become everyday common and is served the year round. It no longer is the trademark of Thanksgiving.

All of these factors, and others, no doubt have contributed to the diminishing importance of Thanksgiving, the one big holiday not related to politics (as is the Fourth of July) or to traditional Christian church calendar (as are Easter and Christmas).

Then, again, maybe the day hasn't changed as much as old-timers think it has.

It could be that Thanksgiving pasts now are blurred just enough by the passing years so that only fond and pleasant memories come to mind.

For, beyond the shadow of any doubt, the best Thanksgiving Days, like the best Christmases and birthdays and other memorable occasions, are when you are young. (11/22/70)

JOE CREASON PLAYS GOLF LIKE SIXTY   From time to time of late I have read learned and persuasive articles touting the game of golf as the perfect way for a party to relax and forget the troubles and assorted woes with which we all are beset these nervous days.

For a long time I held grave doubts about the golfing way of shucking anxieties and cares and tribulations. How golf can cause a man whose wife has just left him, who is up to his armpits in debt, who is about to be called up by a reserve military outfit, and who is hurting from migraine headaches to forget all these things and throw a victory celebration for at least 200 people after sinking an eight-foot putt, was beyond my power of comprehension.

However, the forget-your-cares-with-golf propaganda finally took. And so the other day, after 10 years' absence from the links, I set out to play myself some cow pasture pool, as we used to call the game down at Benton, the only town in Kentucky where I was born.

As a result, I am herewith testifying that all the jazz about forgetting one's tensions and frustrations by trying to knock the cover off a tiny ball that is so expensive it should be put in a safe place alongside family silverware is nothing but purest hogwash.

Instead of forgetting my troubles, this round of golf made me aware of problems I didn't even know I had, viz: mental frustration from hooking drives one time and slicing the next, a sudden awareness of insecurity with iron shots, and concern for my eyesight after losing balls the few times they landed in the fairways.

My 13-year-old son Bill was my companion on this expedition against par and I'm downright ashamed of some of the remarks reflecting on the ancestry of the inventors of the game, the manufacturers of the clubs and the like he heard me mutter.

But that's getting the putt before the drive, to speak in golfese.

I must admit that after having studied at the elbow of Arnold Palmer on TV, I was as cocky as a man who works a crossword puzzle with pen and ink when I stepped to the first tee, which is the batter's box in golf.

I took an over-vitamined swing and not too much happened. In fact, I'm sure I could have teed up a prize pullet and she could have laid a Grade-A egg farther than I drove the ball. I ran out of fingers on which to count the score long before depositing the ball in the hole.

The second hole was little, if any, better. The drive sailed away in as graceful a hook as you ever saw. Some 150 yards forward and to the left it suddenly ran out of steam and dropped like a stricken mallard in a region remindful of the late Mr. Longfellow's forest primeval. That fearsome blow cost me $1.50 plus sales tax since the only thing I found in the woodstand was a bumper crop of chiggers.

Things took a turn for the better on the third hole in spite of my executing what might be called an explosion shot off the tee. Nevertheless, I finally made it to the hole in six, only two strokes over par.

The fourth hole resulted in another six and my confidence mounted to the extent that I could feel troubles rolling from my rounded shoulders like water from a duck's back.

Then came No. Five and all my old troubles and a big batch of brand-new ones came back. Unfortunately, some 25 yards to the left of the tee there is what is described as an abandoned swimming pool. But I know it differently. From the ways the balls I hit were attracted to it, the thing can only be a water-disguised golfball magnet. I left three balls there before making it past, and my score mounted like a fever chart.

The sixth hole is not a long one; as a matter of fact, I've seen tobacco chewers who could (pardon the word) spit that far. However, there is a little creek that crosses the fairway midway of the distance. My drive, of course, made it into the creek with unerring accuracy. I had very little luck with the ball in this lily-padded situation, but I did succeed in pitching a bullfrog, medium size, onto the fairway.

By then I was seeing red. And Red is one person I was in no mood to see since I owe him a $2 cribbage debt from the days we were in the Navy together.

What's more, while I was putting on more trouble by the minute, my son was playing a respectable game. I was in a mood to say the dickens with it all—although I assure you I would have used a much stronger word—and call the whole thing off.

Still I was determined to finish the round if it killed me, and along about then it appeared it just might.

Well, that's the way it went.

My conclusions? Only that I never will be able to forget many troubles playing golf.

My score: you might say I had a Civil War round—out in 61, back in 65. (6/30/62)

DO IT YOURSELF? SURE,   Those concerns that flood the
IF YOU LIVE THROUGH IT   market with their do-it-yourself-around-the-house propaganda this time of year should put me on their payroll. They should pay me never again to attempt any project that can be done cheaply and easily by anyone with an I.Q. of minus four or more.

As a do-it-yourselfer, I am batting pretty nearly 1,000—in reverse. Perhaps the fact that I have no tools of my own and depend on handouts from neighbors has something to do with it. Anyway, I now approach even the simplest home chore with the cocky self-assurance of a man being led to the electric chair.

For instance, there was the time last fall when I painted myself green.

It all started when I decided the front and back doors needed painting. So I bought a gallon of dark-green paint, a brush and a jug of mineral spirits.

I rushed home, climbed into a pair of shorts—no shirt—and retired to the basement. About the time I had pried the lid off the paint bucket, the telephone rang. I laid the lid back on the bucket, and went upstairs.

The conversation ended, I returned to the basement and picked up the bucket to mix the paint by shaking, forgetting that the lid had been loosened. I gave the bucket a sharp up-and-down shake.

There was a glugging sort of sound, and a wave of green paint engulfed me from chin to toe tip. In the twinkling of an eye, my frontal anatomy had assumed the eventual color of a cheap wedding ring.

And, believe me, you haven't really lived until you've taken a bath in mineral spirits.

Before that, there was the episode of the basketball goal. A friend had given my elder son a basketball. But what good, if any, is a basketball without accompanying backboard and goal? A child could build a backboard and attach a goal, I kidded myself as I gathered material in the basement for the job.

The material I wound up with was more than Noah put into his ark. The backboard came out a four-by-six mass mounted on a frame of two-by-fours and bolted to a pair of 18-foot-long four-by-four poles.

There was only one very slight complication: The thing was so heavy I couldn't lift even one corner, much less drag it up the steep basement steps. Moreover, it was much too wide and long to get out the back door.

Then there was the time I almost sawed off at least five fingers on my left hand in trying to make a basement wash table for my wife, who should have known better.

Now it wasn't intended to be a fancy table; certainly nothing that would make Mr. Duncan Phyfe or Mr. Hepplewhite hang their heads. All I meant to do was nail a few boards across a frame and attach it to a set of two-by-four legs.

Since the legs weren't the same length, I borrowed—naturally— a saw to even them up. The only thing around to use as a sawhorse was an old orange crate. I upended the crate, placed the first two-by-four across it, braced it with my left knee and hand, and started sawing like I had good sense.

Things happened in the following order:

The saw struck a knot; I gave it a sharp jerk; the flimsy crate collapsed; the saw flew out of the hole; the saw struck my left-hand fingers, blade down; blood spurted.

One day a downspout pulled loose from the gutter at the corner of the house. With borrowed ladder and blow torch, I embarked upon repair mission.

Mission completed finally, I stepped back a bit to admire the job.

The only thing was, I happened to have been standing some eight feet up on the borrowed ladder at the time.

Once I decided to stop the basement walls from leaking.
I carefully chipped away the concrete at the leaking spots and
filled the gaps with fresh mortar.

The walls didn't leak after that. But the next time it rained and
the water pressure in the ground built, there was a loud cracking
noise, and a network of the neatest cracks you've ever seen
developed in the basement floor.

The latest misadventure came just last Saturday. Minus shirt
and armed with paint, brush, hammer, nails and an eight-foot
stepladder, I set out to paint and repair the rail across the
front porch, which happens to be a good 12 feet up.

I got up on the roof, but then couldn't get back down. It's
amazing how far down a ladder can seem when you're looking
down at it.

My wife rushed to rent half an extension ladder to get me down.

Meanwhile, the sun popped out in full fury. My shirtless back
began to steam. And the only thing more futile than trying to find a
corner in a silo is trying to find shade on a roof.

Delayed by the longest freight train ever to block the Chenoweth
Lane crossing in St. Matthews, my wife was nearly an hour in
arriving with the rescue apparatus. My back was blistered; my
temper matched. In my haste to get down and get the ladder back,
I suspect I left all the tools on the roof.

I'm afraid to check and find out. (5/25/56)

HUSBANDS, ARISE! THROW OFF   Maybe I'm just being like
THE CHRISTMAS SHACKLE!   the nervous clock—all
alarmed over nothing—but I'm of the firm opinion that it's high
time we men stood up on our hind legs and did something about
this being turned into Christmas-time pack horses.

I refer specifically to the unholy practice employed by some
women who drag their husbands along on shopping tours merely to
have them carry the bundles. It's bad enough having to pay for
the bundles, but having to haul them around, too, is double
jeopardy pure and simple.

There's a society for the prevention of cruelty to dumb animals.
And as matters now stand, there's a very great need for a similar
society for the prevention of cruelty to dumb husbands during
that period of the year some wise guy—unmarried, of course—
once referred to as "the joyous yuletide season." Even the chairman

of the board of the Spanish Inquisition thought up few tortures more cruel than those inflicted upon a husband who is carried along as portage bearer on a Christmas shopping expedition.

To prove that, post yourself in the immediate vicinity of one of the larger stores the next time you're out on Fourth Street, especially on a Saturday, between now and Christmas. But heed this warning: Take a station a safe distance from the doorway, else the suction created by the swarms of shoppers passing through the revolving doors easily might suck you through the entrance, past ladies' ready-to-wear and into the depths of men's shoes before you realize what is happening.

Note, while you offer up frequent silent prayers to your lucky stars for being spared a similar ordeal, how the cowed, dejected looking husbands are being loaded this season. The 1949 motif seems to be to hang a large shopping bag over each wrist for the nonbreakable toys, fill the overcoat pockets with the smaller items, and then stack the larger bundles upon the extended arms to a point approximately three inches above the bridge of the nose. There is, as you will note, a limit to everything but the number of bundles a wife can load on her man servant. You'll find them loading down everything but the bags their overworked soul (or cell) mates wear under their eyes.

This belt-to-forehead shipping arrangement, of course, means the husband has some difficulty breathing, while the prime function of seeing is an utter impossibility. There has been some talk in other areas of equipping bundle-blinded husbands with seeing-eye dogs and/or periscopes, but so far that plan hasn't reached Louisville. Anyway, even if he could see, the sidewalks are so crowded there's no place to plant a foot. His best bet under such conditions is to stand perfectly still and allow himself to be swept along by the surging tide of humanity after first leaving a call with the person directly arrears to notify him once he has been swept to his next shop stop.

The disadvantage of this scheme is as plain as the nose on Jimmy Durante's face. There's always the chance that he might hit a whirlpool, get swept completely around and be carried three blocks in the wrong direction before he can do anything about it. There's little or no chance of getting over into the other traffic lane. It would take the entire right side of the Notre Dame line to break through the solid wall of human flesh one finds grinding along Fourth Street these days.

One of the most ironic sights known to mortal man is the dilemma that confronts a partially bundle-bound man upon meeting a female of his acquaintance. He is faced with two choices of action: ignore her or tip his hat. If he pursues the first line of strategy, she'll most certainly take offense and stomp away muttering about "some people . . ."

So being a gentleman if nothing else (that, in my case, is a scoreless tie if I ever saw one) he'll probably elect to tip his hat and 14 bundles. Dropping an armload of bundles under such conditions is enough to make even the most tight-lipped sufferer break down completely and resort to the type of colorful language that usually is associated with mule skinners. For trying to pick up spilled bundles on a Christmas jammed sidewalk is, roughly, the equivalent of trying to row a leaky skiff up Niagara Falls.

Those are just a few of the rigors, risks to both life and limb, to which husbands are exposed by Christmas shopping days.

As I see it through my specs of partiality, there's only one thing to do—organize a two-legged mule train union and go immediately on a three-day workweek. In due time, who knows, maybe we can work our way up to a no-day workweek. (12/16/49)

20 YEARS AND HALF A MILLION MILES HAVE LEFT IMPRESSIONS WITH CREASON   The other day I was lounging at the office, trying my best to look industrious, when it suddenly dawned on me that an anniversary of considerable personal importance was taking place.

That day marked exactly 20 years since I departed *The Ledger & Times* of Murray, Kentucky, and took up typewriter residence in the sports department of *The Courier-Journal*.

In the years between then and now, I have worked, in order, as radio editor, magazine feature writer, Navy ensign who really won World War II, and magazine writer again. Which brings my stirring biography up to date.

Using the same infallible mathematical system which enables me to put two and two together and get four one time and 22 the next, I figure that during those two decades I have traveled well over 500,000 miles through the circulation area of this newspaper.

To retreat behind numbers, I have written more than 1,000 magazine features stories, nearly 1,000 magazine "Grapevine" columns, about 500 Sunday Passing Show, Business and Amusement section articles, and maybe 200 pieces for this space facing the editorial page. And that doesn't include more prewar sports stories and radio columns than I could ever guess.

Although they represent an unprecedented number of split infinitives and dangling participles, I refer to these production figures now because of two other reasons:

1. They illustrate the forebearance of this remarkable newspaper in having put up with me for so long.

2. Some of the incidents arising from stories I have covered are things I'll never forget.

For instance, a memorable quote came out of the very first interview I did after joining the sports staff. I was sent out to see Walter Johnston, the ex-major league baseball pitcher, who was visiting friends in the Shively area.

The talk swung to the batter who had given him the most trouble.

"It was Ty Cobb," he answered. "When he came up, I'd take time out for a conference with the catcher. After that, I'd hitch up my pants, dust my fingers with resin, rear 'way back and throw the ball as hard as I could.

"Then," he added, "I'd run over to back up third base when Ty came sliding in."

I remember going up to the Elliott County hills to do a story about an old man who lived on a farm where shafts once were sunk in an effort to find diamonds. At that time the search for uranium was in full swing and people with Geiger counters were everywhere.

"I'm liable to be rich one of these days," the old man said. "Just yesterday they was a man here with a Goober counter looking for geranium."

The first time I was in a coal mine I heard a remark that has stayed with me. We had been underground all morning and when it came time for lunch I noticed most of the miners ate their dessert first. I asked why.

"Because," one man replied simply, "the roof might fall in."

Shortly after the war, I was sent to Bowling Green to do a story about Ed Diddle, the amazing basketball coach at Western State College, and the powerful team he had assembled. Among other things, we wanted a team picture. As is sometimes the case, in relaying our wishes to the squad, Mr. Diddle's tongue got more than a little red.

"All right, boys," he instructed, "line up here alphabetically according to height."

Another time I rode a railroad handcar 20 miles up the Big Sandy River above Louisa to talk to a man who had 21 children. Nothing unusual about raising such a sizable brood, he reckoned.

However, he did find it downright astounding that his wife could recite all their names.

Along the line of large families, I once went down to Cumberland County with "Bix Six" Henderson on a moonshine whiskey raid. Tucked back in the hills, we came on a family with nine children, all of whom were named for western or country radio singers. These were seven boys named Cowboy Copas, Gene Autry, Roy Rogers, Smiley Burnette, Roy Acuff, Ernest Tubb, and Old Joe Clark, and the two girls named Dale Evans and Little Eller.

I went into southern Indiana some years back to do a story about a man and his wife who, after scrounging for a bare living for 40 years on their poor farm, struck oil. Overnight they had more money than they ever dreamed about; so much, in fact, they couldn't realize what happened.

During the course of their talk, I asked the wife, now that they had money, what she intended to get for herself.

"Well," she reasoned, "I do need a new ax handle."

Down in Calloway County I visited an old storekeeper whose name was, honest, Thomas Jefferson. By way of making small talk, I happened to comment that he certainly had a well-known name.

"It ought to be well known," he replied, "I been storekeepin' around here for 45 years!"

I called on an old mountain farmer who lived far back in the Leslie County hills. He was cordial, but didn't have the faintest idea what *The Courier-Journal* was or where Louisville was located.

"By the way," he said in a faint effort to find common ground between us, "who's the barber in Louisville these days?"

The 20 years in which those, among many other, incidents have been packed have been good years; so good I hope the next 20 are carbon copies. (1/24/61)

INTRODUCTION   *All too often Kentucky and its citizens, both past and present, have been short-changed when it comes to receiving credit for significant contributions to our nation's development.*

Historians have failed to recognize the great contributions which so many of our native sons and daughters have made in helping shape the way of life we now enjoy in America.

One noteworthy example is Nathan Stubblefield of Murray, who is not the recognized inventor of the radio, although he should be. It was Stubblefield who devised a means of transmitting the human voice without wires sometime around 1890, at least five years before Guglielmo Marconi, an Italian, came up with the same idea.

Likewise, John Fitch of Bardstown received the first patent for a steamboat in 1791, 15 years before Robert Fulton put together the plans that resulted in his "Clermont." But we all know from our history books that Fulton is the recognized inventor of the steamboat.

Dad did his best to set the records of history straight. On the following pages are excerpts from his writings which show that the Commonwealth takes a back seat to no one when it comes to historic importance. From these examples, all Kentuckians can draw some degree of pride in knowing their state and its sons and daughters have been important cogs in America's wheel of fortune.

CHAPTER 9

KENTUCKY FIRST AND FOREMOST

You'd think that with all the momentous events that have taken place and that continue to take place it would be unnecessary for two states to lay claim to the same thing.

But there have been rumblings afoot by citizens of Oklahoma that say the first Boy Scout troop in America was started at Pawhuska, Oklahoma, in 1909 when everybody knows—doesn't he?—that the very first troop was at Burnside, Kentucky, in 1908.

But that isn't the only attempt to swipe away one of our credits. Pennsylvania has said that the first commercial oil well in the world was drilled there in 1885, when it really was near Stearns, Kentucky, in 1819.

And Maryland has the audacity to say bourbon whiskey originated somewhere inside its narrow borders and not in the Kentucky county which bears its name. Missouri hints loudly that Daniel Boone is buried in its soil and not at Frankfort, while the same state claims Jesse James robbed his first bank there and not in Russellville.

Finally, Virginia insists the last battle of the Revolutionary War was fought at Yorktown instead of at Blue Licks, Kentucky, 10 months later.

Apparently there aren't enough big ones to go around so competition in the claims business is pretty brisk.

Students at Transylvania College in Lexington are the types who, in effect, would break mirrors, open umbrellas indoors and encourage black cats to walk across their paths with utter disregard for all the bad luck such things are supposed to bring.

For while theirs may be the only college in the land with an honest-to-goodness curse hanging over its ivory towers, Transylvanians aren't the least bit intimidated; in fact, they openly celebrate and honor the man who placed the curse on the college 146 years ago.

The curse-placer was Constantine Rafinesque, an eccentric scientist who taught botany and natural science at the school from 1818 to 1827. At about Halloween time each year, students hold a day in his honor during which they drop by his tomb in the basement of Morrison Hall on the campus for some hint as to the present status of the curse.

The curse goes back to a personality clash between Rafinesque and Horace Holley, president of the school. One day while Rafinesque was out sketching plants, Holley gave one of his rooms to a student and piled his belongings in the hall.

This didn't make Rafinesque hilariously happy and he announced he was leaving. But before departing he placed a humdinger of a curse on President Holley in particular and the college in general.

Within a year, Holley had been forced to resign as president and had died of yellow fever. Moreover, the main college building had burned to the ground and everything in it except, strangely, the papers left behind by Rafinesque had been destroyed.

Rafinesque himself died penniless in Philadelphia in 1840 and was buried in a pauper's grave. But in 1919, Transylvania decided that, curse or no curse, the college had been harsh on him. His remains were claimed by the school and reinterred in the basement tomb that bears this inscription: "Honor to whom honor is overdue."

Later students invented Rafinesque Day and it became a highlight of the college calendar.

But it seems to me there may always have been a small flaw in the celebration. Could be the generations of Transylvanians have honored a total stranger.

You see, there were eight bodies in that pauper grave and the members of the group from Transylvania never were sure if they got the right bones.

What with all the laborious research done by historians, fiction writers, movie and TV producers, you'd think that by now just about every unusual incident of the Civil War would have been brought to light.

Not so. One unusual event that escaped the researchers took place in Kentucky at the time when the pieces were falling into place for the bloody battle fought at Perryville on October 11, 1862, in Boyle County.

The incident was told to me by Mrs. Ollie Crouch Moore of Willisburg, whose father was one of the principals in a bizarre case in which his twin brother was in and out of the Union Army all in a matter of a few hours.

Mrs. Moore's father, Martin V. Crouch, had an identical twin brother, Richard, and they grew up on a farm in Washington County. When the war started, Martin joined the Union, while Richard remained at home.

In October of 1862, an older sister became seriously ill. Learning that Martin's detachment would be marching through the country from Confederate-held Frankort, Richard rode to Springfield in the hope of seeing his brother. Luckily he was able to spot Martin and, during a rest break, tell him of the illness at home.

Martin was anxious to see the sister, but it seemed impossible until he hit on an ingenious idea. Since the brothers looked exactly alike, how about exchanging places temporarily?

The switch was made. Richard climbed into Martin's uniform and took his place in the ranks when the rest break ended, and Martin, dressed in civilian clothes, rode to the family farm.

After spending a few hours with his sister, Martin was able to catch up with his detachment. Another exchange of clothing was made, and the two brothers went their separate ways—Richard back to the farm, and Martin into the battle that developed in the rolling hills surrounding Perryville.

I once heard a sports announcer call attention to the fact that both Jimmy Ellis and Muhammad Ali would be involved in boxing matches.

"By strange coincidence," he adlibbed, "the only two Louisvillians ever to be heavyweight champions of the world."

But the fact of the matter is that Ellis and Ali weren't the only citizens of this fair community to be named heavyweight champion. In 1905 there was a third—Marvin Hart, a shy, modest fellow who was a plumber when he wasn't fighting for prizes.

Hart won his title by knocking out Jack Root in the 12th round on July 3, 1905. But since he came along before the golden era of sports heroes, he reigned in relative obscurity.

His were the days when fighters flailed the stuffing out of one another with unpadded gloves for what amounted to peanuts. In fact, Hart's championship fight, one non-title exhibition, and the 20-round title defense in which he was outpointed by Tommy Burns the next year brought him only $10,000, about what Ali received for ten seconds of his time in Zaire.

Unlike Ellis and Ali, who started under capable teachers, Hart never fought as an amateur, received no instruction in the manly art, and didn't enter a ring until he was 23. After losing to Burns in what newspapers called "the bloodiest fight ever fought in Los Angeles," Hart continued to box on and off until 1910 when he became a plumber full time.

But he was a heavyweight champion and he was from Louisville.

Although I can't abide smart alecks who are forever playing down stories with sarcastic "The-way-I-heard-that-one" type remarks, I feel compelled to talk back—in a humble way, of course— to a short item that appeared in *The Louisville Times* the other day.

The item had to do with a celebration held for Spokane's Mrs. Bruce Dodd, 92, who was honored as "The initiator of Father's Day."

The way I heard that one, the inventor of Father's Day wasn't Mrs. Dodd, but a Kentuckian, Harry C. Meek, a native of Carrollton, Meek is supposed to have hit on the idea of a special day for dads in the very early 1900s after he had taken up residence in Chicago.

It took more than five years for his brainchild to get the boost it needed to put it over. Then the Chicago Lions Club began to push the idea and it took root and spread nationwide.

In its present form, Father's Day doesn't come within a long-distance phone call of what Meek planned it to be. To use his own words: "I envisioned it as a day when fathers and sons could go fishing or take in a ball game."

Instead, the necktie and after-shave lotion people took it over and Father's Day became a carbon copy of Mother's Day, only the gifts cost a little less.

While I am caught up in the credit-giving mood, I should point out that another important annual observance, Memorial Day, was originated by a man with strong Kentucky ties.

The founder of Memorial Day was John A. Logan, a native of Illinois who studied in the law department of the University of Louisville several years before the Civil War. After completing his studies Logan returned home and was twice elected to Congress.

In fact, he resigned his seat in Congress when the Civil War broke out, accepted a commission in the Union Army, and organized the 31st Regiment of Illinois Volunteers, an outfit which many historians credit with a major role in winning the Battle of Atlanta.

Following the war, Logan, who had risen to the rank of major general, became commander-in-chief of the Grand Army of the Republic. While serving in that capacity he hit upon the idea of a national day of tribute to honor those who gave their lives serving in the Union Army.

As a consequence, on May 5, 1868, Logan issued "General Order Number 11," designating the last Monday of May as a "national memorial day to the dead comrades who fought in the Civil War."

There is a downward twitch in the Kentucky-Tennessee line south of Franklin, the seat of Simpson County. And I've heard how it came about, but how legitimate the story is is not for me to judge.

Anyway, according to this story, a substantial landowner whose property would have been split by the boundary agreed upon by the two states in the mid-1790s wanted all his holdings to be in Kentucky.

So, when the two separate teams of surveyors, moving toward each other from opposite directions along the parallel agreed upon as the boundary, reached his land, he made a social announcement. A barrel of good whiskey awaited them under a shade tree a distance south of the line they were following if they agreed with him that his land should be in Kentucky.

Both teams of surveyors immediately veered slightly south and took the shortest route to the refreshment tree.

They got the whiskey and Kentucky got a small triangle of land it didn't deserve.

During the ceremonies in Louisville at which the U.S. postage stamp dedicated to horse racing was officially unveiled, someone happened to mention the Pony Express, the privately operated delivery service that once attempted to provide fast mail service from Missouri to California.

That brief mention moved me to check into the history of the Pony Express. The result was more than just somewhat startling.

I learned, for instance, that the prime mover in the founding of the Pony Express was a Kentuckian, Alexander Majors. Born in Simpson County, Majors had gone west in the great migration following the War of 1812 and, according to Dr. Thomas Clark in his book *Kentucky—Land of Contrasts,* had organized a freight wagon company to Santa Fe.

Majors must have been a most unusual man. Although hard-drinking, loud-cussing men were the breed that made up freight wagon drivers, he didn't believe in drinking, cursing or working on Sundays, and he even bound his employees to a strict blue-law pledge before taking them on.

Later he became a partner in the overland freighting company of Russell, Majors and Waddell. When the firm's business began to drop in the late 1850s, Majors dreamed up the idea of giving it a shot in the arm by providing 10-day mail service from St. Joseph, Missouri, to Sacramento, California, by using a fleet of fast-pony riders. The Pony Express, comprised of 80 select riders along a 1,980 mile route, started in April of 1860.

Sensational as it was, the venture was a financial fizzle. Majors failed to take notice of what was happening along the very route his riders followed and the Pony Express came into existence only a few months before completion of the transcontinental telegraph line. The Pony Express lasted less than 18 months before its riders rode off into the sunset of history.

It may come as something of a mild revelation for me to call to your attention the fact that it was a Kentucky lady who invented Mother's Day and it was in this state that it first was observed in 1887.

I say this knowing full well some of the reference books won't agree with me. Most of them try to convince you that it was a Philadelphia woman, Anna M. Jarvis, who started Mother's Day. But don't you believe it. Mother's Day was originated by Mary

Towles Sasseen of Henderson, and it was she who proclaimed the sentimental merit of such an observance a good 20 years before Miss Jarvis hit on the identical idea.

Miss Sasseen was a teacher at Henderson and as far back as 1887 began observance of a special day for mothers in her schoolroom. Some years later she visited a sister, Mrs. E. W. Olds, in Springfield, Ohio, and introduced the idea in the public schools there. Then in 1893, Miss Sasseen published a pamphlet which set down her aims and objectives. After that she traveled all across the country, speaking before educational groups in an effort to have her day observed more widely.

Miss Sasseen gave up teaching in 1900, married, and moved to Florida. She died six years later, still endeavoring to promote a nationwide day for mothers.

It remained for Miss Jarvis to complete the work and gain the national reputation as founder of Mother's Day. Still, it should be noted that she didn't introduce her plan until one year after Miss Sasseen's death.

Ironically, neither of the Mother's Day pioneers ever knew the thrill of being honored on the day they had started. Miss Sasseen never had any children, and Miss Jarvis never married.

A chilling incident that took place at Georgetown College in 1861 proves the fact that Kentucky, as no other state, was split down the middle by the burning issues that divided the nation during the Civil War.

The incident that was enacted on the Georgetown campus on April 23, 1861, illustrates how the unholy spectacle of father fighting against son and brother against brother was repeated in this state on a massive scale.

For, according to legend, that day the college closed its doors and the student body marched off to war—half going North, half going South.

Although Confederate and Union sympathizers had had mild run-ins previously, it wasn't until April 14, the day after Fort Sumter, that real trouble erupted. That night Southerners hoisted a Confederate flag atop Giddings Hall, the main campus building. Next morning when pro-Union students stormed the hall to take down the banner, fist fights developed.

As the legend has it, once order was restored President Duncan Campbell had Confederate sympathizers line up on the south side of the lawn, Unionists on the north side. Then, at a signal from him, the two groups about-faced and each group headed off in the right direction to war.

That isn't exactly how it happened, but it's close. Minutes of the college faculty reveal this account of the incident:

"April 23, 1861—On account of increasing excitement among the students caused by the agitated condition of the country and by order of the trustees of the college, Georgetown classes were suspended till the first Monday in September. . . ."

The college reopened in September, but on less than full scale. In fact, it closed again (and there was no graduation class the next spring) when Colonel R. M. Gano, a resident of the town, led a Confederate detachment of Texas Rangers into Scott County. He didn't attack Georgetown when he learned that a company of State Guards was drawn up ready to defend it.

As though to underline Kentucky's divided loyalty, the commander of the State Guards ready to resist Col. Gano was Dr. S. F. Gano, an uncle.

Owsley County's government which had been without a home since its courthouse burned in 1967 moved into a new building in Booneville in the spring of 1974.

The occupation of the Owsley County structure is of more than ho-hum significance, since it again brings to 122 the number of courthouses used by the 120 counties in the state.

If that seems about two courthouses too many, the oversupply is caused by Kenton and Campbell counties which have two seats of government and courthouses for each. Kenton County maintains buildings at Independence and Covington, while Campbell County has a similar setup in Alexandria and Newport.

Actually, 122 courthouses for 120 counties isn't any more unusual than Kentucky, the 35th largest state in size, having more counties except Texas and Georgia.

This came about because it once was held that no Kentuckian should live more than a day's ride on horseback from his county seat. As a result, it wasn't long until that simple rule of thumb was shot to, however it is you spell, smithereens, and we wound up with many county seats within easy walking distance of each other.

For instance, Lexington, Fayette County seat, is 18 miles or less from five county seats; Danville, seat of Boyle County, is 9, 11 and 12 miles from the seats of Mercer, Garrard, and Lincoln counties, respectively.

But counties are deemed so important that sporadic efforts to reduce the 120 to a more reasonable (and economical) number have gone over like a lead balloon. And, to be objective in the matter, if the number of counties was reduced, what to do with the tobacco-chewing loafers who are an integral part of the scenery around most courthouses might present an insurmountable problem.

Like the two old-timers who were inspecting the new Laurel County Courthouse after it was opened some 15 years ago. Unfortunately, the cuspidors that were provided for the tobacco-chewers and snuff-dippers in the old building hadn't been put in the place yet.

"This is a right nice place," one man mused, rolling his chew around in his jaw, "but I shore do miss the spittoons."

"I know," replied his friend, "you always did."

The most durable of all sayings relative to the fickle, now-you-see-it-now-you-don't nature of Kentucky's climate is the bearded old clinker that if you don't like the weather, just wait a minute.

That may be an overstatement of the situation, but just barely.

During March and most of April, especially, our weather is subject to such drastic changes without notice that one never knows whether the uniform of the day should be thermal underwear or bathing trunks.

And while many feel that our weather has been particularly undecided in recent years, the weather has always been variable during this period.

Norman Allen of Prestonsburg once told about an old mountain man who was plowing on a March day years ago. The hot sun was beaming from a cloudless sky and perspiration was rolling down his face as he guided a team of somewhat reluctant mules back and forth along the steep hillside. Yet draped across the plow handles was a heavy overcoat.

"Why in the world would you be carrying an overcoat while you plow on a day like this?" a passer-by stopped to ask.

The old-timer paused just long enough to give the stranger
a withering look.

"Anytime," he almost spat, "a man is sich a durned fool he'd
trust Kentucky weather in March from one end of the field
to the tuther, he ain't got sense enough to plow nohow.
Git up, Kate!"

Since there is now an effort in the legislature to name an official
tree for Kentucky, you might be interested in knowing if any
of the so-called National Champion (largest) trees are
located in this state.

According to a late-1970 survey, Kentucky could claim six:
pawpaw—41 feet high, 3' 2" in circumference, Henderson
County; sassafras—1,000 feet high, 17' 3" in circumference, Daviess
County; slippery elm—85 feet high, 18' 3" in circumference,
Henderson County; swamp white oak—94 feet high, 20' 5" in
circumference, Monroe County; sycamore—104 feet high,
33' 4" in circumference, Montgomery County; mountain
maple—68 feet high, 7' 8" in circumference, Muhlenberg County.

"A Night With the Blues," a program honoring the 100th
anniversary of the birth of W. C. Handy, the man credited with
originating that distinctive, low-pitched, wauling kind of
music, was held at Bellarmine College in March, 1973.

There is no particular reason to expect it to have been woven
into the program, but the fact that Kentucky is closely
identified with Handy and his blues is worth mentioning here.

Not only did Handy live for ten years in Henderson, he
also married a local girl and there, in his own words, he changed
from "a hobo into a professional musician" and started a
career that spanned 65 years until his death in 1958 at age 84.

I spent most of an afternoon with Handy a couple of years before
he died and he talked about his Kentucky years at length. A
portly gentleman with a halo of snow-white hair encircling
his head, he then was totally blind and spoke in a soft,
refined voice.

"I didn't write any songs in Henderson," he said, "but it was there I realized that experiences I had had, things I had seen and heard, could be set down in a kind of music characteristic of my race. There I learned to appreciate the music of my people.

"For instance, when I was a little boy in Alabama I sang in the church choir. We sang according to the music, just as the white man had written it. Then, one day one of the singers took one of the notes and dressed it up with a slight inflection at the beginning and at the end and, instead of one note, he actually made three.

"It wasn't until years later when I was playing trumpet in a band in Henderson in about 1895 that I came to appreciate the rhythm as being Negroid and our true expression in music. I think it was then the blues were born because from that day on I started thinking about putting my own experiences down in that particular kind of music.

"I remember," he went on, "how in 1893 the band I was playing with in Chicago went broke and, in starting back to Alabama, I ran out of money in St. Louis. I slept several nights on the river levee and time after time I told myself I sure hated to see the evening sun go down, a phrase I put to good use later.

"I also remember seeing a red-headed woman and a man in a lover's quarrel. I recall hearing the man mutter as he walked away that 'a red-headed woman's done made a fool out of me.'

"Those experiences kept running through my mind until 1914 when I built the lyrics for 'The St. Louis Blues' around them."

All in all Handy wrote 40 blues songs and twice as many spirituals, including the classic "Steal Away, Jesus."

And it all started in Henderson, Kentucky.

Before television, when many people in the hinterlands never had a chance to see a major league baseball player, it was common after the World Series for some of the superstars of the game to travel around the country and appear in exhibition games with local teams.

Louisville was a regular stop in the off-season for the big names during the days when the tube was still a mere gleam in the eye of some scientist.

After the 1928 World Series in which he had led the New York Yankees to a 4-0 sweep over the St. Louis Cardinals, the mighty Babe Ruth came to Louisville to appear in a game involving the two best teams in the city's strong semi-pro league.

Ruth was in his prime then. The year before he'd hit his record 60 home runs and had come back and hit 54 in 1928. A massive host of fans jammed Parkway Field to see the great slugger and it was going to be a great disappointment if he didn't whack at least one ball over the fence.

On the same team with Ruth, and batting just ahead of him, was Reed Miller, a local player of considerable renown.

The game had gone into the late innings and Ruth still hadn't put one out of the premises. With two men out and Miller at bat, the opposing pitcher deliberately walked him to bring up the Babe, who immediately proceeded to knock the first pitch out of sight.

"I have the strong feeling," Miller says in recalling the incident, "that I may be the only player in baseball ever to be intentionally walked to pitch to Babe Ruth!"

With the 100th running of the Kentucky Derby out of the way, it is only fitting and proper that another centennial of still another important sports event to be celebrated in 1975 be pointed up. That event is the founding of the National League of Professional Baseball Clubs.

According to legend, and some hard facts provided by Dick Potter, Louisville photographic historian, the National League emerged from a meeting held in Louisville in 1875.

Up to that time, baseball was being played professionally in a loose, ungoverned way in a number of cities, including Louisville. There was a National Association of Baseball Players, but control over the game was lax and, with gambling and other abuses common, public confidence was lacking.

All of which, again according to legend, led the owners of the Louisville, St. Louis and Chicago clubs to meet in December of 1875 here in the back of Larry Gatto's saloon on Green (later Liberty) Street. Their discussion centered on the formation of an organization that would put integrity into baseball by eliminating, among other things, gambling and liquor selling at the ball parks.

The outgrowth of that meeting was a session of all club owners in 1876 in New York and from that emerged the National League for the purpose of "encouraging, fostering and elevating the game of baseball."

Ironically, Louisville was the first club to have the ax lowered on it when the league set about to live up to its charge. The very first year, 1876, four Louisville players, including a star pitcher, were expelled from baseball for "throwing" a game.

A legend claimed by the largest area of Kentucky and which adds a dash of flavor to the rich and colorful regional history of Kentucky concerns the fabled silver mine of John Swift which he worked here after 1760, the year he left Virginia to explore the mountains to the west. Somewhere in eastern Kentucky he discovered a silver lode which he mined off and on for nearly 10 years, returning to Virginia periodically with samples of his treasure.

The journal Swift kept, and which is reprinted in the privately printed booklet *Lost Silver Mines and Buried Treasures of Kentucky,* written by Paul Henson of Louisville, seemed to indicate the mine was on or near Paint Creek in what is now Johnson County. However, legend also holds that the mine might have been on Lower Devil Creek in Wolfe County, on Laurel Fork of Clear Creek in Bell County, near Hazel Patch in Laurel County, or a dozen other places.

From time to time sporadic attempts have been made to locate the mine. As recently as 1970 two different groups were exploring Wolfe County.

But they, like countless men before them, searched in vain; the cloud-capped mountains still hide Swift's fabulous lost silver lode.

In Kentucky it is said even dogs are found with amazing degrees of intelligence. Tales have been told to me that make me feel some members of the canine corps can ably take my place and I'll walk around on a leash all day.

One such story deals with Shep, a dog of an especially high IQ, that Jimmy Johnson of Campbellsville once knew about. Shep's great talent was in herding milk cows, and he did his chores with dramatic flair.

Late in the afternoon Shep would run by the house of his master and check the clock. If the hour was right, he'd head out in the pasture and, alone, bring in the cows to be milked.

But that wasn't all. As the herd neared the barn lot, Shep would take position at the gate and count the cows as they trooped through. If any were missing, he'd immediately take off and bring in the stragglers.

Well, one morning Shep's master sold a cow to a neighbor. That afternoon when the herd was brought in Shep found one cow missing. The dog started a frantic search. Hours later he found the missing moo-er in the neighbor's pasture and set about trying to make her jump the fence to get back home where she belonged. Nothing the neighbor could do would make Shep cease and desist.

In fact, as proof of the raw intelligence of the dog, not until the new owner showed the bill of sale for the cow would Shep leave!

While Virginia has been called the cradle of presidents, Kentucky can claim the title of the cradle of governors, what with some 115 natives having been elected chief executives of other states. In fact until Otto Kerner was elected governor of Illinois in 1962, Kentucky was tied with Illinois, itself, in the production of governors in that state.

Seven native Kentuckians have served as governor of Illinois. On top of that, Ninian Edwards, then resident of Kentucky, was appointed governor of the Illinois Territory in 1809 before it became a separate state.

The "Ask Andy" column in our newspaper is a popular feature. It provides answers to some of the most difficult and interesting questions one can imagine. However, I did come across one question and answer exchange that was only partially correct in its information.

Asked when chewing gum was invented, Andy replied, in part: ". . . This was about 100 years ago and, even without flavoring, gobs of chicle gum became very popular. About 10 years later the Adams recipe was improved by John Colgan of St. Louis. Colgan thought he could sell more gum in his drugstore if it tasted better. He added some tangy, long lasting balsam flavoring . . . and the first flavored recipe was invented in St. Louis about 90 years ago. . . ."

That part of the answer was OK except that Andy got his geography mixed up. John Colgan was a Louisville, not a St. Louis druggist.

Colgan had a drugstore at 10th and Walnut and, sometime around 1874, he began experimenting with a chicle-based product he called chewing gum and which he gave as a premium for trading at his store. This in time led him to flavor the chicle with balsam from the tolu tree and by 1880 "Colgan's Taffy Tolu Chewing Gum" was catching on.

In 1884, Colgan started the Colgan Gum Company at 938 W. Walnut Street. His success was copied and eventually seven different firms in Louisville were making chewing gum. By 1905 the Colgan firm occupied three floors at 315 S. Seventh and the next year it moved into even larger quarters on West Breckinridge.

Slowly the Louisville chewing gum makers began to fold and by 1917 all, including Colgan, were gone. But by then the flavored chewing gum, which was invented here, was as much a part of the American scene as apple pie and the Fourth of July.

It was only 50 plus years ago that women even could vote in county elections in this state. They'd won the right to vote in national elections in 1920, but not until the next year had the girls been able to help choose local officials.

That year Miss Bess Howard made political history by running for county clerk of Barren County. During the course of the campaign, it was whispered around that a woman just couldn't hold an office like that of county clerk. Think how embarrassing it would be, the whisperers added, if some man had to ask her to issue a bull license.

Well, she won anyway and it wasn't long until she encountered the very situation the whisperers had tried to use against her.

One day a young man entered her office. He seemed to have the embarrassed, ill-at-ease appearance she had come to associate with those wanting to get a marriage license.

"I want to get a license," the man said, blushing head to toes.

"That's fine," Miss Howard said, thinking he had marriage in mind. "Are both parties 21?"

"I . . . I . . . I don't know, ma'am," stammered the man, turning even redder. "This license is for a gentleman cow!"

Well, the Supreme Court has finally agreed to hear the arguments on a boundary dispute between Kentucky and Ohio that has been flaring up periodically for 150 years.

At stake, literally and figuratively, is the Ohio River.

When Ohio became a state in 1803, the boundary between it and Kentucky was set at the low-water mark on the north side of the river, meaning the stream belonged to Kentucky. Ohio now contends the construction of locks and dams has caused the river's low-water mark to creep far up the northern bank, transferring to us a goodly chunk of its real estate.

Thus, the Buckeyes claim, the boundary should be the northern shore of the river as it existed in 1792, when Kentucky became a state; or, better still, the middle of the stream.

Although a special master recommended last year that Ohio's claim be rejected, the state has persisted in what it regards as a sort of holy crusade. Anxiously awaiting the outcome are Indiana and Illinois, since they too say Kentucky is holding territory that belongs to them.

The source of the troubles goes back to 1787 when the Northwest Ordinance set the boundary of the Kentucky District of Virginia as the low-water mark on the north side of the Ohio River. When Kentucky became a separate state five years later, that boundary was settled on without dispute, since then there were no other states across the river.

Because of the locks and dams, no one knows where the low-water mark of 1792 lies today except it's somewhere out in the river.

What is at stake isn't exactly insignificant. After all, as the boundary has been interpreted historically, Kentucky owns the Ohio for more than 660 of its 981 miles.

As recently as 40 years ago, I've been told by those who should know, there were some counties in the mountainous eastern quarter of Kentucky without a single road that was passable the year round.

Consequently, the first automobiles that were imported via rail into the hills could be operated only in the county seat towns.

A story told by William Hazelrigg, Paintsville lawyer and former commissioner of highways, points out how it was back then.

Shortly before World War I, his story goes, a man in Paintsville bought an automobile and had it shipped to town from Ashland. It was the only car in all of Johnson County when it finally arrived, and for a couple of weeks it remained in the owner's yard while he learned by cautious experiment to operate the thing. Meanwhile, people from a wide area came by just to stare at it.

At last the owner felt competent to go excursioning. He drove out of the yard, down the gravel street and out the wagon road that led toward Salyersville in Magoffin County, the next county west. As he swept along at a brisk five miles per hour, people came flying in all directions to see the only car in Johnson County.

About midway between Paintsville and Salyersville, the narrow dirt road made a right angle turn around a rocky cliff, a true blind curve.

There it happened.

At that exact spot the only car in Johnson County had a head-on collision with the only car in Magoffin County.

INTRODUCTION   *At one time or another everyone recalls those days of yesteryear when everything was simpler and life a little more predictable, that time often referred to as "the good old days."*

For it was in those days past that one remembers the girls as being prettier, the education better, and the winters colder than their contemporary counterparts.

The way things were done and the way events were viewed in the good old days also gives rise to some of the funniest tales imaginable. The annual trade fairs, for instance, were an integral part of life in most county seats in Kentucky. Those swap days gave citizens the opportunity to come to town to bicker and barter with one another over the trading of items ranging from pocketknives to horses. Everyone believed himself to be a shrewd bargainer.

Tater Day is the super trade day held annually in Benton, the seat of Marshall County and Dad's birthplace. One year a trader appeared in the jockey ring with a sway-backed horse.

"This is a thoroughbred," he said, "and if I don't get the right price for him, I'm thinkin' of racin' him."

"Well," another trader replied after giving the nag a critical appraisal, "I'll bet you beat him."

THE GOOD OLD DAYS

As some say, newspapers don't practice personal journalism the way they did in the old days. Two shorts from the June 6, 1894, issue of *The Benton Tribune* perhaps explain why:

"The big fat form of A. J. Cox was seen in town Thursday."

"If you don't want your stamp licked by a Democrat, don't mail your letter at the Briensburg post office."

The Kitty League was the professional baseball circuit which flourished for years until its demise in the early 1950s. The league was comprised of teams in western Kentucky, southern Illinois, and northwestern Tennessee. Despite its somewhat primitive playing conditions, the league sent more players to the major leagues than any other Class D loop.

In the Kitty League the unexpected was always expected. Evidence of this fact is provided by Louisvillian Mike Powers, once a major leaguer who managed the Bowling Green club in 1941.

During his year as manager, Powers recalls, the team was playing in Mayfield where neither the playing field lights nor the stands exactly rivaled Yankee Stadium. Among other things, a light wire connected to a pole just off the playing field near third base stretched across the diamond to another pole near first base. The wire, some 50 feet up, passed directly over the pitcher's mound.

In this particular game, Bowling Green was leading by one run in the last of the ninth. The first two Mayfield batters singled and Powers ordered the third man walked to set up a force play at any base.

The fourth batter was Vern Stephens, the league's leading home run hitter, who later starred in the American League. On the first pitch Stephens swung with all his might and the loud, crisp crack of bat meeting ball had the sound of a home run.

However, the screaming line drive struck the light wire that stretched above the pitcher's mound. The ball ricocheted into the glove of the surprised Bowling Green shortstop who stepped on second base to double off the runner there and then tagged out the man coming from first for an unassisted triple play that ended the game.

Repetition can make us such creatures of habit that we expect things to be in the same place at the same time every day. Take the case of a truck driver who Dr. William M. Rowletts of Murray tells about.

Seems this driver had been making the same 40-mile trip from Murray to Paducah at exactly the same time each day for years. However, one day in passing through Benton, my old hometown, his truck and an NC & St.L Railroad locomotive arrived simultaneously at the crossing on the north end of town.

After climbing from his smashed truck unhurt, the driver pulled out his pocket watch.

"Humph," he observed, "it was three minutes early today."

A story my uncle, the late Walter Prince, used to tell about his days in a one-room school in Marshall County before the turn of the century proves that all wasn't enlightenment in the area of education during the "good old days."

The seventh grade had been studying the founding of the nation and the teacher called upon a boy to name a signer of the Declaration of Independence.

"Damned if I know," the boy replied in complete candor.

Unable to believe his ears, the teacher repeated the question and got the same answer.

"That's the most impertinent answer I have ever gotten," he fumed. "You go home right now and tomorrow bring your father with you to school. I want him to hear you give me that answer."

Next morning the father occupied a front row seat.

"Now," the teacher said to the boy, "for the third and last time, tell me who signed the Declaration of Independence?"

"Teacher," he almost sobbed, "damned if I know."

His father leaped to his feet, let out a roar, and cuffed the boy on the side of the head.

"If you signed the damned thing," he snarled, "you own up to it."

Mrs. Semmie Carpenter-Kennady of Elizabethtown recalls the race her father-in-law, J. B. Carpenter, made for a seat in the Kentucky legislature more than 70 years ago. As was normal among political candidates in those days, he avoided any beating around the bush in soliciting votes.

One day he rode into Three Springs, a village in Hart County, and delivered perhaps the shortest, most blunt campaign speech on record to a handful of men loafing outside the crossroads store.

"Hello," he began his speech without ever getting off his horse, "I'm making a hell of a race for the legislature.

"If you vote for me," he concluded as he turned his horse and rode away, "it will be all right; if you don't want to vote for me, you can go to hell!"

My wife's uncle, Harold Robertson of Sharpsburg, tells of an incident in a one-room school in Reynoldsville, a crossroads community in northwest Bath County, more than 50 years ago. The senior citizen of the school was a big, raw-boned boy who, since his IQ rated about -4, had been mired in the first grade for a number of years.

One day the boy was asked to stand and recite the alphabet. He rose, then stood there, staring at the floor without uttering a sound.

"Say 'A'," the teacher prompted several times, but the young dullard remained mute.

After school some of the other children were giving him a hard time.

189

"Why couldn't you say 'A'?" a classmate asked?

"Aw", the veteran answered reasonably, "if I'da said 'A', she'da just wanted me to say old 'B'."

When she was a child, reports Mrs. Jean S. Slaight of Jeffersontown, her grandmother used to tell her about a notorious cusser who lived in her section. This guy was known far and wide for using language which could make a veteran mule skinner blush. When properly prodded he could come up with cuss words that hadn't even been invented yet.

Well, one year a high-powered evangelist was imported to hold a community revival meeting in a local church and, hearing about the cusser, he dedicated himself to changing him. Consequently he spent hours counseling the man, trying to convince him that turning to the Lord would get him through hard times.

Finally, shortly before the meeting ended, the evangelist broke through. The man vowed he was reformed, whereupon the preacher suggested he offer up an immediate prayer for help in the difficult days ahead.

"Dear Lord, you know these are hard times, I got a big family and I need your help bad," the ex-cusser began, getting to the heart of the matter quickly. "I need a barrel of flour, a barrel of salt and a barrel of pepper."

Suddenly he stopped.

"Oh, hell," he picked up after a pause, "that's too much pepper."

As an example of one old-time bill collecting style, consider the method employed by the late Jim Bishop, who once ran a hardware store in Dawson Springs. Mack Sisk of Frankfort recalls that he resorted to a directly indirect way of prodding deliquent charge account customers.

During the warm summer months, Bishop would sit outside on a keg of nails in front of his store, his head resting on his chin, apparently taking a little nap. However, he really wasn't

dozing at all because he was ready with an exact figure reminder
when anyone who owed him passed.

"Why," he drawled without ever looking up, "hello there,
$14.95."

Edwin Carlisle Litsey, the Lebanon banker who shared the
title of Kentucky poet laureate with Jesse Stuart, once was
recalling the old days. Years ago, he mused, a favorite pastime of
what then were termed high-spirited boys (now they are
called juvenile delinquents) was to ring doorbells and run away
before anyone answered.

One day a Lebanon minister was walking down the street
when he saw a small boy trying to ring a doorbell that was just out
of his reach.

"I'll help you, little man," the kindly preacher said as
he pressed the bell.

"Thanks," the kid yelled as he dashed off. "Now run
like hell!"

Newspapers just aren't like they used to be, it is said, and
the change is most noticeable in writing styles. News reporting now
is concise and almost impersonal, whereas once articles
were done in a sort of first-name familiarity with great regard to
the smallest details, including more than a touch of editorializing
at times.

Although I'm convinced that papers as a whole are better
by far today than ever, I won't debate the matter. I'll simply give
you a sample of the way stories were written 50 years ago
and let you be the judge.

This is the way a wedding was reported in an Indiana weekly
paper shortly before World War I:

"Miss Jennie Jones and Bob Henry were married last night.

"The bride is the daughter of Constable Jones, who has made a
good officer and doubtless will seek re-election this spring.
He offers a fine horse for sale in another column in this issue.

"The groom runs a grocery store on Main Street and is a steady
patron of our advertising columns. He has a good line of

bargains in his ad this week. All summer he paid two cents more for butter than any other store in town.

"The young couple was married by the Rev. Josiah Butterworth, who last week called at this office and gave a nice order for printing. He also is going to give some time to the real estate business. Or so say the business cards we recently printed for him.

"Jennie and Bob left on the 10 o'clock train for Chicago to visit her uncle, who, we understand, has lots of money and an incurable disease."

Few football games will be remembered in as unusual a vein as the contest between Morganfield and Corydon High Schools in 1914. Corydon won 18-17 but didn't make a single first down all day while Morganfield was afflicted with acute butterfingeritis. Consequently, three fumbles were recovered and converted into touchdowns by Corydon's Gip Hancock, who was, of all things, a tackle.

Then there was the incident that cropped up the day the first football game was played at Greenville High years ago. Fearing trouble might arise, the superintendent hired the town marshal to keep order.

On the very first play, the marshal, thinking they were having a riot, rushed on the field and arrested all 22 players.

When he was growing up in North Pleasureville, Elizabethtown banker M. L. Underwood lived next door to a country doctor.

One day the doctor was called to see a farmer who was sick. After an examination, he prescribed some medicine and told the family what the patient should be eating.

However, in a few days it was reported he wasn't doing any better.

"Have you been giving him the light diet as I instructed?" the doctor asked the man's son.

"Yes, sir," came the reply, "we been doin' just what you said about a light diet—we been feeding him popcorn."

Since it was over before they were born, the generation just after
mine doesn't know how tense times were during the
depression of the 1930s. That was before Social Security,
unemployment insurance and other things which today help prime
the financial pump.

As an example of how bad times were, down in Grayson County
I heard about a man who walked into Leitchfield one day from
his home in the country and joined the courthouse yard loafers.

"This here depression's about over with," he announced
confidently. "When I was walkin' in, a rabbit run across
the road and nobody was chasin' it."

The coming of the first railroad train to Lawrenceburg in 1888
created great excitement in that community. Elegant words
and phrases were used to describe that dramatic moment when the
train first appeared around the bend.

But perhaps the best comment was offered by an old man
who, seeing the steam-belching locomotive high-balling into view,
took off for the higher ground.

"Get out," he shouted. "They'll never stop 'er."

For some reason the office of jailer seems to hold a fascination
for Kentuckians, and in some years when county elections
are held more people will be running for that job than all
others combined.

Since the post is a seven-days-a-week undertaking and thus
certainly is confining (no pun is intended), I've often wondered
about the great popularity of the office.

Dr. Mahlon Miller, president of Union College, wondered
the same thing when he came to the Barbourville school in
the mid-1950s and found 12 men running for the office of jailer
in Knox County. Being of an inquisitive turn of mind, he
determined to find an answer to the puzzler. His inquiry began and
ended a few afternoons later when one of the candidates,
an elderly gentleman wearing bib overalls and munching a
jaw-puffing chew of tobacco, stopped at the Miller home.

The two men passed the time of day for a few minutes and then the visitor handed Dr. Miller a card and allowed he'd sure appreciate his vote in the upcoming election.

"Tell me," Dr. Miller said, getting around to the question that was bugging him, "since there are 12 of you running, why would anyone want to be jailer?"

"Wal," the old man mused, shifting his chew the other side of his mouth, "when a feller gits too old to foller a plow, all he can be is a preacher or a jailer."

There are those among us, you know, who openly criticize our present system of campaigning for elective office as being archaic, costly, inefficient and sometimes even larcenous.

To prove their point about the latter contention, many critics use the bearded old story of the defeated politician who, in performing a post-mortem on his race, moaned that you just can't trust voters anymore, and he longed for a return to the good old days.

Asked what he meant by his remark, the politician replied, "I mean the good old days when you could buy a vote and it stayed bought."

Sometimes too late we get smart. Charles Smith of Paducah recalls his father telling about a hanging he witnessed around the turn of the century when that was a legal form of capital punishment.

"Anything you'd like to say?" the hangman asked the condemned man.

"Yes, sir," came the sad reply. "I just want everybody to know this sure will be a lesson to me!"

As we get older, everything from the past takes on new dimensions. The girls then were the prettiest, the summers the hottest, the winters the coldest, etc.

Consider the winter William Bell recalls when he was
a boy growing up on a farm in Scott County. We just don't have 'em
like that anymore.

"I recollect that winter," Bell claims, "as one when it was so
cold we had to constantly break the ice on the water for
the stock.

"Why, one day I took a kettle of boiling water out to pour
in the trough for the chickens and it froze so quick the
ice was red hot."

One Sunday years ago Mayfield was entertaining Union City,
Tennessee, in a big baseball game. It was the last of the ninth,
two men were out and the score was tied when the batter hit a ball
far over the centerfielder's head for what appeared to be the
game-winning run for Mayfield.

But as the runner rounded third base, a huge English bulldog ran
out from the crowd standing along the third base line, caught the
runner and pinned him to the ground some ten feet from home plate.
Meanwhile, the ball was retrieved and relayed to the catcher,
and the runner was tagged before he could divest himself
of the dog.

"Nothin' in the rule book to cover this," the umpire ruled after
due deliberation. "It's an act of Providence—the runner's out!"

Old-timers in Mayfield still talk about the big fight.

One of the best stories dealing with farmers that Henry C. Givens
of the Soil Conservation Service in Ohio County heard involved
two men who once owned adjoining farms in Ohio County. One of
the farmers was hard working and exacting. His land was carefully
tended, the fence rows were cleared, and all the buildings were
in exact repair.

The neighbor was just the opposite. In fact, he could have been
named Hydromatic since he was completely shiftless, and his
farm showed it. The land was badly eroded and grown up with
vines and bushes and the buildings were about to collapse.

However, with such a stand of bushes, the lazy farmer usually
did have a bumper crop of blackberries growing on his place.

One year his hard-working neighbor, noticing the lush berries had not been harvested, decided to pick some. But while he was doing so, the owner of the farm appeared and indignantly told him to leave the berries alone.

"I'm sorry," the industrious guy said, "but since no one will pick these berries and they'd go to waste, I didn't think you'd mind."

"All I got to say," snarled the shiftless farmer, "is that if you didn't keep your place so damn clear you could raise your own berries!"

Years ago in spring and fall, mule herders moved across the western part of the state with large numbers of beasts they offered for sale or trade. Needless to say, the herders were a rather rough lot and often were unaccustomed to many refinements of gracious living.

When overtaken by night, they'd simply stop at the nearest farm and ask to be allowed to spend the night in a spare room, barn loft or any place vacant.

Late one night a herder stopped at an exceptionally nice farm home, was taken in, fed, and after supper invited to sit with the family in the parlor. The herder immediately took out a twist of home-cured tobacco, bit off a chunk, and began to munch on it.

The farm wife, noticing the move, left the room and returned with a large hand painted spittoon which she placed near the herder's chair without saying a word. When it became necessary for him to spit, however, he glanced at the ornate spittoon, then turned and spat amber on the floor on the opposite side of his chair.

The wife arose and, still without saying a word for fear of embarrassing the guest, moved the cuspidor to the other side of the chair. Again it became necessary to spit and again he spat on the floor opposite the spittoon. Once again the wife moved the receptacle.

By then the herder was bewildered by the switching around.

"Ma'am," he said gently, "if you don't quit movin' that fancy bowl around, I'm liable to accidentally spit smack in the middle of it."

Back in Breathitt County where he was born, recalls Franklin D. Rice of Louisville, a circuit court case that had drawn a full house of spectators was being tried by a crusty old judge around the turn of the century.

A fancy-dressed lawyer from Lexington who had been imported by the defendant was summarizing his case in long, multi-syllable words that were too much for the judge to handle. Right in the middle of the summation, a mule that was hitched outside the courthouse began to bray loudly.

"All right now," shouted the judge, rapping for order, "just one of the jackasses at a time."

Some years back while in a reminiscing mood, George McCormick of Vincennes took pen in hand and recorded some of the many stories he recalled as a boy that were told to him by his grandfather, an Indiana country doctor.

He'd sit by the hour, McCormick said, and listen to the strange cases his grandfather had encountered in practice.

One concerned a middle-aged maiden lady who came to the doctor with a most curious complaint.

"Every night when I go to sleep," she said, "I dream that a young scamp is chasing me."

As the interview continued, the young scamp was identified as a handsome local fellow that owned an enviable reputation as a ladies' man.

"I can fix that fast," the doctor said confidently as he reached in his satchel and pulled out a bottle of harmless sugar pills. "Take two of these when you go to bed at nights and you won't be troubled any more with that fellow chasing you in your dreams."

Some days later the doctor met the lady on the street and asked how she was doing.

"Them pills worked wonders," she reported. "That man ain't chasing me no more in my dreams. But you know what, Doc, I sure do miss that young scamp!"

Mrs. Burgess Parks of Lexington recalls her father, the late Clyde Willis, telling her a story that points up the fact that back in the good old days, as well as today, whiskey could be bought on every street corner. This incident took place in Pleasureville years ago.

Back then, she recalls him starting this particular story, whiskey was sold by the gallon at general stores, but the customer had to bring his own jug.

One day a well-known local character strode into a store in Pleasureville and firmly placed the two jugs he was carrying on the counter.

"Give me a gallon of whiskey and a gallon of molasses," he said.

After a slight pause, he turned back to the storekeep.

"On second thought," he vetoed himself, "just fill 'em both with whiskey. My kids make such a mess of the molasses."

When she was growing up in Harrodsburg, Mrs. Catherine Hughes remembers horse drawn vehicles were about the only means of transportation.

Also living in town at that time were two old maid sisters who were inveterate funeral goers. Any time a person died in the community, the sisters were at the service and their buggy, drawn by their sway-back horse, always was in the middle of the procession to the cemetery.

As a matter of fact, they went to so many funerals that eventually their old horse became hooked on such functions, too.

One day while the horse was grazing in the yard, a funeral (which, for some reason the sisters had missed) passed by the home.

Whereupon old Dobbin clomped through the gate, took his place in the procession and, true to habit, followed it to the cemetery.

Some years back, when James Stevens of Dawson Springs was principal of the elementary school, it seemed that one kid in the first grade might become eligible to vote before he earned promotion to the second grade. After the boy had made three runs at mastering "Goldilocks and The Three Bears," the A, B, C's, and

the other requirements of the first grade, Stevens decided he
might as well send him on to the next rung on the educational
ladder.

So he called the boy into his office to send him on his way
with a rousing pep talk.

"I'm promoting you to the second grade," he told the boy.
"I hope you'll work and study hard and take advantage of this
chance to move up the ladder of success."

Apparently psyched up with a new-found desire to forge ahead,
the boy resolutely marched across the hall to the second grade.
Half an hour later, completely disillusioned, he was back in
the principal's office.

"Mr. Stevens," he said in a deep foghorn voice, "I spent three
years learnin' all about them three bears, but damned if they ain't
got a new story over there in that other room."

About 75 years ago Kentucky was famous for the stands of virgin
hardwood that covered the mountainous eastern quarter of
the state.

Kentucky hardwood demanded top prices in England for
ship beams, in Italy for fine furniture, and in France for wine
casks.

However, since railroads hadn't yet penetrated the area where
the scenery is filled with all the high hills, getting the timber to
market posed a problem. The most reliable method was to
tie logs together into massive rafts and float them to market.

Riding a log raft to market was the only time during the year that
many mountain men got down to the flatlands. Some of them
had no formal education and were not very citified, yet they were
seldom easy prey for the sharp dealing buyers.

Sometime around 1900, Henry Baker, then only 18, jockeyed a
raft from Perry County down the North Fork of the Kentucky River
and the main stream to market in Frankfort. He was young and
fresh from the hills but he was not about to be taken to the
cleaners.

In order for the board feet to be figured and the price to be
paid, a notorious buyer scrambled out on his raft and called out the
dimensions of the logs which Baker, standing on the bank,
jotted down in an entry book.

"Watch that buyer, boy," an experienced rafter warned him. "He'll give you the wrong call on those dimensions."

"Don't worry," young Baker replied. "You don't think I'm puttin' down what he's callin' out, do you?"

Some people just can't pass up an opportunity to brag a bit.

State Sen. William Sullivan of Henderson tells about two old gents who were sitting on the bank of the Ohio River.

"Wonder how old this old river is?" one man wondered.

"I don't know," the other replied expansively, "but my Daddy helped when they digged it."

Those who offer themselves for elected office may think they run into unprecedented harassments and distractions these days, but I have the strong feeling that waging a campaign isn't as frustrating as it was years ago.

Before television and radio became an integral part of campaigning, candidates met at large gatherings appropriately called "speakings" and openly debated each other. Since most speakings were out of doors and without the benefit of loud speaker systems, you can imagine some of the problems candidates faced.

Marshall Espie of Louisville recalls the disruptions one candidate for judge ran into at a speaking in Union County more than 40 years ago.

"Ladies and gentlemen," the candidate began.

"Ain't no women here," a man interjected from the back of the crowd, "and mighty few gentlemen."

"Gentlemen," the candidate rephrased his start in a low voice.

"Louder, man, louder," a raucous voice interrupted him once more.

"Gentlemen," he began a second time, raising his voice a couple of octaves.

"Louder, louder!" again came the call.

"Gentlemen," the candidate shouted at the top of his voice,

"when time is no more and Resurrection Day has come and the Angel Gabriel is blowing his golden trumpet, I'm sure some damn fool in the rear will rise up and shout, 'Louder, Gabriel, louder!' "

In Knott County, I heard about the mighty throng that gathered along the banks of Troublesome Creek the day it was announced that the area's Number One reprobate was to be baptized.

Since the man was unmatched in the amount of moonshine whiskey he had made and consumed, the fights he had picked and his generally unneighborly manner, there were skeptics among the witnesses who doubted he could ever mend his ways.

The preacher conducting the service saw fit to hold him under the water for an extra second or two.

"And now," the minister proclaimed once he'd pulled the convert up, "your sins are washed away in this water."

From the rear of the throng on one bank came a spontaneous remark that was perhaps in the mind of many:

"God help the fish."

It's hard to imagine now, but radio once was the mysterious marvel of the age, a fact pointed up in a story told by J. A. Miller of Russellville.

Back in the 1920s, few people understood radio, how it worked, or why. Just as a family in an apartment building in the city settled down to listen to President Calvin Coolidge, the set went on the blink. One of the boys rushed across the street to get someone to come over and work on the radio.

When the kid reached the street, he heard the president's voice coming in over a set in a neighbor's apartment. Sadly he walked back upstairs.

"Nothing wrong with our radio," he reported. "Them people on the first floor just got that speech first!"

Once upon a time—and not too many years ago, really—a home-grown baseball team was as important a fixture of every crossroads town as the general store.

Needless to say, the diamonds were not exactly maintained like Yankee Stadium. The infield might be skinned down to the raw earth, but the outfield would be often covered with knee-high weeds and grass. It was on such a field that a Bath County team was playing one Sunday.

When he took his position in the first inning, the right fielder was stomping down some of the bigger weeds when he came across a fruit jar full of moonshine whiskey that had been cached there and apparently forgotten.

Turning his back to the diamond, he took a deep swig. He replaced his find but continued to nip as the game progressed. By the time the game was half over, he was reeling more than somewhat as he jogged to and from his position.

It wasn't until the eighth inning, when a batter lofted a towering fly, that a ball had been hit in his direction. He circled uncertainly and camped where he thought the ball would fall. It came down, smacked him flush on the top of the head, and bounded away. Teammates rushed to attend the stunned fielder.

"I seen two balls comin'," he reported once he had been revived, "and I caught the wrong one."

Once upon a time, white flannel trousers were the "in" thing with all the dudes. Morrison Hicks, Louisville, tells about a wealthy guy who had gotten tar on his favorite pair of white flannels and who had instructed his servant to get it out—the tar that is.

"Did you try ammonia?" he asked after all else failed.

"No, sir," the hired hand replied, eyeing the pants enviously, "but I know they'll fit me."

As I've implied so many times before, basketball is almost a religion in Kentucky, and E. Hampton Barnett, a Methodist minister in Pikeville, shares a personal experience that tends to prove the point.

Years ago when he was serving a church in Carlisle, schoolteachers were in short supply and the Rev. Mr. Barnett was pressed into duty during the emergency. His job was to teach and coach basketball in the lower grades.

However, the basketball season had barely started when a revival meeting was scheduled at his church and the Rev. Mr. Barnett had to miss school and basketball practices for several days in succession.

One afternoon a special service was held for young people. When the evangelist made the call for those who wished to make their confession to come to the altar, Barnett was surprised to see about a dozen little boys leading the procession. As they knelt at the altar, he stooped beside them to instruct them in making their confession.

Barnett was stopped in mid-sentence by one boy who seemed to be speaking for the group.

"Coach, I didn't come up here to git religion—I done got religion," he whispered loudly. "I come up here to ask you when are we gonna practice basketball again?"

WHAT'S HAPPENED TO CLOWNS WHO PUT LAUGHS IN BASEBALL?   Here it is World Series time again, and the lid is about to be nailed shut on another season of baseball.

In spite of the pulse-pounding windup in the National League, generally speaking this was a pretty dull season for screwball incidents. Except for Ted Williams trying a couple of times to spit on heckling fans, no other player even batted .200 in the monkeyshines department.

What I mean is: there wasn't a single out-and-out, 100-proof clown playing baseball this year.

Which is a far, far, far cry from the old, anything-can-happen days.

Compared to the old-timers, the 1956 crop of players had about as much color as so many three-toed sloths. They were little more than mechanical robots who played baseball, period. Off the field, they wrote books on batting, endorsed breakfast cereal, posed for cigarette ads and counted their money.

There was practically no curricular or extracurricular tomfoolery like in the old days.

Ask yourself, for instance, did a single player this season try to catch a fly ball on his noggin? Did even one player steal a base already occupied by a teammate? Did any pitcher call for time at a crucial stage of a game to watch an airplane winging overhead?

The answer to each question is a loud, ringing, "No." Yet the ball players of earlier, less sophisticated eras did all those things, and more. Unlike the dear, dead days, when a ball game was punctuated with much comic relief, the highly professional conduct of today's players has taken the belly out of baseball.

Perhaps only one current player even vaguely resembles the clowns of yesterday. That player could be only Yogi Berra, star catcher of the New York Yankees.

To illustrate, there was the day in 1948 when Berra made a rare unassisted double play at the plate.

With one out and a runner on third, the opposition tried a squeeze play. But the batter bunted poorly. Berra grabbed the ball in front of the plate, tagged the runner before he had taken two steps, whirled and tagged the runner coming in from third, then whirled again and tagged both the umpire and the batboy.

"I wasn't takin' no chances," Berra explained later. "I just tug everybody in sight!"

For all that, however, Berra couldn't have clowned in the same league with old-timers like, say, Babe Herman.

Now Herman was a great hitter, but he took his life in his hands when he played in the outfield. One afternoon he circled confidently under a high fly ball, grabbed at thin air and kabong!—stopped the ball smack on the noggin.

The story also is told about Herman and an encyclopedia salesman.

"Your children can use this encyclopedia in school," the salesman insisted.

"Listen," said the indignant Herman, "my kids is healthy and they walk to school—they don't need none of them cryin' encyclopedias."

Then there was Dave Harris, a real screwball with Washington in the 1930s. One day he stole second with bases filled. He charged into the base with a nifty hook slide while the Washington runner occupying the station glared down at him. The Washington manager was furious.

"But, Skipper," Harris apologized, "I had such a helluva lead, I just couldn't help it!"

One of the clown princes of baseball was "Lefty" Gomez, once a star pitcher for the Yankees. In the 1937 World Series he was pitching and the Giants, National League champions, were making menacing gestures in the seventh inning. The heat was on, but good.

Suddenly Gomez heard the drone of an airplane motor. Calling time, he stepped off the mound and squinted into the sun to watch the plane pass overhead. Then he resumed pitching and retired the side without damage.

Another real comedian in his playing days was Casey Stengel, now Yankee manager. In 1918, he was traded to Pittsburgh after five seasons with Brooklyn. The first time the teams met in Brooklyn there was polite applause when the ex-Dodger came to bat. Just as politely, Stengel tipped his cap to the crowd— and out flew a sparrow.

The minor leagues have had characters galore. One was a centerfielder for Mobile in the Southern Association when night baseball was first introduced. The Mobile lights were nothing to write home about and the player had a habit of carrying an apple in his hip pocket. Those factors teamed for a most unusual incident.

It was the last inning, two men were out, and Mobile was leading by one run when an opposing batter hit a terrific drive into the dim light of centerfield. The ball cleared the fence with plenty to spare. But the Mobile centerfielder, thinking fast, suddenly reached into his pocket, pulled out the apple and held it up, pretending it was the ball. Then he ran off the field. The umpire called the batter out and the game ended with Mobile winning.

John King was an outfielder for Houston in the Texas League. In Dallas, he always was a prime target for the bleacher wolves, who set up a howl every time he made a move. One day as he took his position, he was given the usual reception.

Without warning, King wheeled, reached down inside his shirt and pulled out a passel of meat scraps.

"Here, you wolves," he shouted gleefully, throwing the pieces of meat into the bleachers, "eat this!"

No, sir, they just don't make baseball buffoons like that nowadays. (10/3/56)

INTRODUCTION   For those who have ventured to taste it,
Kentucky has a flavor which is distinctively its own. Dad was
intrigued with the Commonwealth's small towns and annual
events, but especially with its people, and he felt that Kentucky
owed its reputation to the efforts and accomplishments of its hardy
citizens.

People who have played leading roles in world politics, business,
and the arts were born and bred in Kentucky. Vice President Alben
Barkley, Colonel Harland Sanders, and author Jesse Stuart, among
others, have represented, personified, and described Kentucky as
only a native offspring can.

On the opposite side of the ledger, Dad felt compelled to write
about the celebrated criminals and ne'r-do-wells, including Jesse
James and William Quantrill, who got their starts in Kentucky.

The average Kentuckian also has had a great deal to do with the
wide diversity which exists in the state. Religious groups that
use deadly rattlesnakes in their services are to be found here, as
are moonshiners who ply their trade in the hollows and backwoods
of the state and have made their own distinct contributions to
Kentucky and its legends.

The list could go on and on. But it is easier for you to read the
tales that follow and form your own opinion.

CHAPTER **11**

KENTUCKY THROUGH AND THROUGH

TWILIGHT OF
THE GODS
Americans dig nostalgia and this passion for
looking back has created the illusion that most
of our distinctive national figures, the true giants, lived in
the past.

In rating our political figures, we usually start with Washington
and work timorously from past to present by way of Jefferson
and Lincoln. Business tycoons of today are measured against the
likes of Carnegie, Astor and Rockefeller and found to be pale
shadows of the genuine item.

Without intending to mean-mouth the present, let me add a bit of
fuel to the past-over-the-present fuss by drawing a bead on four
distinguished and distinctive Kentuckians who represent a
generation, now nearing its sunset, that may never be duplicated.

For these four Kentuckians are survivors of times far different
from today, times when a dominating personality, rugged
individualism and bulldog tenacity were more the marks of the
successful man than in today's relative faceless, stylized and
somewhat sterile society.

The four are politicians John Sherman Cooper and A. B. (Happy)
Chandler, basketball coach Adolph Rupp and fried chicken king
Col. Harland Sanders, who, around the world, just may be the
most familiar Kentuckians who ever lived. All of these men are
in their 70s and 80s now, and likely we'll never see their
ilk again.

It is highly unlikely, with political campaigning turning more and
more to the impersonal, mass approach dictated by television,
that the one-on-one, handshaking, backslapping approach of
a Cooper or a Chandler can succeed in a statewide election today.

Moreover, a new, more sophisticated and more questioning breed
of athlete has appeared on the scene since Rupp began rewriting

the basketball record books with his dictatorial, do-as-I-say-and-don't-ask-why technique of coaching.

As for Sanders, the man whose success with finger-lickin' Kentucky fried chicken ushered in the era of take-home food, just bear in mind that at age 66 his business was sold at auction and he was reduced to living on Social Security, but at 80 he was a millionaire many times over.

What was it about these men that made them far different from those who have followed in their footsteps?

All had in common the broad characteristics previously mentioned; each was unique unto himself. It's almost as though each, long ago in the misty past, sat down at a drawing board and designed himself. What emerged was a character, molded to fit a slower, less precast era, a character that exploited fully the distinctive and considerable talents of the individual.

Thus, Cooper made full use of his halting, homefolks speaking style, Chandler of his unflagging energy and elephant-like memory of names and faces, Rupp of his massive ego and ability to turn a colorful phrase, and Sanders of his cooking talent and physical likeness to the Kentucky colonel of the caricatures.

To understand the individualistic nature of these men, and perhaps appreciate the contribution each made to Kentucky, look at them separately.

Cooper: No politician in Kentucky, a state that thrives on partisan politics, ever has been able to take on the mantle of nonpartisanship the way the 73-year-old Cooper did during his career as county and circuit judge, U.N. delegate, ambassador and United States senator.

Republican born and bred, he nevertheless was not one to be distracted by a party label. He clung to his party's basic beliefs, but was quick to question it when he thought it had strayed afield. He followed his own conscience, voting the Republican line when it seemed right to him, but often as not supporting the other side or charting a course all his own. It was in working with Democrats, in fact, that Cooper pushed through some of the key measures which bear his name.

In 1970 he joined Democrat Frank Church in drafting the Cooper-Church Amendment to bar further U.S. military action in Cambodia; a year earlier he teamed with Philip Hart, another Democrat, in sponsoring amendments aimed against the Safeguard antimissile system.

"I vote as I see fit," Cooper said. His motives and sincerity seldom were questioned, and he came to serve Kentucky longer in

the Senate than any other man in history except the legendary
Alben W. Barkley, another Kentuckian who was from his
generation of giants.

Although when Cooper first became active in state politics
Kentucky was heavily Democratic, three times he was elected to
fill unexpired Senate terms and once he was elected to a full
six-year term.

A tall, warm, friendly man with a perpetually wrinkled look,
Cooper was born in Somerset and blended the down-to-earth
qualities of the Kentucky mountaineer with the urbanity of the
Easterner by graduating from Yale in 1923 and from Harvard Law
School in 1925.

Cooper tells how it was when he came back to Somerset to
practice law. His shingle had been out some time, but he still was
waiting for his first customer when a long-time friend burst
into the office.

"Johnny," he said excitedly, "a woman just ran smack into my
car. It was her fault and she admits it!"

The more the friend described the mishap, the more apparent
it was that this indeed was an open-and-shut case. Cooper admits
his mouth watered in anticipation of the nice fee he'd get for
handling the matter in court.

"Now, Johnny, we've been friends for years," the aggrieved
friend concluded. "Tell me straight: Where can I find myself a good
lawyer to take this case?"

Cooper wasn't an orator and he knew it; he'd stumble through a
campaign speech and come away with most of the crowd openly
sympathetic because he sounded so much like one of them.
Many of the flashier, more articulate opponents he defeated over
the years vowed it was the sympathy vote that did them in.

To a degree, maybe. But Cooper's success was due more to his
disarming honesty, his sincerity, his conscientiousness and his look
that so inspired confidence that Democrats would flock to vote
for him.

Like many a successful politician before him, Cooper had—and
still has—a deep and abiding sense of humor and a wealth of
folksy stories. These he relishes telling, but often, not being a
politician stand-up storyteller in the mold of Barkley, the punch
line is lost because, anticipating what is coming, he starts chuckling
himself before getting to the climax.

A statesman of the highest order whose years as ambassador to
India still are pointed to as a highwater mark in the diplomatic
service, Cooper long has been an eagerly sought guest at

Washington parties, but by his own admission he'd much prefer sitting with the whittlers and tobacco chewers outside the Pulaski County Courthouse at Somerset.

Only 29 when he first was elected county judge, Cooper quickly rose to prominence in statewide Republican circles. He was regarded as a comer, and he made the prophets look good in the way he became almost an interparty figure.

Despite his success in politics on the national and international level, Cooper often has commented that the real interest in politics in Kentucky is in the races for local offices. A story he tells points up the fact that even the dispensing of justice sometimes can be clouded by partisanship.

When he ran for re-election as county judge, a massive rally was held in Somerset for him on the night before election. During the rally a fight broke out among his supporters and those backing his opponent, and a number of men were thrown into jail.

Early the next morning several of Cooper's boosters called on him and suggested that some of the brawlers be released in time to vote.

"Actually," Cooper told them, "I plan to let them all go."

"No, don't do that," his supporters urged in unison, "just let our friends out!"

Chandler: Recently turned 76, Chandler still has iron in his arms, steel in his grip, sunshine in the famous ear-to-ear grin that earned him his "Happy" nickname, instant recall of names and faces, and the willingness to belt out a few bars of "Gold Mine in the Sky" or other of the songs he used in vaulting to political prominence more than 50 years ago.

The last Kentuckian to serve twice as governor, Chandler, like Cooper, is something of a political maverick who more often than not had the leaders of his own party supporting his Democratic opponents in primary elections before rallying behind him in the general elections—since everybody loves a winner.

The fact is, Chandler made his best races against those who were holding office. "I've always run best against the 'ins,' " he has said many times.

It was his opposition in 1934 to the sales tax enacted by Gov. Ruby Laffoon that catapulted Chandler, then relatively unknown, from lieutenant governor to governor in the first place. And from that time on he seemed almost to court controversy.

By taking his cause directly to the people with whom he communicated so well, Chandler usually came out on top after jumping the political traces.

One time he didn't was in 1938. Then governor, he sought to take the senate seat held by the legendary Barkley, the undisputed "Mr. Democrat" of Kentucky politics. Not only did Chandler lose the race, but he was virtually read out of the party, denounced as a turncoat and accused of tacit support of both Republican and Dixiecrat candidates.

But Chandler obviously always operated under a lucky star.

Shortly after Chandler lost to Barkley, Sen. M. M. Logan died. Chandler resigned as governor, was appointed to take the seat and later was elected to the full six-year term which terminated in 1945 when he resigned to become commissioner of baseball.

Moreover, to prove the Chandler magic still worked, after being fired as baseball commissioner in 1951, he came back to Kentucky and once again was elected governor in 1955.

A fiscal expert whose terms in Frankfort were highlighted by tax reform and economy measures that left the state treasury with a healthy surplus, Chandler was at his best in eyeball-to-eyeball campaigning. He could set out alone, visiting stores around a courthouse square anywhere in the state, and wind up with a small army of people following him.

The man has a magnetic personality that attracts people to him. The complete extrovert, he still is uncomfortable if even one hand in a crowd remains unshaken.

A Chandler political speech—and he was making them as recently as 1971 when he made an unsuccessful bid for a third term as governor—was a real production. Chandler has the ability to run the emotional gamut from modesty to sarcasm to rage to bubbling optimism in the course of one speech. One minute he'd have his audience howling at his salty description of an opponent; the next minute he'd bring tears to their eyes as he recounted his many battles fought against the "ins" on behalf of the common people. He then usually would round out the show with a song or two sung in a voice which still shows the professional training which, during his student days at Transylvania College, enabled him to pick up a few bucks by singing at central Kentucky revival meetings.

Being an inveterate sports fan—he once played semi-pro baseball and coached football—Chandler takes great pride in his accomplishments as baseball commissioner. "I started with the players' pension fund, don't you know," he says, using a phrase, which with "podner," has become his trademark, "and I broke the color line when I approved Brooklyn calling up Jackie Robinson, even though the other owners were against it 15 to 1.

Satchel Paige, the great black pitcher, told me once that he'd have won 30 games for 30 years if I'd been commissioner when he was in his prime."

He had the ability to express himself in colorful phrases: "Mamma and I have been married nearly 50 years and we've always gotten along because I do what she tells me to do the first time."

Rupp: Although he actually was born in Kansas and came to this state by way of a high school coaching job in northern Illinois, in his 42 years of producing winning basketball teams at the University of Kentucky, Adolph Frederick Rupp, 73, became as much a part of Kentucky tradition as bluegrass, bourbon whisky and country ham.

In the course of winning a record 874 games and losing only 190 and picking up four NCAA championships and more than 20 Southeastern Conference titles in the process, Rupp literally forced basketball in the South to step into the 20th century.

Until Rupp came along, southern colleges played a dull, low-scoring brand of ball that stirred what few yawning fans they could lure into crackerbox-size gyms to massive apathy. But when Rupp's UK teams started beating the sneakers off them with an exciting, disciplined, fast-break game that brought the spectators to their feet screaming for more, eventually the other schools took step to keep up.

The Rupp method was more revolutionary than merely teaching a newer, faster version of basketball; he encouraged shots which once had been called "show offs." That is, he didn't hold that the two-hand set shot was the ultimate. If a player felt like shooting one-handed or free-wheeling them in with his back to the goal— as French DeMoisey, an early Rupp All-American, did—that was fine. As long as the shot went in. Rupp's idea was to open up the game and to win.

He did both.

Soon the teams that UK competed against in the South, prodded on by Rupp's jibes that playing some of them was "like kissing your sister," began to follow his example as an alternative to further humiliation.

Consequently, today the SEC is one of the nation's strongest basketball leagues, and some of the largest and finest playing arenas in the nation are south of the Ohio River.

Rupp isn't known as "The Baron" for nothing. A master organizer, he has an ego to match his king-size career winning record. It was his style to let his players know from the minute they reported to him that he was the coach as well as the judge, jury and executioner when it came to interpreting the iron-bound rules he laid down on training routines, eating habits, dress and personal conduct both on and off the floor. Consequently, even a Rupp practice session was a study in discipline and the judicious use of time.

Because of his dominating personality, a personality which in today's more permissive times might have players rebelling, Rupp perhaps never was as close personally to his players as, say, his contemporary, the late Ed Diddle of Western Kentucky University. But Rupp's men respected him and they put out because they knew he was a winner.

By combining his winning ways, a twangy Kansas drawl, an ability to turn a colorful phrase and a natural outspokenness, Rupp soon became what is known as "good copy" in the news trade. He could (and can) produce a quotable quote with the speed of his team breaking down the floor.

Item: When asked what it was like to send a team against Notre Dame at South Bend, and, when students filled all available seats in the old arena, he fired back: "Who could beat a team with all 4,000 spectators in the place saying 'Hail, Marys' and praying against you?"

Item: After having been branded a "carpetbagger" for recruiting talent in what a Big Ten coach regarded as his personal preserve, Rupp later was invited to make a speech in the area. "My text," he said after his introduction, "will be: 'A Carpetbagger in the Holy Land.' "

Item: Once when UK was in New York City to play, Rupp was asked during an interview what steps he would take to improve basketball. "I'd raise the hoop to 12 feet and remove the banking board," he replied. After the excited New York reporters had rushed away to file stories about the revolutionary suggestion, Rupp was asked if he really meant what he'd said. "Hell, no," he grinned, "but anything for a column!"

Rupp's first 7-foot player was a Georgia farm boy, Bill Spivey, who became an All-American but who weighed a feathery 167 pounds when he came to Lexington in the summer of 1948. Later that summer when he departed to coach the U.S. team in the Olympic Games, Rupp left Harry Lancaster, his assistant, behind to put pounds on Spivey's lank frame.

He was, the coach decreed, to have malted milks with eggs in them three times a day. And Lancaster was to write him periodically to give him a progress report.

"Spivey is up to 180," Lancaster wrote in his first report.

"Spivey is up to 190 . . . 200 . . . 210," he added in subsequent reports as the summer wore on.

Finally the big question became too much for Rupp to bear, so he fired off a cablegram to Lancaster which read:

"I know Spivey can eat. Can he shoot a basketball?"

It was entirely in keeping with Rupp's style that even his retirement from UK wasn't done in conventional fashion. When he reached 70 and, in keeping with across-the-board university policy, retirement became mandatory, there was a widespread movement to force UK to make an exception in his case. Rumors had it that the matter might be taken to the state legislature. But in the end policy held, and the winningest coach in history stepped into retirement.

Sanders: If Horatio Alger ever had tried to turn the true story of 84-year-old Harland Sanders into one of his rags-to-riches novels, he no doubt would have been drummed out of the fiction writing corps.

Moreover, Sanders rose from failure to make his mark at age 66, a time when Alger had his make-believe heroes settling into an easy chair and enjoying the fruits of their hard-working salad years.

Born in poverty on a southern Indiana farm, Sanders practically educated himself and started to work after the sixth grade to support his widowed mother and younger brother and sister by hiring out on a neighbor's farm for $2 a month.

During the next half century he tried a variety of things—service in the Army, railroad laborer and fireman, insurance salesman, operator of a service station and cooking, an art that always had appealed to him.

The service station he operated for 20 years or more on U.S. 25, a main north-south highway on the edge of Corbin, Kentucky, and to which he eventually added a small restaurant and later a motel, drew trade because Sanders advertised "Free Air" for motorists' tires, a new service at that time. And the restaurant drew trade because of one item he served—fried chicken cooked using his mother's recipe with a few "secret" herbs and spices of his own added to the batter.

Served with hot biscuits and honey, Harland Sanders' fried chicken was a success despite the admission on the menu under the price which read: "Not Worth It, But Mighty Good."

No small part of the modest success of the Sanders Motel and Restaurant was the character he created for himself—that of the goateed, mustachioed Kentucky colonel in the white suit. Once assumed, and armed with a Kentucky colonel commission, that role would be one that, through good times and bad, Harland Sanders would develop into his personal trademark worth millions.

Just when the motel and restaurant were doing well, with tourists driving miles out of their way just to stay with Sanders and partake of a meal or two, things took a turn for the worse. In 1955 he had refused an offer of $164,000 for his motel-restaurant-service station in Corbin. Less than a year later it was announced that I-75 would be built some seven miles away, which meant the traffic that had been passing his place would be diverted. The value of the Colonel's place dropped immediately; in less than a year business in general had tailed off so drastically that the complex was sold at public auction.

At age 66 Harland Sanders was down again. But he still wasn't out.

With his first Social Security check of $105 and the money from the auction of the Corbin property, he set out to do something he'd long thought of trying—market "Col. Sanders Kentucky Fried Chicken" as a take-home food. To do this, he proposed setting up franchised outlets all over the nation to prepare chicken according to his patented recipe. In return for his own designed pressure cooker, an ice chest containing dressed chickens and a supply of flour containing his mixture of 11 spices and herbs, franchise dealers would pay him a royalty of 5 cents per order served.

The selling of his idea wasn't easy. The Colonel and Mrs. Sanders drove thousands of miles, slept many a night in their automobile, before the first franchise was sold in Salt Lake City, Utah.

During the next nine years he located 600 franchises and then in 1964 sold his company for $2 million and hired himself back at a six-figure salary as a public relations man for the new firm.

By 1969 Kentucky Fried Chicken, Inc., the name assumed by the chain, was the largest commercial food service operation in the nation and the colonel's face was smiling from atop more than 3,000 stores all over the world.

But the Harland Sanders story doesn't end there. Today he has his own food company in Canada, he operates a place near Shelbyville called "Claudia Sanders, The Colonel's Lady Dinner House," the likes of which he'd like to open elsewhere, and he has a national-debt-size suit filed against Hublein,

Inc., the conglomerate which bought out the firm that took his original operation.

Claiming his name, image and picture have been misused in promoting products he had nothing to do with, Sanders has sued Hublein for $122,386,000.

Some may say Harland Sanders has become obsessed with just making more money. But few share more generously with the less fortunate than he. Half of what he makes from his Canadian company goes to charity and scholarships. In addition, he is one of the major donors to the Salvation Army, perhaps his pet charity, the Boy Scouts, Lincoln Memorial University and various other causes.

Which isn't a bad image for a man who, like Cooper, Chandler, Rupp and many unnamed others of his generation, represents a rapidly disappearing breed of determined, self-reliant, hard-working and extremely capable men, the likes of which we may never see again. (9/21/74)

HE DWELLS IN LONELINESS   That first look at Hensley Settlement is downright startling, about as startling as opening a pearl and finding an oyster.

Maybe the rough route you follow in getting there adds to the surprise. You spend two long, hot hours in scrambling up the almost sheer, 3,000-foot-high side of the mountain, one of those two-steps-up-and-one-step-back slopes so common in eastern Kentucky.

But by clinging to the rocky, narrow, poorly defined path—the only way up—you finally make it to the saddle of Chadwell Gap, a rough break in the mountains in northeastern Bell County near the Harlan County line. You pause there and rest a second, panting like an overloaded locomotive, while small streams of perspiration snake down your back.

Below, almost straight down, you see traffic crawling along Virginia Highway 58, the road you took earlier that morning out of Middlesboro. The top of the rickety coal tipple near the foot of the mountain where the car was parked barely is visible in the wilderness of trees.

To the north, the timber-sided hills seem to spread out in even ripples like a roll of blue-green velvet. From where you stand, their slopes appear amazingly regular and unbroken. And

to the south, the rough face of the mountain rises up over the gap
another 500 feet or so, the remaining distance you have to
drag your tired feet.

As you drum up energy for that climb, you wonder, for
approximately the 100th time, if it is worth the trouble. You doubt
that Hensley Settlement will really be as it was described
by Howard Douglass of Middlesboro, secretary of the Cumberland
Gap National Historical Park Association. He said it was a
place where a lone resident, remaining from a once-sizeable group,
still lives as mountain people did many years ago. Once over
that last hump, however, your doubts evaporate like a drop of
water on a hot griddle.

For what you see there is something entirely different. It
almost makes you rub your eyes and gasp in disbelief.
There, spread out before you on the very top of this near-
perpendicular mountain, is 500 acres of land that is gently rolling
and in spots almost table-flat. Much of the land has been
cleared and fenced, and in places uneven rows of brown cornstalks
stand as evidence that the fields had once been cultivated.

Over on your left is a three-room log cabin, made
entirely by hand, including even the rough wooden shingles of
the roof. It has a rough, soot-blackened field-stone chimney jutting
out from one side, and a porch, supported by a pile of flat
creek rocks at either end. A split-rail fence, sagging and rotting
away in places, encircles the cabin. Behind the cabin is a
smaller log barn. Straight ahead are another log cabin and barn,
almost exact carbon copies of the others. Farther on are
still more, some 20 in all, all uninhabited except for one.

This is Hensley Settlement, once the home of more than 100
people. Now it is a ghost settlement where only 70-odd-year-old
Sherman Hensley lives alone.

Although it is less than 10 miles as the crow flies northeast of
Middlesboro, this little settlement is unbelievably remote.
Few outsiders ever have fought their way up that steep path and
through the gap to reach it. No automobile horn ever has
punctured the stillness, no electric light ever has cut the
nighttime darkness of the mountaintop. There the Hensleys lived
for years in a quiet, 500-acre world all their own.

And there Sherman Hensley continues to live, alone
except for two cur dogs, a cow and the mule that is his means of
transportation up and down the mountain.

You walk on past a couple of the vacant cabins. The
chinking is falling from between the logs, many of the wooden

shingles have blown away, and the sagging, half-open doors creak in the soft wind. On the other side of a small clump of giant trees you see a patch of chin-high corn and another log barn. A pair of snarling dogs, yellow fangs bared and back bristles erect, set up a terrific racket as your steps are heard. Leaning over the rail fence, squinting suspiciously as he looks your way, is a tall, gaunt man, wearing a battered felt hat and clean, faded blue shirt and trousers. A bright silver pistol in the holster on his belt glistens as the sun strikes the butt.

Howard Douglass, a rather short citizen whose energy would be the envy of any jumping bean in Mexico, knows the man to be Sherman Hensley. Douglass dealt with Hensley over the acquisition of his property for Cumberland Gap National Historical Park. In reaching terms and getting all the papers signed, Douglass was in the settlement before.

"Hi there," Douglass shouts as you stop there on the edge of the wood lot. "This is Howard Douglass from Middlesboro, Mr. Hensley, and I have a couple of newspapermen with me from Louisville."

At a sharp command the dogs stop their growling and crouch on their bellies in the tall grass at the side of the path. The man in the battered hat grins and comes forward. As he takes your hand warmly and invites you down to the house "to set a spell," the dogs fall in with the spirit of things and lick your hands as you walk along. The man in the battered hat leads the way along the edge of the corn patch, through another wood lot to the largest of the cabins you've yet seen.

He opens the heavy door and stands back as you walk in. The cabin has three rooms, one a combination bedroom and sitting room, another a smaller bedroom, the third a kitchen. The front room has a tremendous stone fireplace along one side. Firewood, neatly stacked and ready for a match, is inside the fireplace. The furniture consists of two steel-framed beds, a chest of drawers, two tables and several cane-bottom chairs.

But it's the construction of the cabin itself that holds your attention. Some of the handhewn logs in the walls are as much as three feet thick. The boards in the floor, also hand cut and dressed, range up to 36 inches in width.

Sherman Hensley walks over to the chest of drawers, takes off his pistol and lays it inside.

"Always carry that," he says. "Never can tell what you might run into, bein' up here by yourself."

You wonder about this tableland set here in the middle of sheer precipices and rugged terrain. You wonder why people happened to settle there.

"My wife's daddy held a land grant to this land," Hensley explains as though reading your mind. "I'm from Wallins over in Harlan County myself and came here after I married her—47 years ago. When he died, she inherited the 500 acres."

He walks out of the cabin and leans against a fence post as he continues in a low, slow voice. "We had five sons and six daughters and whenever one married, they'd take over a plot of ground, build a cabin and set up housekeeping."

As he explained it, it was as simple as that. The essentials were there—plenty of trees and enough strong backs to hack those trees into logs for a cabin. And there was flat, fairly fertile land where a man could plant himself a crop and garden and raise a few pigs for meat.

The cabins sprang up, one by one, until there were some 20 in all. With kids coming on all the time, a school was opened. It was a compact, independent, almost self-sufficient world in which the Hensleys lived there atop their mountain. They raised most of the things they ate except salt, flour, coffee and a few related items. Complete cycles in the history of the family were recorded there as children were born and some of them died and were buried in the little graveyard across from the schoolhouse. Mrs. Hensley died in 1937 and was buried in one of only two graves whose stones bear lettering. The others are marked by unlettered field stones.

Whenever the Hensleys had business in Middlesboro in Kentucky or Ewing in Virginia or any of the other nearby towns, they'd go down to the foot of the mountain on muleback and hitch a ride or hike the rest of the way. No other means of transportation was available down the hill, not even a wagon could get over that path.

But times change, even in so remote a place. During World War II, starting about 1942, there was a movement of the Hensleys and their in-laws down the mountain. Some of the men went into the Army, others took war jobs.

"After the war," Hensley says sadly, "none of 'em seemed to want to come back. They stayed where they was and now they're scattered all over."

As you listen, you can almost feel the loneliness of the place, the loneliness of the man. Sounds carry far there on the mountaintop. While you listen to Hensley the excited yelps of his dogs as they flush a rabbit drift from the distance. Only that, the sound of his voice and the whisper of the wind through the tall trees break the stillness.

Where shouting children used to romp and play outside the little schoolhouse, only berry vines now are growing. There have been no classes for nearly five years. Inside, everything is in ruin. Desks are overturned, the rough slate blackboard is cracked, books are turned inside out. There is no sign of life except for the field mouse you see timidly poking its head from under a faded, torn *First Reader* in a corner. The scene is equally as lonely outside. Fields in which corn once rustled in the breeze that forever seems to move across the mountaintop are dotted now with large locust trees. No smoke comes from the chimneys of cabins, forsaken by families whose men now mine coal or clerk in a store or maybe stay in the Army.

Only Sherman Hensley stays on, living much as he did when he first arrived 47 years ago, as the sturdy, reliant mountain people did long before that.

And so a mountain settlement has about run its course, about been reduced from an isolated little world where bright-eyed children once romped through the woods and where the fields were carefully tended, to a place where only an old man lives alone and where the fields are growing over.

Only one chapter remains to be written in the story. That will come when Cumberland Gap National Park is a reality and Sherman Hensley, like his children before him, leaves his mountaintop and moves down into some valley. Then Hensley Settlement will be no more. A curious table-top plot on the very peak of an almost perpendicular mountain will be deserted and, perhaps, forgotten. (9/17/50)

THERE'S NO SUCH ANIMAL AS A TYPICAL KENTUCKIAN   Say, have you noticed how the word "typical" has become an almost indispensable part of everyday language, a sort of linguistic standard equipment, you might say?

Everywhere you turn nowadays you're face to face with something or other that's typical—Typical Home, Typical Small Town, Typical Boy and/or Girl, Typical Married Couple or, as the boys at the poolroom might say, Typical Schnook. Without using the word "typical" freely one just isn't, well, just isn't typical, that's all.

Typical may have just seven letters, but it's used to cover more territory and subjects than the British flag. Perhaps the most common use of the word at the local level is in reference to a shadowy figure no one ever really saw—Typical Kentuckian. I doubt that one person in 10,000—including myself —really knows what he's talking about when he falls back into that phrase.

What, to get down to brass knuckles, is a Typical Kentuckian?

Ask anyone fitting those two words together to explain what he means and he'd probably flounder like a fish out of water for an embarrassing moment or two. Then he'd doubtless come up with one or the other of two tattered and well-worn descriptions in an effort to make himself clear.

The first probably would be of the venerable, goateed and habitually half-crocked old colonel, sitting on his veranda, julep in hand, dreaming of how the mortgage on the old home place will be lifted as soon as the one remaining colt frisking across his rolling bluegrass acres comes through and wins the Derby, as it has done in so many movies.

The second most common picture the typical conversationalist has of the typical Kentuckian is built around the grossly mistaken idea of what the people of the mountains are like. You know what I mean. The idea is pretty general that mountain folks are gaunt, bearded, feuding citizens with short tempers and long rifles.

But neither of those descriptions are, I feel, even second cousins by marriage to a typical Kentuckian.

To start with, both the old colonel and the mountaineer are children of somebody's imagination. I've never seen a man who fitted the old colonel picture. And I've seen few mountaineers who look like what most people think they should. In spite of what's been written about the mountain people, you'll find them as enlightened and civilized as in any other part of the state. Sure, some of them can't read or write. But you'll find complete illiterates on the Haymarket in Louisville and in Irishtown in Lexington.

Kentucky is far from being a unified region and that makes trying to bestow a typical label on one sort or type of person all but impossible. Though known as the Bluegrass State, Kentucky divides naturally into at least six sections, each of which differs sharply from the others in geography, culture, economic ways and means, and social habits. It has been said, in fact, that no state can be more accurately characterized by its sectional variations than Kentucky.

Largest of the six regions is the mountains. The land is thin and not suited to extensive farming. Coal mining, and timbering to a lesser degree, is the main source of employment. Next comes the Knobs, an area with large wooded areas, such as the Cumberland National Forest.

Then comes the Bluegrass, the central Kentucky land of horse farms and burley tobacco. After that is the Pennyrile, an area that ranges from gently rolling farms to cliffs and scarps and where livestock and a variety of farm produce is raised. The Western Coal Field, next region in size, is one of the nation's fastest growing coal producers. Smallest of the six is the Purchase, lying between the Tennessee and Mississippi Rivers. Farming is the principal industry and strawberries is one of the main cash crops.

Varying as the state is, then, it isn't correct to draw a character, even a mythical character, from any one region and label him typical of the whole state. The coal miner in Pike County is no more typical, and at the same time just as typical, of all Kentuckians as the horseman of Fayette County, the steel worker of Boyd County, the cattleman of Wayne County, the corn farmer of Todd County or the strawberry raiser of Marshall County.

Truth of the matter is, there's really no such animal as a Typical Kentuckian. (2/17/50)

U.S. AGENTS
RAID A STILL
It was a typical midsummer Sunday morning with the sun burning down round and hot from a cloudless blue sky. The meadows had been soaking wet with dew earlier, but the sun was rapidly steaming every blade of grass dry. It still was fairly cool in the thick woods.

Except for an occasional bird call and a hollow thumping noise up ahead that sounded like hot weather thunder far in the distance, the stillness of the Marion County woods seemed almost thick enough to slice with a knife.

I lay flat on my stomach and peered open-mouthed through the bushes down into the little creek.

Less than 100 yards in front of me, two men were busier than ants at a picnic. The one in the slouch hat was tinkering with a kerosene burner which gave off the thunder-like thumping

noise when it worked. The other fellow, the one with the
thick blonde hair, was dipping water from the creek and pouring
it into the oil drum boiler under which the kerosene burner
blazed spasmodically.

Arranged in a line behind the boiler and connected to each
other by a series of Rube Goldberg pipes and tubes were three other
barrels. On the opposite side of the little creek were eight
50-gallon wooden barrels, each of which gave off an unmistakable
sweet-sour odor.

The men were making moonshine whiskey.

The small talk was quite heavy as they worked on,
blissfully unaware that their lawbreaking—the producing of
untaxed whiskey—was being watched by five persons. Three of the
interested spectators were Treasury Department Alcohol Tax
Unit investigators. The other two were there just to watch the
revenuers in action.

Mark Holmes, a giant of a man who'd played three years of
varsity tackle when Auburn was a football powerhouse
of the South in the early 1930s, lay at my side downstream from the
moonshiners. Charley Summers, head of the raiding party,
and Tommy Miller, *Courier-Journal* photographer, had
worked along the brow of the little hill above the creek to a
point on the east side directly above the men. Quinn Pearl
crouched in a thicket directly across from Summers. Pearl had
scouted ahead when we stopped an hour before to see if
the still was running.

The burner blazed up again and in a few seconds the strong odor
of kerosene mixed with the smell of sour mash in the
barrels. Soon the boiler of the steam-type still would be hot
enough to produce the steam, which in turn would heat the mash
in the still itself, the nearest of the three barrels to the boiler.
The alcoholic steam rising from the mixture of mash and
steam in the still then would pass through the brass tubes into the
middle barrel, the thumper, and from there into the third
barrel, the condenser.

A sweat bee buzzed noisily around in jerky circles and finally
settled on the tip of my nose. If this had been a movie, that
probably would have been my cue to sneeze loudly and give away
our presence. Nothing so melodramatic occurred. I simply
lay there and thought thoughts reflecting directly on the
ancestry of the little insect as it sank its spurs several times into
my schnoz.

The men at the still froze a moment as the hoarse baying

of a hound dog started up from the creek behind them.
But they resumed their distilling when the barking stopped.

There was less than a minute to go before 9:25, the time the
agents had set as the time they'd flush out the moonshiners, when
Summers tried to slip down closer to the two-strand barbed
wire fence at the top of the creek bank. The sun reflected for just
an instant on something, maybe his badge. But that was
long enough.

The blond-haired fellow dropped his bucket and, without
so much as a parting goodbye to his partner, came out of
the creek bed toward where Pearl crouched with the speed of a
jack rabbit equipped with overdrive. It didn't take the man
long to figure something was up. He, too, took off and by the time
they'd hit the top of the ridge, was almost abreast of his
partner.

Meanwhile, Summers had come tearing down the hill,
screaming like a "locoed" Commanche Indian.

"Stop, Williamson," he yelled as he ran. "I saw you! I know
who you are."

By then the figures were making Olympic sprint time up
the long-abandoned wagon road that bordered the creek.
Summers, still yelling at the top of his voice, was hot after them,
while Holmes and I were heading toward the excitement up
ahead.

As the two men sped up the road, Pearl leaped out of the
bushes and brought the man in the slouch hat down with
a rib-rattling flying tackle. The blond fellow disappeared into a
heavy briar thicket with Summers still after him.

Holmes took charge of the man who had been downed.
Then Pearl, limping badly because he had struck his right knee
on a rock when he made the tackle, set off to help Summers, who
could be heard thrashing through the underbrush.

The man they'd nabbed still was gasping for breath from
the force of the sudden stop he'd made. The first thing Holmes did
was search him. He was carrying nothing but a battered
pocketbook which produced a driver's license made out to
Marion R. Mattingly.

It was some time before the man had enough breath
to talk. Then it came out in a torrent. It turned out that he normally
worked at a distillery not far from Loretto, that he had been
laid off and needed a little money, that he was married and had
three children, that this was the first time he'd ever tried
to make moonshine, that he'd take a vow that this also was the

last time, and that he hoped they wouldn't put him in
jail on Sunday.

Before long, Summers and Pearl reappeared empty handed. The
blond man had disappeared. However, Summers, who had
been almost close enough to him in the bushes to read his palm,
had identified him. They had gone to his house, which was less than
a half mile away, and had found several clues there—a number
of gallon jugs and a barrel in the yard and a package of rye,
used to seal the top of the still, and some cornmeal in a
battered old car beside the house. In addition, the car's tire
treads matched those they had found in the soft mud near the still.

(The man who had escaped, Dave Williamson, gave himself
up the following morning. Both were released on $300
bail.)

Almost immediately, Summers and Pearl set off to get the
truck in which we had ridden over from Lebanon, the county
seat some 15 miles away. We had left the truck hidden off
the main road a good two miles from the still. It was an hour before
they returned. Then, after making an inventory of items at the
still, they wrecked everything in sight. Six hours after
we'd left Louisville, 400 gallons of mash—which in another two
hours would have become approximately 50 gallons of
illegal whiskey—had been poured into the creek, the barrels
had been smashed, and the boiler punctured beyond repair.

And so, another still was stilled.

Although moonshine still hunting has been pictured as
something of a hit-and-miss part-time thing, it's anything but that
the way it's practiced by the Treasury Department boys.
They work at the job full-time and a raid is the climax of detailed
and careful scouting and planning. That's the reason agents were
able to raid and destroy 267 stills in Kentucky last year. A
total of 376 persons were arrested and 46,325 gallons of mash
seized in those raids. If made legally, government tax on
mash and whiskey taken would have been $69,808.50.

The raid on the Marion County still, which, ironically, was
located on property owned by the Dant distilling interests,
was a perfect example of how carefully the revenue agents plot
their moves. They had discovered the still the preceding
Friday night. But since they were more interested in taking the
operators than merely in tearing up their equipment, they
had left it alone and marked it for future reference. From the
condition of the mash, they figured the 'shiners would run
off the bottled dynamite about Sunday morning.

They were extremely cautious in approaching the still. They stuck to the woods and avoided crossing any open expanses. Before moving in on it, Pearl scouted ahead and came back to draw a diagram of the still's location, obstructions in reaching it, and the positions each agent should take. Then a definite time to flush out the moonshiners was set.

Although all agents wear pistols, they are seldom used these days in the Marion County area. They're more for effect than anticipated use. The 'shiners, at least in the Marion-Taylor County section, are a rather peaceful lot and violence seldom crops up. That's in contast, however, with the way it used to be. Not too long back, it wasn't at all uncommon for an agent or a 'shiner to be shot at fairly regularly. That being a strong Catholic section, several priests met with the agents and then with the known moonshiners and a sort of armistice from shooting was worked out. That agreement seldom, if ever, is violated by either side in that area now. The agents are seldom rough. Usually, in fact, they're very considerate. While the moonshiners are pretty placid in their dealings with the agents in this game of moonshining hares and hounds, they get rough with each other at times. Let them suspect that someone has turned informer and the result is violence.

Moonshining, like all occupations, has changed over the years. Now stills are so expensive to set up and the ingredients so costly that not many small operators can get started anymore. Instead, they work stills for big-time operators who own a chain of several. Wages paid still workers range from $15 to $30 a day, but the work is only for a few days at a time.

Their business may be definitely on the shady side of the law, but the moonshiners have sort of code of ethics. It's unwritten law that the owner of the still will care for the family while a man taken at his still is in jail.

In case you're interested, a common recipe for moonshine is 25 pounds of corn meal (this is used now instead of corn because it breaks down faster), 50 pounds of sugar, and half a pound of baker's yeast in a 50-gallon barrel filled almost to the top with branch water. After fermenting, or "working," for about 72 hours, the mash is ready for the whiskey-making process.

The whiskey, then commonly called "white mule" because of its lack of color and the power of its kick, comes from the condenser crystal clear with a strength of around 120 proof. It is sold for about $4.50 a gallon at the still, usually in gallon jugs or fruit jars. Sometimes it is given a legal-liquor color by adding food coloring or by having charred oak chips thrown into the mixture when it is in the condenser.

Although there seems to be no shortage of legally made liquor, there is a demand for moonshine for several reasons. For one, it is less expensive. And, two, a lot of people who were introduced to moonshine during prohibition have cultivated a taste for it.

There are 27 agents scattered throughout Kentucky with headquarters at Louisville. W. H. Kinnaird, a veteran of the business, is investigator in charge. Uncovering moonshine making is serious business and the selection of agents is done very carefully. But in spite of all the dead seriousness of the work, a lot of funny things pop up.

"Big Six" Henderson is an agent in the Bowling Green section. Some years back he had been trailing a known 'shiner for months without luck. Then one night Henderson lay in the bushes within spitting distance of the man as he prepared to run off several gallons. The 'shiner chuckled to himself as he labored. As the first whiskey came off, he laughed and said aloud:

"Wouldn't old Henderson like to see me now!"

The moonshiners call the car that the agents out of Louisville drive the "dead wagon." Not long ago Summers was at his home in Lebanon when a 'shiner given a ride in the dead wagon only a few weeks before stopped by and asked if he could borrow $2! And he got it, too.

All of which proves the revenuers are diplomats as well as sleuths. It isn't every officer who can arrest a man and leave him feeling he can drop around later for a small-size loan. (8/8/48)

COTTONMOUTH POSSE   The waitress was too polite to come right out and say it, but the look she aimed at the five customers branded them unreconstructed liars.

The look had its beginnings with a routine passing-the-time-of-day question.

"What are you all doing?" she had asked the khaki-pants-and-old-shirt-clad diners at the filling station-cafe in Lewisburg.

"We're going snake hunting," one of the group answered.

The ice-cube glance and the biting way she mumbled, "Smart alec!" made it as plain as the nose on Jimmy Durante's face that she wouldn't have believed any of the five on a stack of Bibles as high as the jukebox.

But the visitors were indeed going snake hunting. And, more to the point, they were going snake finding.

Less than 30 minutes from Lewisburg over backcountry roads they were going to prove the books wrong by finding cottonmouth moccasins, a highly poisonous snake, in an area 100 miles east and slightly north of the outside limits where such critters are supposed to be in Kentucky.

In four hours of swamp wading, they were to see a dozen or more cottonmouths and catch five, one of them perhaps record size for this state.

The five who made the expedition were Richard Dooley, a graduate herpetologist (that's a big word for reptile expert) who runs the Kentucky Animal Land and Reptile Garden at Park City; Burnis Skipworth, the third district supervisor for the State Department of Fish and Wildlife Resources; George Laycock, a Batavia, Ohio, free-lance writer and photographer who specializes in outdoor-style pieces, and two newspapermen from Louisville.

The Louisville newspaper gent with the handful of cameras was Warren Klosterman. The one with the handful of big sticks and a yellow streak down his back had best remain unidentified.

The cottonmouth search was through an area of second growth timber and scrub brush not far from Mud River in the so-called Coon Range section, almost astraddle the Muhlenberg-Butler County line.

The land is low. Overflow from the river keeps 50 or more acres standing in stagnant water from ankle to hip depth.

Locally the place is called Old Duck Pond, even though it doesn't even vaguely resemble a conventional pool.

Contrary to what might be imagined, there were at least three legitimate excuses for the trip. Not particularly in order, they were:

1. To add native entries to the reptiles Dooley displays at his Park City location.

2. To prove that Dooley and Skipworth weren't seeing things last fall when they found four small cottonmouths in the swamp.

3. To remove any doubt that cottonmouths can be found outside the Purchase, the Kentucky area to which they supposedly are limited.

Those in the cottonmouth posse were along for one reason or another.

Dooley, who really knows which way is south in such matters, was there to catch the snakes; Laycock, the writer-photographer, was to record Dooley catching snakes for one of his magazine clients; Skipworth was to take motion pictures of Laycock taking pictures of Dooley catching cottonmouths for use on the outdoor program he conducts on a Nashville TV station.

Klosterman, the newspaper photographer, was to take pictures of Skipworth taking movies of Laycock taking pictures of Dooley catching snakes; and the other newspaperman, the cautious one, was to write about Klosterman taking pictures of Skipworth taking movies of, etc.

There was seldom, if at all, a dull moment.

It would be entirely safe to report that, aside from Dooley, perhaps there never before had been assembled a more reluctant band of cottonmouth catchers. The wild horses have yet to be corralled that, under normal conditions, could have dragged the other four into cottonmouth country.

Dooley kept the group as nervous as relatives at a will reading on the way over from Park City, where they had assembled. He told what ugly tempered creatures cottonmouths are, how well they blend into their surroundings, and how nasty their bite can be. The latter observation he drew from personal experience. He was nailed by a cottonmouth three years ago.

"Actually," Dooley said, "the cottonmouth is the most difficult snake in the United States to identify since it looks so much like many others.

"They resemble copperheads and various common water snakes. Usually they are a dark brown, heavily bodied snake with a pronounced head, and when wet the brown color is interlaced with black patterns."

The surest way to tell a cottonmouth from a common water snake is to observe it in water, Dooley continued. A nonpoisonous snake will swim with just its head out of the water; a poisonous snake inflates itself like an inner tube and floats with its whole body on top of the water.

"Many people are entirely wrong about snakes that live near the water," Dooley said, "in that they call water snakes 'moccasins.'

"There is no such thing as a nonpoisonous water moccasin. The word moccasin designates a poisonous pit viper.

"Water moccasin, then, is the correct name for the cottonmouth, which sometimes also is known as the 'lowland moccasin,' while the copperhead is called the 'highland moccasin.' "

It was, however, in talking about cottonmouth bites that Dooley almost had a mutiny among his companions.

"Don't worry," he kept reassuring them, "the mortality rate is less than five per cent even when there is no medical care."

An adult three-foot cottonmouth, he said, can inject 10 to 15 drops of venom when it strikes. It is a peculiarity of the species, perhaps because of the snake's singularly unwholesome habitat, that a bite usually develops gangrene.

On such a happy note the group neared Old Duck Pond.

The cottonmouth roundup started almost immediately after the party entered the swamp.

All but Dooley had changed into the snakebite-proof waders before heading into the swamp. He wore a pair of sneakers and carried nothing more lethal than a short snake stick.

The group had slogged only a short distance through foot-deep water and two-foot-deep mud before Laycock spotted the first cottonmouth. It was coiled four feet away in a thick clump of marsh grass. Dooley moved cautiously up from behind and hooked the metal open loop of his snake stick under the snake's body.

Before he could pin down the head and make the catch, the madly striking three-footer slithered away.

Minutes later the first catch was made. The snake, another three-footer, was pinned down on the edge of a pile of brush and deposited in the leather case Dooley carried.

During the next two hours, numerous other cottonmouths were spotted, but because of the difficult going only three were caught.

By then the mosquitos were getting thicker and more hungry and the hunters were getting tired.

The group had turned and was heading out of the swamp toward the car when the real excitement began. Suddenly Dooley almost froze in his tracks, then moved slowly toward a large hollow log that lay in the shallow water.

"The granddaddy of them all is in there," he said excitedly, leaning over and peering into the log.

"I can barely reach him with my snake stick. Give me room because he's a big one and I've got to get a firm hold on him when I pull him out."

For several minutes he probed into the log to make sure that when he pulled the snake out it would emerge tail first. That way he could pin the head and get a safe and firm grasp behind the jaws before trying to lift it out.

"Got him!" Dooley exclaimed after considerable grunting.

The snake he lifted from the log was enough to provide nightmares for a month. The rusty brown critter was more than four feet long, as big around as a man's upper arm. He weighed nearly six pounds.

Dooley's grip back of the head, which was at least two and one-half inches across, had forced open the jaws, clearly revealing why the species was called cottonmouth. The inside of the mouth was filled with a white, almost frothy membrane. Two long, hypodermic-like fangs were visible in the upper jaw.

The fangs dripped venom in an almost steady stream.

"This fellow is red-hot," Dooley said. "I'll bet this is as big a cottonmouth as ever has been taken in Kentucky. I've seen very few in Louisiana or Florida that were larger."

It wasn't until the swamp was a good way behind that the noncatching cottonmouth catchers breathed easily.

"All we have to worry about now is the strap on that case coming loose," Skipworth sighed in relief.

"I'm still dizzy from all that looking in circles I did back in the swamp," Laycock said. "I'd take a step, then look around in a complete circle before taking another step."

Dooley didn't say anything.

He was sleeping placidly. (6/7/59)

MERCY HITS THE TRAIL The routine would have caused most anybody else to drop out for a long rest cure.

But to Nancy Boyle and the other nurses of the Frontier Nursing Service, it hadn't seemed unusual—just part of the day-to-day job they do in the mountains of eastern Kentucky.

Nevertheless, the routine showed such disregard for time and physical hardships that it would be difficult to explain what it is that drives those who work in the field for the Frontier Nursing Service.

Perhaps it is a deep sense of wanting to serve; perhaps it is the romantic appeal of the service; perhaps it is the desire to get thorough background in nursing under difficult conditions.

Whatever her reason, Nancy Boyle makes her rounds like this:

It isn't quite 6 o'clock this particular morning, and the sun still lies behind the mountains to the east. But Miss Boyle is ready to ride. Her saddlebags are packed. Her horse snorts impatiently to leave the nursing service hospital halfway up Thousandsticks Mountain overlooking Hyden, the seat of Leslie County.

The narrow valley of the Middle Fork of the Kentucky River in which Hyden is located is enveloped in thick fog. Vapory swirls rise as Miss Boyle rides up the steep hill behind the hospital and heads toward Hell-for-Sartin Creek and Possum Bend Nursing Center 15 miles to the north.

A fox squirrel barks sharply from a tree. A jet black towhee chatters noisily. The faraway caw-cawing of a rain crow echoes through the hollow below. The horse and rider wind higher and higher up the rock-studded path toward the ridge top.

Nancy Boyle is on her way to the Possum Bend Nursing Center to join Mary Hewat, a nurse-midwife, for two days before returning to the Hyden Hospital for floor duty. The nursing center, located near the Post Office of Confluence, is one of six outposts scattered through the remote, often roadless, 700-square-mile region covered by the Frontier Nursing Service in Leslie, Clay and parts of Perry and Owsley counties. More than 10,000 persons live in the area. A majority of them are beyond the reach of doctors or any kind of medical care except that of the FNS.

Besides the six nursing centers—and the FNS headquarters at Wendover—there are seven smaller outposts where clinics are held weekly. Possum Bend Center serves about 78 square miles bounded roughly by Hell-for-Sartin, Wilder and Trace Branches, Sugar and Camp Creeks and the Middle Fork River.

There are 30 nurses and nurse-midwives in the FNS. Although their main work is to care for children and women in childbirth, they give bedside nursing to all ages and do general preventive health work. This care is brought to patients regardless of where they live. When her jeep bogs down, the nurse rides a horse. When the horse is unable to go farther, she walks.

Full information is kept on all pregnant mothers. An examination is made by the doctor who heads the FNS hospital in Hyden at least once during pregnancy. The doctor determines if deliveries should be made in the hospital or if they can be made safely at home by a nurse-midwife.

Before Mary Breckinridge founded the FNS in 1925, the only doctors were "yarb" (herb) doctors. "Granny women" delivered babies for their neighbors. The mortality rate was high.

In contrast, there are these FNS figures for last year: 9,609 sick persons attended; nurses at centers received 22,642 visits; bedside nursing given to 1,015 persons; 4,379 assorted shots given.

The nurse-midwives attended 459 women. There were 455 live and four stillbirths and no maternal deaths. During the 28 years, 9,476 babies have been delivered with only 11 maternal deaths. Which is by way of background on the FNS.

By now Nancy Boyle reaches the top of Thousandsticks Mountain and lets her horse rest. The sun is high. Civilization seems—indeed, is—far away.

From there to the outpost clinic buildings on Bull Creek, the going is downhill. Up to now there hasn't been a single house along the way.

However, at Bull Creek, where children are gathered at the little stone schoolhouse, there is a cluster of houses, many of them converted log structures. On down Bull Creek, and all the way to the Hell-for-Sartin clinic, houses are frequent, even though there is nothing faintly resembling a road.

The Hell-for-Sartin outpost, a small log building, lies ahead across an open field from the schoolhouse.

Mary Hewat, the English nurse-midwife who has been in this country only since April, is conducting her weekly clinic. A group of mothers and children sit on the porch waiting their turn. At recess, children from the school come over to be weighed, have their throats swabbed, and leave messages from their mothers for Miss Hewat to please stop by on the way back out.

Miss Hewat, who could weigh no more than 110 pounds with full saddlebags and her thickest English accent, is giving shots. She has driven to the clinic in a jeep. Although there is no road, she drove the five miles up the creek bed, almost bone dry from the summer and early fall drought.

Nancy Boyle leaves her horse for Miss Hewat and goes the rest of the way to Possum Bend in the jeep. Miss Hewat follows, and they meet at Possum Bend for lunch.

After lunch, Nancy Boyle takes the jeep for calls in the Moseley Bend section. Mary Hewat saddles another horse and rides up Wilder to visit some newly born babies. The nurses visit new babies daily for the first ten days and once a month for a year. They also make periodic calls on families in their areas to check on general health.

Moseley Bend is farther down the Middle Fork. Nancy Boyle fords the river—there's no bridge for miles—and drives as far as possible. Then she walks the last quarter of a mile to a cabin tucked in the head of a hollow. She asks when the mother would like to take two of her children to the hospital in Hyden to have some troublesome tonsils removed.

Then she visits the Joe Stidham family. They live across the river at a point where it is a wide stream. She rows a flat-bottom boat over and finds three in that family are going to have tonsillectomies. The operations are given free at Hyden.

The next stop is at the Thomas Campbell cabin up a hollow far off the dirt road. On the way the nurse calls on a young mother, not yet 30, who hasn't been to Hyden, the county seat, for three years.

Eighty-year-old Thomas Campbell stops shucking corn to "talk a spell." His wife is "complaining a leetle," he says. One of her ankles is swollen. It's caused, he figures, from standing so much while canning the 400 or more quarts of fruits and vegetables she put up this year.

It is pitch dark before Nancy Boyle starts for the center. During the afternoon alone she has made more than half a dozen calls.

Back at the center, she and Mary Hewat rub down the horses, feed them and start their own dinner. The day's work finally done, they sit around a fire in the living room and talk.

Nancy Boyle is from Pennsylvania and has been with the FNS for 18 months. Before that she took three years of nursing training. She is not a midwife, but is a registered nurse. She became interested in the FNS during a high school career conference. All the romance and adventure of the service whetted her appetite. After nurse's training, she wrote for and received an appointment.

Mary Hewat is from the Bedfordshire section of England and has been nursing for 11 years. She read of the FNS in a magazine and the idea of being a Florence Nightingale on horseback attracted her. She applied for a place and within four months was in this country.

At first she had trouble understanding the Possum Benders. They, in turn, thought she talked the "quarest." But now she picks many old English expressions from their conversation.

For instance, an ailing child is said to "puny around." Instead of offering help, they volunteer "holp." A pain may be "punishing so bad I don't know how I'll live." A common present is a "mess of beans in a poke." Locusts make the best "fence postes."

Both nurses are up by six the next morning. Nancy Boyle leaves at eight o'clock for the subsidiary clinic on Grassy Branch. Miss Hewat again saddles her horse and rides out for calls up Trace Branch.

At Grassy, near the Perry County line, the building is open and a fire burns in the grate. A large group of mothers and children are waiting. Most of the children are delighted when they spot Ted, the big airedale dog that is Nancy Boyle's constant companion.

The Grassy clinic is of logs and has a wooden shingle roof. It is across the narrow, deep rutted dirt road from Grassy School. The school is so big this year it has expanded into the nearby log

Church of Christ.

By noon Miss Boyle has seen more than 30 children and several adults. On the way back to Possum Bend she makes two house calls.

In the afternoon she returns to Hyden and duty at the hospital. This time Miss Hewat drives her in the jeep, taking the round-about, dusty state road that winds up the river from Confluence. The last seven miles of the road is used by so many coal trucks that a dense haze of dust hangs over it. The dust is so thick that vehicles always are driven with headlights on as a safety measure.

Houses are thick along the road, and there is no way to keep out the dust, which has been called "a positive health menace." The attention of state highway officials has been called to the situation. Thirty-two coal trucks are counted moving back towards the mines in just the last seven miles.

No sooner has she cleaned up than Nancy Boyle is on duty at the hospital. Mary Hewat is on her way back to Possum Bend. (11/29/53)

SNAKE HANDLERS   Although poisonous snakes—rattlers, copperheads and moccasins—have been used in religious faith demonstrations in the Kentucky mountains for 20 years or more, it wasn't until 1937 that the outside world was first told of this practice. Since then meetings of the snake handlers—who call themselves the Holiness branch of the Church of God—have been strictly big news and the cultists have been all but smothered under the flood of publicity.

Some of the stories written about them, their leaders say, have been fairly factual. But a vast majority, they moan, have not been anywhere near the truth.

For instance, the Rev. Oscar Hutton of St. Charles, Virginia, a native Kentuckian who is credited with teaching snake handling to most of the 1,000 or more cultists in this state alone, claims no one ever has explained in an impartial, unbiased manner what their religion is, what they believe and what—if anything—it is based upon.

"They've pictured us as fanatics who should be in the asylum," he said, "but they've never tried to tell our side of the story."

This, then, will be an attempt to set down in so many words

the doctrine of the cultists and at the same time to show what kind of people they are. This will not be a defense of snake handling. I am not a believer; in fact, my nervous system still is tied up in knots even a Boy Scout couldn't untangle following my recent visits to cult demonstrations. But I saw things at those meetings which left me gasping with amazement and for which I have no logical explanation.

The first thing most people want to know about the snake—or as they say, the serpent—handlers is, what are they like?

Well, they're the kind of folk you meet throughout the mountains. No, that isn't exactly true; perhaps they're more friendly than most and are quicker to invite you into their homes. Probably 95 per cent of the men work in the coal mines and the women at home care for large families. Their homes aren't exactly palaces, but most of them are comfortable, with electric lights, electric refrigerators and radios.

As a class they aren't particularly well-educated. But as one man put it, "We all can read the Bible, and that's what is really important."

The next question that always is asked is, what are their religious beliefs?

That's hard to answer. Actually the doctrines in which they place enough faith to handle poisonous snakes like house cats are a mixture of several different faiths. These doctrines might be broken down into six points:

1. They do not believe in the use of medicine during illness. Faith alone can cure, they contend.

2. At times during services they speak in the "unknown tongue" and roll upon the floor, much like the so called "Holy Rollers."

3. They, like most Protestants, believe in an organized church— that is, an organization of deacons and elders whose duty it is to call upon and talk with sinners.

4. They believe in church rule, meaning that if a member still pursues his sinful ways after the deacons and elders have talked to him, he should be banned from the church until he sees his mistakes.

5. They believe in baptism by immersion.

6. Specifically, the snake-handling portion of their doctrine is based upon passages found in John, fifth chapter, 12th through 17th verses; James, fifth chapter, 13th through the rest of the chapter; Mark, 16th chapter, 15th verse through the rest of the chapter.

While there are other groups known both as Holiness and Church of God, only this particular sect believes in snake handling.

The snakes, according to Mr. Hutton, are symbols which prove they are willing to risk their lives to prove "the power of God." The cultists do not handle the snakes until they have called upon God, as they put it, to "make this serpent submit to Your will" and until they "feel the power" themselves. After that, they say, the snake's jaws are locked and they are harmless to those who believe.

Most bites are received, Hutton claims, when the snakes are handled before they are "in the power."

"The serpents must be handled when you feel the power of God moving in you," he says.

Strangely, few people are bitten in taking up the snakes despite the fact that they are coiled and ready to strike. It is in passing them from person to person that most bites occur. That, it was explained, is due to the fact that some of the cultists along the line may not feel the power 100 per cent.

Contrary to popular belief, snakes are not a part of all Holiness services. Four meetings usually are held each week, on Wednesday or Thursday night, Sunday morning or afternoon, and Sunday night. Sometimes snakes will be used in all the services, sometimes in none.

Two other questions always asked are: Do the cultists use any trickery in handling the snakes, and are they really poisonous?

The answer to the first part of that question is, "I don't know." The answer to the last part is an emphatic and underscored "Yes."

Perhaps there is a trick to handling the snakes. But it seems strange that hundreds of supposedly unlearned people would know such a gimmick. Perhaps the snakes are hypnotized by the chanting and singing and near-hysteria that precede the handling.

However, the snakes seem anything but happy when they are dragged from the boxes. The rattlers are lashing out in all directions and their tails are buzzing angrily. Yet—and I saw this with my own eyes—the wildly thrashing snakes often become limp and seemingly lifeless after the cultists have mumbled their incoherent prayers over them.

You need very little convincing that the snakes are poisonous. One look at the rigid, swollen, right hand of Faye Nolan, the 12-year-old handler who was bitten by a rattler at a Cawood, Kentucky, meeting on September 28, will convince even the most skeptical that snakes do have fangs and they pack a powerful, often deadly, wallop.

Few of the cultists have gotten by without at least one bite.

Mr. Hutton has been bitten four times. Raymond Hayes, who will stick his head into a hot stove or hold a blowtorch to his forehead to show the "power of the Lord," has been bitten 31 times, once on the top of his head. But he never has lost a day of work, he says. Hayes has been bitten so many times, in fact, that now he can't even tell he has been struck until some time later. His first realization is a tingling sensation on the tip of his tongue. Yet he, like the other true believers, never has accepted medical attention for a bite or any illness.

"How can a doctor know how to heal you if God, who made us all, can't?" asked Hutton. "In the Bible it says call for the elders of the church in sickness. It didn't say call for the doctor."

Some years back Hutton's wife, a nonhandler, became sick with typhoid fever. After the fifth day she was so sick that neighbors threatened to have Hutton arrested when he refused to call in the doctor. All he did was keep ice water for her to drink, and pray. For 20 days she lay between life and death, but on the 21st day, he says, the fever left her suddenly and she got out of bed and cooked breakfast.

Most Holiness meetings are held in the little unpainted churches you find clinging to the sides of the hills in almost every hollow in the mountains. But some big sessions, like the one two weeks ago near Harlan, are held out of doors during the summer. However, much of the effect of a demonstration, the mood and the atmosphere, is lost in the light of day.

Indoor meetings build up a mood that defies the imagination. They have to be seen to be believed. Such a meeting opens with the "saints," the believers who are saved, seated behind the pulpit, facing the "sinner people." It opens with a song or two, the accompaniment for which comes from guitars and the rhythmic crashing of cymbals and tambourines.

Then the "saints" all kneel on the floor and pray aloud. If there is one of their number who is ailing, he may be brought forward and they will attempt to cure him by the laying on of hands upon him. Preaching starts, after which more songs build up the atmosphere for the climax. By then the cultists are shouting, stomping, chanting and some may be speaking in the "unknown tongue."

Finally, the singing becomes an undistinguishable mumble and the throbbing regular beat of the cymbals and tambourines gives a weird jungle-like touch to the whole scene. The blinking lights and the packed church add to the general effect.

The moment the vicious, ugly snakes are lifted from the boxes is like something you've seen before only in a nightmare. The dull, dead buzz of the rattlesnakes can be heard above even the beat—that constant beat—of the cymbals. The cultists, some praying, hold the snakes high over their heads or place them around their necks. And, right before your unbelieving eyes, the snakes appear to stop much of their hissing and twisting. Soon they appear to hang limp and lifeless.

The handling actually has consumed no more than 10 or 15 minutes of the three-hour long service, yet to you, the skeptical outsider, it seems like eternity.

Psychologists and students of mass hysteria probably have scholarly explanations for the fact that so seldom are handlers bitten. They no doubt would contend that it is the excitement of the moment which creates a sort of hypnotic effect on both the cultists and the snakes making it possible for them to handle and be handled. The cultists themselves say it is faith alone. Whatever it is—hypnotism or faith—it takes an awful lot of it to make a person overcome his or her natural fear of a snake and pick it up.

At the recent Harlan demonstration, Faye Nolan handled the same snake that had bitten her just three weeks earlier. It was apparent that she was badly frightened; her mouth was a fine white line and her good hand shook visibly. Yet she overcame her deep-rooted fear and reached into the box and brought out the rattler.

Some say the cultists are exhibitionists, that they handle the snakes only because it attracts attention and gets their names and pictures in the paper. Hutton, however, points out that snakes were being handled in faith demonstrations long before a single line had been printed about it.

"I handled serpents 15 years ago," the 53-year-old native of Knox County said, "but the first time anything ever was written about it was 10 years back. Actually, we'd rather nothing ever had been printed about it because it has caused laws to be passed against serpent handling. On top of that, most of the things that are written are lies."

There is no denying the fact that most of the cultists are anything but shy when a camera is aimed their way. They'll pose with their snakes and usually move around to a better spot for the photographer. This they explain by saying once they feel the "power" they can pose, stand on their heads or stuff the snakes inside their shirts without being bitten.

State laws in Kentucky, Virginia and Tennessee make it unlawful to handle snakes in religious services. The Kentucky law, passed in 1940, states that "Any person who displays, handles or uses any kind of reptile in connection with any religious service or gathering shall be fined not less than $50 nor more than $100."

Cultists have been arrested, fined and jailed, but instead of discouraging them it has made them more determined. Now the handling of snakes has become a sort of divine crusade and they feel they are being persecuted for their religious beliefs much like the early Christians.

O. V. Shoupe, a Cumberland, Kentucky, preacher, is a good example of how determined the cultists are. He has been arrested 50 times and jailed nine times for handling snakes in Cumberland. Then when he preached on the streets, an ordinance was passed against using loudspeakers on Sunday nights. After that he attempted to preach in front of his car but, so his story goes, he was forced to close his Bible and get out of town. Not to be outdone, he moved beyond the city limits and preached.

Some years back a cultist was arrested and fined. He refused to pay the fine and was sentenced to 35 days in jail. Every night he would hold a one-man preaching service in his cell. He'd pray, sing and shout for hours. Finally, the strain was too great for the other prisoners and the jailer. The man was told bluntly to get out of jail and go somewhere else. But he refused to leave. The jailer compromised finally by leaving his cell unlocked at night so he could go out and do his singing and shouting at regular Holiness meetings and then return.

"We should get more veterans interested in this," said Joe Helton, a Harlan garage mechanic who spent 43 months overseas, "because they're trying to destroy over here what we fought for over there—the right to worship as we please."

Many of the cultists claim it is other Holiness people, folk who once believed in snake handling, who are creating most of the opposition to them.

"Hypocrites who once believed as we do are leading the persecution," said Hutton. "They say they have religion but they don't because they once saw the light and now they are going against the word of God."

In reality the Holiness people who believe in snake handling as a symbol of their faith are divided into two groups. On one hand are those who are headed by Hutton. And on the other hand are the so-called Newlights.

As far as Mr. Hutton knows, snake handling started 20 years ago on the Black Bottom section of Harlan County. It was there that he learned it. Now it has spread throughout the mountains, but

Harlan County remains the center. He says he knows about
12 persons, men and women, who have died of bites received in
services.

"We don't have a thing against other churches," Hutton said.
"We're just worshipping God as we think best, and we all will be
judged by the deeds we commit here on earth. An unlearned,
crippled person like me should do his best to further the kingdom
of God."

"The whole Bible is good," he continued, "and we don't deny any
of it. We have enough faith in the Lord to risk our lives handling
snakes. Even unbelievers aren't afraid of them when the Lord
locks their jaws."

But from the other side of the room came this comment from
Mrs. Hutton:

"I'm afraid of them any time." (10/26/47)

THE AUTHOR WHO   There's nothing in the rules that says a
WRITES SO TRUE   guy who writes a book need equip his
typewriter with a magnetic compass so as never to stray from the
truth, the whole truth and nothing but the truth within the
pages he pieces together.

Even a great many of the advertised all-fact-and-a-yard-wide
historical novels aren't much more than second cousins by marriage
to the real, 200-proof truth. Usually those books have fictional
characters wandering through an authentic chapter of history,
reacting to real or imagined situations as the author supposes they
might have done.

All of which makes the works of Jesse Stuart, the tall Greenup
County ex-schoolteacher who towers head, shoulders and short
story above all competition as Kentucky's most prolific writer,
stand out like an icebox in an igloo.

For Stuart, a literary Midas who turns the things around him not
into gold but into interesting, readable pieces, has used very real
people and events indeed in his more than 1,100 published poems,
500 or more short stories and nine novels. Practically all of those
works have been set in Greenup County, where Stuart was
born and where he lives in a beautiful, semi-remote valley called
W-Hollow. Not so much as one poem has a setting outside of
Kentucky.

This ability to turn even insignificant local events and legends into short stories and even book-length novels never has been mirrored more clearly than in his latest effort, a book called *The Thread That Runs So True*. That book, published in September by Scribners, is an autobiography of the dozen years Stuart spent as a schoolteacher, a period during which he rose from an isolated, one-room grade schoolmaster to county superintendent.

Just as Stuart is no ordinary writer, so also was he no ordinary teacher. Schoolwork was—and still is—like a religion to him, and he gave himself completely to that religion, fighting, literally and figuratively, with his fists and with his wits for new ideas, for better pay for teachers, for equal opportunity for rural students, even though at times it caused him to lose friends and risk his very life.

Stuart was a restless kind of schoolteacher, one whose stomach was all but turned by the obstacles faced by students in rural schools. He worked Siberian-salt-mine hours in trying to right the many inequalities. As a result he was branded a born troublemaker, a malcontent who was out to wreck the school system of his own county because he dared preach the gospel of consolidation and because he advocated elimination of the trustee system whereby, often, a man who couldn't so much as write his name exercised control over a school.

This latest book, then, is nothing more than a chronological audit of his experiences as a teacher. He has set those experiences down in the plain, everyday language that is his trademark. Nowhere does he resort to added color or events; rather, he depends entirely on true incidents and real people. Yet, in spite of his lack of outside stimulus, the story never drags; it has enough humor, human interest, action, suspense and gall-bitter irony to hit the reader like the kick of a healthy mule.

And because of the message it carries, because conditions Stuart faced still are present in schools today, educators the land over have saddled the book with enough bouquets to smother a Derby winner. Dr. Joy Elmer Morgan, founder of the National Educational Association, has referred to *The Thread That Runs So True* as "the best book on education written in the last 50 years."

Strangely, though, in the tremendous volume of bravos he has received there isn't a line from the Kentucky Department of Education. That in spite of the fact that the book is entirely about Kentucky people and schools, many of which still are in use.

That very fact, however, is another thing that makes Stuart more than somewhat unusual as writers go. He's a perfect example of how people can be so near the forest they can't see the trees. For his works are much better known in other states than in Kentucky, the state about which all are written. He was the author of four books, including *The Man With the Bull Tongue Plow,* one of just 12 volumes of poetry included on Dr. Henry S. Canby's list of "100 Best Books of America," before most of the people in Greenup County realized he was a writer. To them he still was a schoolteacher; to a lot of them a troublesome teacher, at that, because he wanted to change things.

In reality, it would seem that *The Thread* would make wonderful ammunition for one of those documentary, crusade-flavored movies Hollywood seems to be brewing up these days at the drop of a testimonial dinner. The book has everything the movie makers claim to want in a "cause" picture and, in addition, at least one trait a great many lack—complete honesty. It is entirely without artificiality, without exaggeration in events, places or people, as those in Greenup County who are familiar with the facts will tell you. Actually, such a movie could be filmed in a great extent at the very schools about which the book is written.

The little one-room frame building where Stuart first taught at the age of 17, when just a junior in high school himself, still stands alongside the country road a few miles from Hunnewell in southern Greenup County. It was there, on a blistering hot July day 25 years ago, that Stuart reported to conduct classes after his sister, Sophie, the appointed teacher, had been beaten up and literally run off by a six-foot, 20-year-old first grader. It was there, in that cramped little room, that Stuart received his trial by fire, facing that same bully and beating the tar out of him in a fist fight that marked him in the community as one teacher who was there to stay. It was there for six months that he taught all eight grades, 54 classes in all every day, for the princely salary of $68 a month.

And it was there that he determined never again to go courting in a white suit. That decision came after a blind date had been made for him with the pretty teacher at another rural school some six miles away. Since his only transportation was bunion-mobile, he set out after supper that fateful night dressed in his best—and only—white suit. But news of his coming traveled fast. A mile or so away from his destination he was ambushed by a large band that resented an outsider calling on one of its own. Armed with tomatoes and aged eggs, the band chased him all the way back to the farmhouse where he boarded. After that he vowed never to wear a white suit at night because it was a fine target.

If you think Stuart exaggerated in his book, take a trip today down that same rutty country road leading to the first school he taught. Keep going until you come to Cane Creek School, the place where Stuart started his career. The building is weather-beaten and badly in need of repairs and paint just as when he, a tall, gawky mountain boy who was determined to be the first in his family to get a college education, went there in 1924. There still is just one teacher for all eight grades, which means she is able to give each of her 50 or so classes only 10 minutes of her time each day.

Until this year there hadn't been a school at Cane Creek for three years simply because there was no teacher willing to go there for the money offered. The only lights are coal-oil lamps. There is no inside handle on the front, the only, door. The teacher has no modern visual aid gimmicks. On top of that, in bad weather it's impossible to travel the last half-mile to the school in an automobile.

The children at Cane Creek are as bright-eyed and as eager to learn as those in the best equipped city school. But by no stretch of the most elastic imagination does the comparison continue after that.

A hot lunch program at Cane Creek? Only if a child leaves the sack containing his biscuit and bacon sandwich in the sun.

Running water at Cane Creek? Nothing more than the crystal clear little mountain stream that chatters noisily along the west side.

Playground equipment at Cane Creek? Only the roots and low swung branches of the tall sycamore trees that tower over the tin roofed school.

It is disadvantages and inequalities such as those faced even today by Cane Creek pupils that Stuart strikes out against in his book. It was because of them that he advocated, 25 years ago, consolidation. It was that fight for consolidation, through which pupils in remote, poorly equipped schools like Cane Run would be transported at county expense to larger, modern, centrally located schools, that caused so many people to rise up and protest against him as a dangerous critic of cherished institutions.

Not many real names are used in the book. But the very real names of the very real people who figure in the very real incidents are camouflaged under a very thin veneer. For instance, Greenup County is referred to as Greenwood County. Ashland becomes Auckland, Greenup High School becomes Landsburg High, the Tygart River becomes the Tiber. Warnock High, the first high school he taught, becomes Winston, and so on. Except for this slight alteration in names, nothing else was changed.

While more than 12 years of Stuart's rags-to-comparative-riches career goes into the 293 pages of the book, he was only 11 months in the actual writing. He first began toying with the idea as far back as 1937, but it wasn't until late in 1948 that he got around to the writing. In the intervening 11 years, an awful lot of water went under the bridge.

For one thing, Stuart had followed his *Man With the Bull Tongue Plow* in 1934 and *The Head o' W-Hollow,* a book of short stories in 1936, with a second collection of poems and six novels, including the best-selling *Taps for Private Tussie.*

All during that time, he says, he'd been wanting to do something that might bring to list the cause, the hardships of the country teacher. *The Thread* is the result. Right now another Stuart book, *Hie to the Hunters,* is waiting for release in April. That novel, like all the others, is Kentucky through and through, and there were offers for rights to it from movie makers even before it was finished.

Incidentally, you might wonder what, if any, significance the title has to the book. That line, *The Thread That Runs So True,* belongs to a schoolyard game called "The Needle's Eye" which Stuart found his pupils playing at the first school he taught. The verse goes like this:

> The needle's eye that doth supply,
> The thread that runs so true,
> Many a beau have I let go,
> Because I wanted you. (1/15/50)

CREASON'S INCREDIBLE KENTUCKY   Kentucky is an incredible state in many wonderful ways—its varied topography, the regional differences in its people, the sharp contradictions to be found here, and the images the very name of Kentucky stirs up in the mind's eye of people the world over.

The accents, for instance, vary from Deep South to mountain twang, and the language spoken by the early mountain people— still found in a few isolated spots—was straight out of Elizabethan England. It was colorful, expressive and picturesque.

Like the old man explaining his rare good health: "Why," he

said, "I ain't never been to a tooth dentist or a eyeball doctor in all my days!"

Or take the way the name of Kentucky tickles the imagination. Kentucky is, at one and the same time, the land of country ham and bourbon whiskey, of picture-postcard bluegrass farms and mist-topped mountains, of beautiful women and fast horses, of goateed colonels and rugged mountaineers.

Kentucky is also a state with quaint and unusual place names. There is a Spider and a Webb; an Ever and a Ready; a Bengal and a Lancer. Then there are the likes of Nonesuch, Hell for Certain, Rabbit Hash, Monkey's Eyebrow, Marrowbone, Will Die and Shoulderblade.

Equally incredible is the fact that so many towns are located in other than what would seem the correct county. Harlan is in Harlan County, Pikeville is in Pike County and Shelbyville is in Shelby County. But Cumberland is not in Cumberland County, Grayson is not in Grayson County and Allen is not in Allen County.

This is one of the most regionally diversified of all the states— 40,000 square miles of terrain, ranging from steep mountains to table-top bottomland. It is a state in which some of the most lush and fertile land in the world is found, and in which vast regions are covered with thin, stingy soil that defies cultivation.

Like the land on which they settled, the people of Kentucky also are incredibly contradictory. This is a state of warm hearts and hot heads; of gentleness and violence; of hard drinking and teetotalism; of great erudition and appalling illiteracy; of great statesmanship and great ballot-box stuffing.

It is a state that has produced two presidents of the United States, four vice presidents, 105 natives elected governors of other states, and a long line of famous statesmen, while also drawing to it the likes of Simon Girty, the James Brothers, William C. Quantrill, the Harpe Brothers, Jack McCall, the murderer of Wild Bill Hickok, and others of the worst scoundrels of all time.

To appreciate why Kentuckians are so unusual, it is first necessary to know more about this incredible state and the role it played in the history of America.

To start with, Kentucky's shoe shape is symbolic of the part it has played in the nation's history. For this state was the shoe the country wore in stepping from the cramped eastern seaboard into the Middle West and eventually all the way to the Pacific Coast. Kentucky was the first state organized west of the Appalachian Mountains, and both routes of civilization moving westward touched it. One route was down the Ohio River, which forms

Kentucky's northern border for 660 miles; the other route was overland, through Cumberland Gap and across the heart of the state.

The pioneers who settled Kentucky were religious men and women who made great contributions to the religion of the land.

These pioneers also were interested in education. The first school in the "West" was started at Fort Harrod in 1776. Transylvania, now in Lexington, was the first college chartered in the "West"—1780. The University of Louisville is the oldest municipal university in the nation, dating from 1798. The first Catholic college for women in the "West" was Nazareth College near Bardstown, founded in 1814. William Holmes McGuffey started writing his now-famous elementary textbooks, the McGuffey Readers, while teaching at Paris, Kentucky, in 1823.

The early schools provided at best a spotty introduction to the mysteries of reading, writing and arithmetic. Often the itinerant teachers weren't exactly Phi Beta Kappas; but they didn't need to be. Like the early bluegrass "perfesser" who persisted in using "seen" incorrectly. The parents of some of his students met to discuss his capabilities. One man rose to his defense. "I'd a heap rather have a man say 'I seen' when he seen somethin' than to say 'I saw' when he ain't saw nothin'," he said.

Kentucky rose to fast prominence as a state once it separated from Virginia. By 1810 it was the fourth leading industrial state, with more than 2,000 manufacturing concerns.

Because of its early prominence, Kentucky was the only state ever seriously considered for relocation of the nation's capital. After the British had burned Washington during the War of 1812, a resolution was introduced in Congress, meeting in New York, to move the capital to the point in the nation farthest west. That point was the village of Red Banks on the Mississippi River in Kentucky. Engineers descended upon the frontier settlement, changed its name to Columbus, and laid out and planned a town which was expected to grow to 150,000 within 15 years. However, before anything else could be done, the war ended, and the capital was rebuilt in Washington.

Thus, Kentucky had left its mark on the nation early. But what about the people who had done these things? Where had they settled between the first coming of Daniel Boone into the state and, say, 1840?

Most of the people who had come into Kentucky—and they were Scotch and Scotch-Irish mainly with a sprinkling of French, Dutch and Germans—had pushed overland via Cumberland Gap toward the rich bluegrass land Boone had described so glowingly. But many had stopped in the mountains and had settled in the pinched valleys and far up the remote hollows in the eastern quarter of the state.

They had settled there because that region reminded them so much of the highland section of their native Scotland. There, in that remote setting, they raised large families and established an independent way of life that remains the trademark of Kentucky mountain people. In this almost impenetrable domain, the people preserved the way of life, the language, the customs of their forefathers. To this day, the purest strain of Anglo-Saxon blood in North America is found in the highland section of Kentucky.

Pioneer life in the mountains was simple. Social life centered on such basic things as weddings, funerals, election and revival meetings. Circuit-riding preachers were so far away that they only made it in twice a year. When they came a big protracted meeting was held and during that time weddings were performed for all those who had been tied up by the local "squire" and funerals were preached for all those who had died since the preacher last came by. And those who had joined the church since the last meeting were baptized in a mass ceremony at the nearest creek.

The story is told about one notorious reprobate who was induced to cast his lot with the church. When the circuit rider came in the next time, he was among those to be baptized. Because of his reputation, he was saved for last. The preacher pushed him under the water and held him just a bit longer than was customary.

"My friend," the preacher asked the gasping convert once he was let up, "are you happy right now?"

"Well, preacher," came the reply, "I ain't what you'd call damn happy—just happy, that's all."

The law likewise was far away then, and over roads that consisted of creek beds or almost impassable trails across the mountains. Place in such surroundings proud and fiercely independent families who were given to brooding over family insults and injustices and the results were the feuds which once ravaged the hill country.

Most of the settlers passed on through the mountains, however. They were anxious to get on to the Bluegrass. There the aristocracy of Kentucky developed. There the goateed, julep-sipping, horse-loving Kentucky colonel of the caricatures was born.

The rich bluegrass soil was particularly suited for two things— the breeding of fine horses and the growing of burley tobacco.

Thoroughbred breeding as an industry is older than Kentucky, the first purebred horses having been produced before the state was formed. Today the largest concentration of thoroughbred breeding farms (more than 135) in the world is centered within a 25-mile radius of Lexington. No other state stands close to Kentucky in the breeding of fine horses. Since 1900, about three-fourths of all money won on American race tracks has been won by Kentucky-bred horses. The Kentucky Derby, started in 1875, is the oldest continuously run horse race in the world, and 70 of the 91 Derby winners have been native-bred horses.

As for tobacco, half the burley grown in the US is raised in Kentucky. Kentucky stands second among the states in production of tobacco of all kinds.

The Bluegrass region also became famed for still another native product—bourbon whiskey. Corn whiskey using limestone water first was made in Bourbon County, from which it took its name. The exact year and the identity of the distiller is buried in the misty haze of time, but most historians set the year as 1789 and the distiller as Elijah Craig. Incidentally, Craig was a Baptist minister and one of the founders of Georgetown College.

While as early as 1815 more than 130,000 persons had come to Kentucky via Cumberland Gap alone and had settled mainly in the Bluegrass, not all the early settlers had entered the state by the overland route. Many thousands had come down the Ohio River on flatboats and had put ashore at Limestone (now Maysville) or at the falls, now Louisville.

Because of its position at the falls of the river, where goods bound up or down the stream had to be unloaded, moved around the rapids and reloaded into barges, Louisville soon became an important city.

The first national bank in the South was opened in Louisville. Here also the first iron foundry, hemp factory, boatyard, gas company and paint manufacturing plant in the "West" were opened.

Louisville has retained its importance as an industrial and business center. Today it is among the 15 largest manufacturing cities in the nation, with such significant plants as the world's largest home appliance manufacturing center, world's largest wheel-tractor plant, and the world's largest bathtub factory. It is also a leader in paint, varnish, cigarettes, synthetic rubber and processed foods. The world's largest printing house for the blind is located in Louisville.

But not all those who came into Kentucky during the pioneer days stopped either in the mountains, the Bluegrass or in the middle Ohio River region. Many pressed on west to settle in the flatland along the lower Ohio, Mississippi, Cumberland and Tennessee Rivers.

This is the Purchase section of Kentucky, so called because it—eight Kentucky and 20 Tennessee counties—was purchased by Andrew Jackson from the Chickasaw Indians for the federal government in 1818. It wasn't until 1818, then, that the far western tip of Kentucky was opened for mass settlement. Once settlers entered the region they developed a way of life there that was unlike any other part of the state.

Their particular way of life was dictated by several factors—soil, climate and lines of communication being prominent among them. Through all these factors, the Purchase was drawn closer to the Deep South than to the North or even to the rest of Kentucky.

The climate was warmer on the average by several degrees than the rest of Kentucky, and the soil was adapted to the growing of cotton, soybeans, and livestock. And the rivers, the only means of transportation, all eventually led South—the Cumberland and Tennessee into the Ohio, the Ohio into the Mississippi, and the Mississippi into the Gulf of Mexico.

So by 1840 all parts of Kentucky had been settled. The state prospered in those early days but trouble lay heavy on the horizon. The clouds of civil war were forming and Kentucky, true to its incredible nature, would be caught squarely in the middle.

Being the independent, free-thinking people they were—and are—Kentuckians were divided by the issues that divided the nation. Most felt closely drawn to the South and the Tidewater region of Virginia and the Carolinas by family connections, but most held an almost reverential feeling about the federal Constitution.

Kentucky was a slave state, but the leading Kentucky slave owners had been among the first to advocate emancipation. As early as the mid-1830s efforts had been started to free the slaves.

The result was divided loyalty in the state. That, plus Kentucky's strategic location as the state lying squarely between the North and the South, gave it a role in the war unmatched by any other state.

Significantly, one of the factors which historians today credit with bringing on the war resulted from a social visit a young girl from Ohio named Harriet Beecher Stowe made with friends in Mason County around 1832. While there, this young lady saw an old slave sold on the village auction block and she was so distressed by what she had seen that more than 20 years later she, then married, wrote an inflammatory novel called *Uncle Tom's*

Cabin. This so cemented opinion in the East and the North against slavery that war was certain.

It was fitting that both Civil War presidents—Abraham Lincoln for the North and Jefferson Davis for the South—should have been born in incredible Kentucky only one year and less than 100 miles apart.

When war came, Kentucky was the true border state, the only state in which the grisly spectacle of father fighting son and brother against brother took place on a massive scale.

More than 100,000 Kentuckians were drafted for federal service, and more than 43,000 volunteered to serve in the Confederacy. Sixty-seven natives of the state were Union generals, while 38 were Confederate generals.

Kentucky, in the end, cast its lot with the Union. But months after that decision had been made, Frankfort was captured by Confederates, making it the only capital of a Union state to be seized by the South during the Civil War. It was captured in September of 1862 and held for a month. During that time, the Kentucky legislature operated from the Jefferson County Courthouse in Louisville.

The last two years of the war pointed out the incredibly contradictory nature of Kentuckians. Until 1863 Kentucky never had showed any serious anti-Union feelings, even though a provisional Confederate government had been formed late in 1861 and Kentucky was the 13th star in the Confederate flag. During the first two years of war, Kentucky never had failed to meet its quota of men for the Union Army or to raise its share of money for the war effort.

But a series of circumstances, including the suspension of the writ of habeus corpus, the declaration of martial law in some counties and the interference in local elections by military officials, caused Kentucky to change sentiment. As a result, the state refused to ratify the 13th amendment which ended slavery, and at the end of the war there was such strong feeling in Kentucky against Union officials that the same reconstruction acts placed against the seceded states of the South applied also for Kentucky.

These points are significant because they tend to underscore what an incredible state this is. Maybe Kentuckians are an incredible breed because this is an incredible state. Maybe it's the other way around. (8/29/65)

Index